THE COMPLETE GUIDE

Consulting Contracts

Herman Holtz

Enterprise · Dearborn
a division of Dearborn Publishing Group, Inc.

Publisher: Kathleen A. Welton
Acquisitions Editor: Patrick J. Hogan
Associate Editor: Karen A. Christensen
Senior Project Editor: Jack L. Kiburz
Interior Design: Lucy Jenkins
Cover Design: The Publishing Services Group

Published by Enterprise•Dearborn,
a division of Dearborn Publishing Group, Inc.

Printed in the United States of America

94 95 96 10 9 8 7 6 5 4 3 2 1

Library of Congress Cataloging-in-Publication Data

Holtz, Herman
    The complete guide to consulting contracts / by Herman Holtz.
      p. cm.
    ISBN 0-7931-0670-2
    1. Business consultants—Handbooks, manuals, etc. 2. Negotiation
in business—Handbooks, manuals, etc. 3. Contracts—Handbooks,
manuals, etc. I. Title.
    HD69.C6H6196 1994   93-32033
    001'.068'D7—dc20   CIP

Table of Contents

List of Figures

Foreword

Any independent consultant has a great need for a comprehensive and yet highly practical explanation of contractual business relationships. Ask any law student what subject has the least glamour and excitement, and the answer will surely be contracts. Ask that same student what area of the law is the predominant element of business intercourse, and the response will most certainly again be contracts.

Service contracts (i.e., legal agreements), the consultant's agreement, the doctor's implied agreement of the performance of the proper standard of care and the accountant's agreement to exercise good accounting practice are all service contracts between the consumer and the professional who represents himself or herself as worthy of trust and confidence in his or her professional field. Most, if not all, professions, through their respective associations, develop standardized agreements, waivers and disclaimers that set forth the parameters of contractual obligations and responsibilities to clients and patients. As the author points out, the consultant often does not have the service of an association or lawyer available to review his or her individual agreements. Therefore, the independent consultant must anticipate the intricacies of a proposed contract.

When special projects and causes demand the retention of a consultant, those who seek these services wish only to establish a relationship that will be beneficial to both parties, unencumbered by dissent, differences or misunderstandings that could jeopardize the basic purpose of the consulting agreement. The consultant's responsibility is to convey honest and reliable projections of his or her ability, eliminate hyperbole and end up with an agreement that is fair and equally satisfying. Consultants must, in simple terms, tell the preparers what terms they desire, what may be expected of them, and what they propose to deliver under the contract.

The author quite properly stresses the elements of negotiation in the consummation of a consulting contract. Negotiation is not for the timid. It's an art form that is a part of the insight and general knowledge of legal minds. However, the art of negotiation also involves common sense, a form of bargaining, the ability to recognize the fallacy of a proposition presented to you and the courage to propose a counterposition where there is work to be done, results to be achieved and compensation to be paid for your services. I applaud Mr. Holtz's position of "defensive" negotiation. Heed it well. Time will develop your skills of negotiation.

In the sale of real estate the seller's asking price is the starting line for negotiation. The seller knows that he or she must be prepared to consider a lesser offer by a prospective purchaser. The prospective purchaser knows that whether or not the seller is motivated (i.e., being pressured by circumstances to dispose of the property) will dictate the amount of the offer he or she makes. If the seller is aware of a special interest by the prospective purchaser, he or she will act accordingly in accepting or rejecting the proffered amount. This is negotiation.

Follow the author's admonition and bargain defensively, without rancor or aggressiveness, to the end of reaching an accord acceptable to both parties. Supreme Court Justice Oliver Wendell Holmes once wrote, "Freedom of contract begins where equality of bargaining power begins."

The Complete Guide to Consulting Contracts presents the reader with a guide to the preparation, consideration and finalizing of a fair and positive agreement that will protect mutual interests. Whether you are in the consulting field at this time or contemplating entry into the field, this book will assist you in developing a reputation for fair dealing and thus a greater and more positive acceptance for your expertise.

Max M. Goldberg

June 1, 1993

Max Goldberg is a native of Washington, D.C., was educated in its public schools, is a graduate of the National University of Law and was awarded his JD degree upon graduation from George Washington University Law Center in 1941. He soon qualified for and was admitted to practice in all local and federal courts in the Washington area, the federal and state courts of the State of Maryland, the U.S. Court of Military Appeals, the D.C. Court of Appeals, the U.S. Court of Appeals, and the U.S. Supreme Court.

Max Goldberg retired from practice in August 1989 and now resides in Bay Harbor Islands, Florida, where he remains active in community service.

Preface

Few professions, not even consulting, are the victims of as many bitter jokes as is the legal profession. Perhaps that is because most of us must turn to lawyers in unpleasant circumstances, such as in accident cases or in litigation where we are either plaintiffs or defendants. One of these stories concerns an attorney who lamented that in a recent case concluded successfully, his client realized almost as much money as he did. Apocryphal as this story is, there are many cases where seemingly endless litigation results in great dissipation of awards in legal fees and many related costs. And even when we sue and win, we may find our victory to be almost Pyrrhic, where the cost of winning largely nullifies the victory. It is thus not only often best to settle out of court but to avoid litigation to begin with, if at all possible; it is best, that is, to avoid having cause for litigation.

One way to minimize the probability of litigation is to negotiate and write effective contracts with clients, associates, suppliers and others with whom you have business relationships. However, as valuable and necessary as good business judgment is, it takes more than that to do this well. There are many specific legal considerations that often go well beyond the bounds of good judgment, or that which we call "common sense." The law does not always "make sense" to the lay mind; sometimes it may appear to defy all common sense. But it is, nevertheless, the law, and it is the final arbiter, as determined by the statutes and the courts, when that becomes necessary.

As an independent consultant, you are a businessman or businesswoman with all the normal concerns and responsibilities involving business relationships with others. But it is likely that you are also an independent contractor—that is, you work under contract. It is thus understandable that you frequently raise questions about and discuss negotiating and interpreting formal written contracts with clients and others. The most common questions I have heard discussed among consultants are as follows: Should I have a formal written contract with every client? Should I have a standard contract form? Should I have a lawyer draw up my contracts or at least help me develop a standard contract form? This book will answer these and other related questions with the help of experienced legal experts.

As an independent consultant, you ought to know at least five things about or related to contracts:

1. What a contract is and is not
2. How to read and interpret a contract defensively
3. How to negotiate and write a contract
4. The hazards of working without a contract—that is, without a proper *written* contract
5. The hazards of trying to develop and enter into a bulletproof contract (perhaps, even, the futility of trying to make any contract totally foolproof)

The last item in this list is probably the least appreciated one. Far too many individuals appear to believe that the purpose of a written contract is to provide their absolute protection from predators and others who have less than honest intentions. But this is an ingenuous and mistaken view. Working without a contract, written or otherwise, is not wise, but it is not the greatest hazard connected with contracts. The greatest hazard is entering into any contract with someone whose honest intentions and general integrity you mistrust. Thus, the contract you believe you must make an impregnable fortress for your own protection is a bad contract. There is no bulletproof or impregnable contract, no contract that can protect you 100 percent. Even if there were such a contract, the probability that you would have to protect yourself—perhaps litigate and even fight a battle in court to defend your rights—makes that a bad contract. The more experience you have with contracts, the more you will discover that the honest intentions of contracting parties are at least as important as the careful wording and ordinary safeguards built into most contracts.

Never enter into contract with anyone who appears to lack good intentions. The purpose of a written document is not to compel the other party to live up to his or her promises but to preserve the agreement in such a form that its preservation does not depend on that volatile human memory, should it be necessary to refresh your minds or should parties other than the original negotiators and signers—e.g., assignees, arbitrators, lawyers and judges—be forced later to administer or otherwise become involved in matters requiring precise knowledge of the original agreement. Only by what is written in the document can those individuals know what the original agreement and intentions were.

Nonetheless, you cannot avoid entering into contracts in any business—and especially not in the consulting business, which is essentially contracting work. Consultants work as temporary employees in many cases, sometimes by choice, and they are often forced to that status by the policy of the IRS and by legal interpretations that increasingly contest and disallow contractor/self-employment status for many consultants working on their clients' premises. Despite the many challenges by the IRS under Section 1706 of the Tax Reform Act of 1976, independent consultants are independent contractors in many, if not most, of their assignments and projects. Except for those special cases where they choose to be temporary employees, they are sometimes prime contractors or subcontractors but are most often in a contracting status by the nature of what they do, even when the IRS insists that they are temporary employees for tax purposes.

This is not a problem that affects all independent consultants and may or may not be a problem for you. The problem arises most often and is most acute for those consultants who undertake long-term assignments—assignments for many months—as opposed to those whose assignments are usually for a few days or weeks, especially consultants who accept assignments via third parties (i.e., brokers). The consultant whose typical assignments are long-term may have only one or two clients during the course of the year, whereas the one who typically undertakes short-term assignments will probably have a dozen or more. This is part of the reason for the IRS' tendency to insist on temporary employee status for some consultants, rather than independent contractor status.

You may, therefore, contract directly with clients, but you may also contract with brokers, job shops, subcontractors, cocontractors, suppliers, distributors and perhaps even others. Some consultants (e.g., computer specialists) also find it necessary to write licensing agreements. And as a consultant and contractor, you must become knowledgeable about the role of a written proposal as part of a contract. It is a common arrangement that is important to your success in marketing as well as in contracting effectively.

In short, what you don't know about contracts can and will hurt you—all too often. However, it isn't practical for you to retain lawyers to help draw up every contract you negotiate, draft or sign. Nor is it practicable for you to have and use your own standard contract forms for every possible application unless your work is unusually specialized such that every assignment is almost identical with every other one. Even then, there are problems in using a standard contract form. For one thing, some clients—especially large organizations—have their own standard forms that they require you to accept. Or they may write formal purchase orders or execute simple letters of agreement. All these documents are contracts, of course. You must appreciate what makes these contracts legal and binding—that is, the elements that make any agreement a binding and enforceable contract. Enforceability is a very important consideration.

On the other hand, it is essential that you learn how to avoid falling into legal traps. These traps are not necessarily set for you deliberately; many are the simple result of ignorance or carelessness when drafting agreements or are the consequences of working on handshake agreements. Either way, they impart expensive lessons and can be avoided.

The objective in this book is not to impart legal training, although legal points will be covered. What is needed is a practical education in business contracts that goes beyond mere exposition of the points of law regarding contracts. Technical legal discussions, in fact, would be unproductive and would range far beyond the limits of interest and usefulness for you as an independent consultant. You will be advised to seek professional legal help when serious legal questions arise. This book addresses only those contract concerns you are likely to encounter, are required to deal with or are capable of dealing with alone. These include typical situations that require written agreements, the kinds of contracts and agreements you are apt to encounter or need, the major elements of every contract, how to negotiate contract terms and how to draft contracts. Thus, contracts will be discussed in terms of typical working situations, negotiations, solving problems and the avoidance of problems.

At the same time, you must avoid the trap of trying to be your own lawyer in serious matters where the counsel of a professional, qualified attorney is necessary. That will also be covered here, and you will be urged to seek qualified counsel in such cases.

One problem in writing this book was deciding where to establish the bounds of coverage because there are so many other areas that infringe on and influence the legal considerations of the contractor-client relationship and other concerns that arise in consulting. These may include questions of incorporation, copyright, trademark and patent law, mechanic's lien, tax status and other related legal concerns. Much of this is in the domain of other books addressing areas of special concern to consultants and specialists (who may or may not call themselves consultants but do the same kind of work under the same kind of conditions that consultants do). Thus, I exclude all material (except briefly in passing) that is not directly concerned with the agreements you ordinarily make with clients and others in the course of conducting a consulting practice.

The nature of consulting is such that it calls for offering you a large number and wide range of model contracts, formal and informal, with discussions of each and guidelines to help you select the most appropriate model for a given use and modify it adequately to meet your specific need. This book is therefore a reference book, to be turned to frequently. It is organized in 13 chapters and is designed for ease of use in finding the right models.

Included in a listing of resources is a bibliography of related books that furnish useful references on related matters; a list of computer software programs, both commercial and shareware, to help you draft suitable contracts and letters of agreement for every situation you are apt to encounter; and other references that might be useful in the future.

What Is a Contract?

If contracts were truly agreements, they would not end up in bitter court battles, as they so often do.

LAY AND LEGAL DEFINITIONS

It is easy and yet difficult to define the term *contract*. The layperson is likely to use a common term, such as *agreement,* as a definition and refer to a written instrument. Legal experts tend to shun such one-word definitions as oversimplifications and to explain that what is on paper is a *statement* of the agreement, not the agreement or contract itself. To avoid the hazard of misleading simplification, legal minds use and prescribe the use of many clarifying and qualifying terms, including *promises, offer, acceptance, consideration, meeting of the minds* and *assent,* among others. Many of these terms bear special meanings for the legal mind. There is also the matter of common law (also known as case law) in comparison to statutory law; the two legal bases affect the governance and enforceability of contracts. The question of enforceability of contracts is obviously an important factor that is at the very heart of the idea of contracting. You will encounter references to it again and again.

The challenge here is to convey to you, a businessperson and lay reader, an adequate understanding of contracts and negotiations that will lead to clear and enforceable agreements. It's too easy to become trapped in legal technicalities and philosophical abstractions or be led astray by special legal terms and concepts. We, both author and readers, are not lawyers, but we must understand the legal principles by which to negotiate and document contracts that will support precisely the exchange we intend. (Yes, let's never lose sight of the fact that a contract involves an exchange and the hope that it is always a fair exchange.) Thus, we must first gain some insight into what lawyers and law professors mean by the terms they use in connection with contracts and contract law. We cannot—nor should we try to—escape completely the argot of the legal profession.

How Practicing Lawyers Define Contracts

Lawyer-authors writing how-to books about their profession for the layperson tend to write about contracts by first raising and answering the question, "What is a contract?" Retired lawyer Harper Hamilton (a nom de plume for John Cotton Howell, who has written under his own name also) writes in his self-published *The Guide to Business Contracts,* about the difficulty defining contracts in lay terms without running afoul of legal quibbling. He points out that a contract is essentially an agreement that includes a valid and legally acceptable offer and an acceptance of that offer, with a valid consideration, entered into by parties having the legal capacity to contract. He also notes that while verbal agreements that meet the conditions stated are legal contracts, there are certain kinds of contracts that are required by law to be in writing (statute of frauds) or if oral, to be certified in writing as an agreement.

One area of dispute among lawyers, Hamilton notes, is what constitutes the consideration in a contract. As laypersons and businesspeople, most of us usually think of money as the only consideration, but many other considerations can be offered in exchange for goods or services. The consideration may, however, be other goods or services offered in exchange or even the abandonment of an earlier claim, the withholding of an action or settlement of some other matter in dispute.

In his book *Write Your Own Business Contracts,* the lawyer E. Thorpe Barrett also observes in an opening chapter titled "The Prerequisites of a 'Good' Business Contract" that a contract need not be in written form to be binding and enforceable. However, he points out that for practical purposes, all contracts should be in writing. Most lawyer-authors and experienced businesspeople appear to agree with this observation. (It may be an apocryphal story, but the late movie mogul Sam Goldwyn was long ago quoted as saying, "A verbal contract is not worth the paper it is written on." That quote has been long preserved as one of the many "Goldwynisms.")

Academic Definitions and Legal Principles

Practicing lawyers, even if retired, are likely to be more pragmatic than technical or philosophical in explaining contracts to lay readers. However, they are not the only writers on the subject. If we turn to authors who have written academic texts for law students (rather than for the enlightenment and guidance of businesspeople and other laypeople), we get into several layers of legal considerations and complexities. We are not studying law here, but it is necessary to understand at least some of the basic legal principles concerning contracts. Authors Rate A. Howell, John R. Allison and Robert A. Prentice, introducing the subject of contracts in a rather massive and typical law textbook, *Business Law Text and Cases,* sort contracts into several classes, including *express, implied* and *quasi contracts; bilateral* and *unilateral contracts; valid, voidable* and *void contracts;* and others classified by equally technical words. Probably the most useful and certainly the most easily understandable classification is *formal* and *informal contracts.* Aside from that, these authors make another, finer point of distinction about contract definitions. They raise the question of enforceability of contracts by the courts, pointing out that from a practical viewpoint, we must distinguish contracts as enforceable and nonenforceable. Enforceability requires that an agreement be a "serious" one (as distinct from a social obligation, such as a luncheon date) and that it include the following essential elements of contracts: a consideration, legal capacity to enter into contract and legality of what is agreed to under the terms of the contract (just as was noted by author Harper Hamilton in his own book). But in the more formal *Business Law Text and Cases,* the authors (all law professors) stipulate that their coverage is with reference only to contracts the courts can and will enforce—that is, those that are truly binding legally. These are the contracts with which this book is primarily concerned.

Authors Daniel V. Davidson, Brenda E. Knowles, Lynn M. Forsythe and Robert J. Jesperson, all law professors who collaborated in *Comprehensive Business Law, Principles and Cases,* offer similar classifications of contracts in their chapter "An Introduction to the Law of Contracts." The opening declaration in this book says that the law of contracts is probably the most pervasive aspect of law impinging on a person's life, including a variety of everyday activities (such as writing a check and buying insurance). These authors state that a contract can be defined as a "legally binding and legally enforceable promise or set of promises between two or more competent parties." In a simpler definition, they say that a contract is a promise for which a remedy is provided if the promise is breached.

NOTES ON SCOPE OF COVERAGE

Note that E. Thorpe Barrett believes that all contracts ought to be in writing. Most writers on the subject of contracts (and even on recommended good business practice) appear to agree with that position, even when they do not say so explicitly. As a businessman and experienced contractor, I share that opinion. I shall therefore be referring to written contracts in all cases in this book, unless noted otherwise. But since this book is addressed to and written primarily for independent consultants (including other service contractors and related service providers), the major emphasis will be on the types of contracts with which such entrepreneurs are normally concerned—that is, contracts involved primarily in the provision of professional services, rather than goods. Nonetheless, it is not possible or even desirable to confine all coverage to consulting and service agreements. We cannot avoid completely the discussion of contracts involved in the manufacture, storage or sale of goods or goods and services. To give you a good understanding of contracts and negotiations in general, it is necessary to consider contracts and negotiations involving physical property—goods—as well as those involving only services. But there are other considerations.

In many cases consultants do negotiate for and provide goods, as well as services, to their clients as an ancillary activity, and they must thus provide for this in the original contracts. Moreover, even when your consultation involves providing services only, your client may be a manufacturer or supplier of goods, and your services may entail involvement of some kind in the client's operations such that it requires you to understand contract law, practices and negotiations as they affect your client's interests. But not all the contracts into which you will enter will be with your clients. You are a business owner, as well as a professional practitioner, and will be the buyer or lessee in many transactions, entering into contracts in that capacity. You may very well wish to involve associates in projects occasionally and will thus enter into subcontracts, limited partnerships, consortia, or other agreements to work or do business with people other than your own clients.

Bear in mind that the main objective of this book is to discuss contracts that cover the many situations you may encounter in the provision of consulting services, primarily those covering delivery of services and compensation, but also the broad aspects of contracts and negotiations involving physical property and agreements on matters other than services per se.

CLARITY AND SIMPLICITY OF AGREEMENTS

In both the engineering and business worlds, any fool can devise a complex system to solve a problem or serve a need, as dramatized and illustrated so satirically by the late Rube Goldberg with his many complex and amusing inventions.

True genius lies in clear thinking to find simple answers. The simple answer is almost always far more effective, more efficient and certainly more trouble free. For example, we have yet to improve on the simple paper clip. That is why it remains the most popular item of its kind and has not been improved, except for the most minor modifications. The same principle applies equally to work systems. For example, when billing errors became a troublesome problem in one office, the cause proved to be the use of an unnecessary worksheet in preparing invoices, which required the extra work of transferring numbers from time records before transferring them once again, adding too many opportunities for error. Billing directly from a redesigned time record, thereby simplifying the procedure, reduced the work and solved the problem. Simplification solves many problems that arise from unnecessary complication.

The principle is as valid in the field of contract writing as it is elsewhere. Writing on the subject of contracts for laypeople engaged in business, Harper Hamilton and E. Thorpe Barrett express firm belief that all contracts should be written in the clearest and simplest language possible. Both state clearly that the main or most frequent problems with contracts arise from the failure to have crystal-clear agreements and state them with equal clarity in the writing.

In 1993, the U.S. Supreme Court handed down a ruling on a tax case regarding an anesthesiologist who claimed his home as a deductible item. The decision reversed the earlier decisions of the tax court and the court of appeals. In the opinion the Supreme Court made the point that their decision depended on the dictionary definitions of the word *principal,* as used in the statute's reference to "principal place of business." (The opinion cited Webster's third edition of the *New International Dictionary* [1971] as its authority for defining the word *principal.*) The Supreme Court's opinion also cited the phrase *place of business* in the statute as grounds for its decision. It went on to state that had the statute used the words *principal office,* rather than *principal place of business,* its decision would have been to uphold the lower courts.

Did the legislators writing the Tax Reform Act of 1976 deliberately choose the words *place of business,* rather than *office,* aware of the semantic consequences? Did they intend to discriminate between an office and a principal place of business or even consider that someone might later make such a discrimination? We shall never know, although it is doubtful that they could have anticipated the consequences 16 years later of their choice of language. It is thus quite possible that the law is not being applied as Congress intended it to be applied and may actually be defeating the intent of Congress in writing that law. Nonetheless, the written opinion of the Supreme Court can justify its decision on semantic grounds, demonstrating once again that our words are quite often not absolute or precise in meaning but are usually open to differences of interpretation, even when chosen with great care and much thought.

When disputes arise, you cannot depend on what you think was implied or understood tacitly, on what you claim is generally accepted practice or on anything other than what was written, how it was written and how the words are defined by the authorities in that field. Nevertheless, always remember that it is the agreement, not the paper and words, that constitutes the contract. (We tend to forget that too often when we make casual reference to "the contract.") Thus, the need for absolute specificity and clarity has two dimensions:

1. We need to be highly specific and absolutely clear in our own minds about what we want and what we agree to do for or give to the other party. That means specific and clear in *all* details.
2. We need to be highly specific and absolutely clear in transcribing and describing this agreement on paper, including all details.

It isn't enough to be clear in your mind as to what you are agreeing to without being sure it is identical with the understanding of the other party. If the two of you are not clear in your understanding of your own and the other's commitments, you will not produce a bulletproof contract. Human memory is faulty, and depending on one's interests, it is often selective. Handshake contracts are too often deadly mistakes, especially when one of the hand shakers decides that he or she is an aggrieved party and the victim of a violated agreement. However, many written contracts are not much more effective than a handshake because they are so broad or vague that they are wide open to a broad range of interpretations. Neither a court nor an arbitrator can judge what the details of the original agreement were, and the result is almost surely a compromise that satisfies neither party. The only way to avoid this hazard is by being absolutely clear in both the agreement and the written documentation of the agreement.

An Example

It is quite easy to deceive ourselves into believing that we have agreed to something in writing when, in fact, we have agreed to something entirely different. Here is one example of how easily you can intend to agree to one thing but actually agree to something quite different:

A writer of books signed a contract with a literary agent that called for the agent to represent the author exclusively, a rather typical arrangement for freelance authors. The agreement was to become effective only after a trial period in which the agent would prove himself by making a first sale for the author. Thus, the agreement specified a certain book that the author was writing. It was not *any* book but a book that was clearly and specifically identified by its highly descriptive title.

The agent was to be given three months to make the sale. He would get the customary 15 percent of the proceeds of the sale, and the author would, of course, get the remaining 85 percent.

The contract included the usual "best efforts" promises and called also for reimbursement of all related expenses—travel, per diem, postage and other—"out of revenue from the sale." And it specified that upon making the sale, the contract would be extended for four years from the date of the first sale.

What neither party realized at the time was that the contract was worded so that the extension applied to representation for only that one book named, whereas the original intention was to authorize representation for all books written by the author for the next four years.

Another unrelated weakness in the contract was the clause relating to reimbursement of expenses. It called for reimbursement "out of revenue" but whose revenue—the author's 85 percent or the agent's 15 percent? And whose expenses—the agent's or the author's?

None of this came to light until the day when the author wanted to discontinue the arrangement, long before the four years had elapsed. Until then the two had maintained an arrangement each had thought they had agreed to, but that arrangement had not been truly represented in writing. (That was particularly remarkable because one of the signatories was a professional writer who might have been expected to detect the faulty wording of the agreement.)

Levels of Detail and Variables

Specific and *clear* are relative words. They must be interpreted in the context of their usage and the practicality of their application. One would not—truly could not—enter into an agreement involving millions of dollars without ample written contracts and formal legal representation, even when the law does not require that contracts be in writing (as it does in most states for certain types of transactions and agreements). For example, when one contracts for the building of a property or construction of equipment, the contract must include *specifications*. These will usually include textual parts' descriptions, drawings, parts lists and whatever are normally accepted standards for the required quality or characteristics of such parts. That probably will include standards such as those for the hardness of steel, the types of stone, fabrics, degrees of tolerance in measurements, prescribed inspections, tests and whatever else the buyer believes is appropriate and necessary and the supplier is willing to provide.

Such details are not appropriate in the case of relatively minor purchases. You don't write specifications for standard commodities, such as a commercially available model of some piece of equipment or standard item offered to the public at large. Neither do you ordinarily retain a lawyer to write formal agreements for the sale of a VCR or the hiring of a house painter, although the wise homeowner asks for a written estimate from a house painter or other tradesman to document the agreement in some manner.

In the business world, however, you might draw up a formal purchase agreement, but it is more common to issue what is known as a *purchase order* for such goods or services. This is usually a standard, preprinted form that acts as a simplified kind of contract, and in many cases—e.g., federal government agencies—the buyer issues the purchase order in triplicate and requests the supplier to sign and return one copy, thus constituting agreement and acceptance. (The purchase order stipulates the goods or services and the consideration, which is usually money.)

It is possible that depending on the nature of what you do as a consultant, a simple purchase order, letter of agreement or letter of understanding will serve as a formal contract. As a consultant, however, you perform a custom service; that is the nature of consulting. In consulting, the work is normally contracted for: you are typically an independent contractor. Thus, contracts are a normal condition of your business relationships with your clients. But it does not end there. In business you are a buyer as well as a seller, and you probably will have occasion to award contracts to suppliers. If you have and use associates to help you with assignments that require extra help or if you are called upon to help another consultant with an overload of work, you are wise to draw up a contract specifying all the terms of the association.

You can thus see the multiple circumstances in which you should be a party to a formal agreement and a participant in the negotiations leading to it.

BOILERPLATE VERSUS CUSTOM CONTRACTS

Many practitioners use standard or *boilerplate* contracts for most of their assignments. These usually are simple contracts that only require filling in a few blanks for each application. The fact that they are uncomplicated and cover relatively small projects does not make them less binding or less important. At the same time, we must adopt a kind of "let the punishment fit the crime" standard of judgment; it doesn't make a great deal of sense to devote many hours of negotiation and writing effort to writing a contract for every small project of a few days' duration. Thus, consultants whose typical projects are small are most likely to use boilerplate, fill-in-the-blank contract forms. In fact, the purchase order (referred to in the previous section), is a boilerplate contract. It may be a form, such as the one in Figure 1.1, or something even simpler, such as Figure 1.2 (my own purchase order). Those who buy regularly and in quantity, such as manufacturers or retailers, are likely to use convenient forms such as Figure 1.1. Those who buy only occasionally, as I do, are more likely to improvise a purchase order on a letterhead.

Figures 1.3 and 1.4 are two other examples of simple, fill-in-the-blank contract forms that require little text, except for write-ins, and serve as contracts for small and informal transactions. There are, however, fill-in-the-blank contract forms that are far more complex and are all text, some of which have many pages with exhibits, seals and witnessed signatures. Figure 1.4, for example, could be broadened and amplified by additional sheets of specifications, exhibits or other ancillary data. You will see more examples of these forms later and may even use some of them as models, adapting them to whatever are your own needs.

PURCHASE ORDER

No. 101

HRH Communications, Inc.
P.O. Box 1731   Wheaton, MD 20915-1731
301 649-2499   Fax 301 649-5745

Date:

To:		Ship to:		

Qty	Unit	Description	Price	Total

Accepted by: _____

Tax:	
TOTAL:	

NOTE: Purchase order number must appear on all packages, invoices and correspondence.

Figure 1.1 A Typical Preprinted Purchase Order Form   9

HRH Communications, Inc.

P.O. Box 1731   Wheaton, MD 20915-1731

301 649-2499   Fax 301 649-5745

PURCHASE ORDER

May 22, 1994

Account #H3267ABN954

TO: A&P Computer Systems, Inc.
     12232 Floppydrive Circle
     Silicon Valley, CA 99999

   Please ship one Model 1788 CD ROM drive to above address and bill our regular account.

(Signed)

Figure 1.2 An Informal Purchase Order Made Up on a Letter

HRH COMMUNICATIONS, INC.

INSERTION ORDER	Date:
	Account Manager:

Advertiser:	Agency:
Contact:	Contact:
Address:	Address:
City/State:	City/State:
Phone:	Phone:

Size

- O Spread
- O Full Page
- O 2/3 Page
- O 1/2 Page
- O 1/2 Vertical

- O 1/2 Horizontal
- O 1/3 Square
- O 1/3 Vertical
- O 1/4 Square
- O 1/9 Square

Art

- O New
- O Pickup _____

Position

- O Cover 2   O Cover 3   O Cover 4   O Page 1
- O Other (specify)

_____

_____

_____

Issue

O Jan	O May	O Sep
O Feb	O Jun	O Oct
O Mar	O Jul	O Nov
O Apr	O Aug	O Dec
O special (specify)		

Frequency

O 1   O 3   O 6   O 12

Special Instructions

_____

_____

_____

_____

_____

Billing

Basic Rate	
Color Chg	
Position Chg	
Gross	
Agency	
Net	

Authorization:

Date: _____   Signature: _____   Title: _____

Figure 1.3 Advertising Insertion Order   11

AGREEMENT

This agreement is entered into this day of _____, 19__ between

_____ of _____

city and state

_____ and _____

of _____.

city and state

The parties agree as follows:

1.

2. This agreement is the entire agreement, with/without attachments, is the entire agreement between the parties and may be amended or altered only in writing, signed by both parties. This Agreement is governed by the laws of the State of _____.

By_____   By_____

name   name

_____   _____

signature   signature

12   Figure 1.4 A Basic Contract Form That May Be Amplified

2

The Major Items to Address

There are certain minimal requirements to constitute a written agreement as a valid contract, but there are also more subtle requirements, not rigidly defined. These can make a great difference in the effectiveness of the final document as a legal instrument.

THE BASIC REQUIREMENTS

The following list reviews and sums up the six specific items discussed earlier that are necessary to establish an agreement as a contract within the legal definition:

1. A valid offer
2. Acceptance of the offer
3. A valid consideration
4. Legal competence of the parties
5. Legality of any actions promised
6. Writing, if required by law

Theoretically, a contract comes about when one party approaches the other with an offer and the other accepts the offer. That would be the case in a simple, everyday transaction, such as the sale of some commodity. But in most transactions that call for a written contract, the contracts are negotiated; that is, an offer is not accepted immediately, but the party to whom the offer is made demurs and makes a counteroffer or asks for better terms. Negotiation or bargaining ensues. Each party wants to reach an agreement but only on acceptable terms. If agreement is reached (i.e., the parties each accept the other's offer), a contract has been concluded, even if formalization has not yet come in writing.

To qualify as a contract, the two parties must be legally competent—of legal age, of normal intellect and otherwise qualified to enter into contract—and the actions the parties promise to perform must be legal actions. If what the contract covers is illegal, it is not a valid contract and cannot be enforced. You cannot be held or hold the other party to a contract if the other party is not of legal age or if what one or both of you promise to do is illegal in some respect. That can be tricky, however. Legality may be a subtle technicality so that what originally appeared to be a perfectly legitimate and respectable undertaking is, in fact, not so.

An agreement to cooperate in smuggling drugs or defrauding a third party is an agreement to do something criminal and so invalidates the agreement as a contract. (Such an agreement would be, in fact, a conspiracy, not a contract!) But there are many far more subtle illegalities and prohibitions that might make a contract null and void when revealed.

Suppose you sign a contract with a builder to build an extra room onto your house for an office. Unfortunately, you soon discover that the builder you signed with is not properly licensed, has not gotten proper building permits or is planning to do work that violates local zoning rules and regulations. The contract is null and void, and neither of you can enforce it legally, although you might very well get involved in lawsuits, especially if money has changed hands or one of you has invested in preparatory work and commitments. No contract can overrule or prevail over the laws and powers of the governments—federal, state and local. If you have doubts about the legality of anything proposed in a contract, it is wise to check on it before signing.

ENFORCEABILITY

Enforceability is a concept that may have more significance as a legal abstraction than it has as a practical safeguard. Enforcing a contract may prove to be a Pyrrhic victory. Thus, you should never enter into a contract, any contract, no matter how well written and how heavily surrounded by legal moats and walls, if you are not satisfied that the other party sincerely wants to make an honest exchange of the considerations and means to honor the contract completely. Despite this, a contract is not worth much if it is not legally effective—that is, if the other party cannot be held to its provisions. The best contract has both factors working to make it a success: the parties sincerely intend to live up to the agreement, and the contract is drawn with proper legal safeguards in place.

In Chapter 1, you read discussions and opinions from several authoritative sources about what a contract is and what it is not—an *enforceable* contract, that is. Most contracts include many items that are not absolutely required to make it enforceable, but there are certain items that are absolutely necessary, as a minimum, to make any contract enforceable. In this chapter we will be discussing the general requirements of most ordinary, garden-variety contracts—what many refer to today as "plain vanilla" contracts. They include contracts of the most basic nature, as distinct from the much more complex, multipage contracts entered into by large organizations agreeing on large undertakings. Contracts of that nature, to be discussed later in several chapters, with all their ribbons, bows, witnesses, corporate seals and notary seals, are another matter with more complex requirements.

Stripped to essentials, the contract is deceptively simple in its requirements—in its *minimum* requirements, that is—to qualify as a legally binding agreement, one that is enforceable. However, that isn't saying a great deal, for the word *enforceable* is an abstraction, a concept that can be quite different in practical application than in theory. What can be enforced is whatever can be deduced from the wording of the contractual document as to the original intent of the parties and the applicability of the law, both common and statutory, as it can be defined or inferred from the contract language. Thus, the degree to which the language is clear or unclear will affect most directly the enforceability of the contract. In general, all that is required for a contract to be valid and enforceable is a reasonably clear statement of considerations and identification of the contracting parties, entered into in good faith by legally competent parties.

THE CONSIDERATION

Perhaps the first question raised about the legal standing of a contract—the enforceability of the contract—concerns the consideration. The *consideration,* defined in my ordinary dictionary as *recompense,* among other things, is critical in validating a contract. It is what each party will do for the other party. Remember that a contract is an agreement to make an exchange of some sort—that is, there is a consideration for each party, whether the exchange or consideration is money for goods, money for services, goods for goods or services for services. On the other hand, the consideration may be withholding or foregoing some action in exchange for something. I may agree to drop my lawsuit in exchange for some other consideration.

Thus, there is a consideration for each party. The question of consideration really embraces what the offeror gives of value in exchange for what the other promises to do. Unless there is that consideration accepted, there is ipso facto no agreement and therefore no contract. If either party fails to keep his or her promise, the contract is violated, and the other party can seek a remedy in court, ordinarily. (On the other hand, the contract may provide some specific action if either party fails to carry out his or her obligation under the contract.)

Note carefully that the consideration for each party is what he or she is to gain from the contract or what the other party promises to do or deliver. It may or may not be one's direct or complete motivation in entering into the contract, and it may or may not represent a fair value. The law normally does not presume to judge what is a fair exchange, as long as the two parties are legally competent to enter into contract and do so willingly and with full knowledge of what they and the other party have agreed to.

Because it must include in its description a specification of what each party promises to do in exchange for what the other party promises to do, the consideration is really the heart of the contract. However, there are other considerations that also are of great importance. There is, for example, the necessity to identify the two parties accurately—to specify in some detail what is to be done, when, under what conditions and other details—if the consideration is to be absolutely clear. It will not be easy to determine whether there is a contract violation by either party and enforce the contract if the descriptions of the considerations are not absolutely clear. The majority of contract disputes arise from unclear language and differing interpretations of what was agreed to.

IDENTIFICATION OF THE TWO PARTIES

Once it was a common practice in formal contracts to have an introductory paragraph that named the two parties and stated that the first party named would be "henceforth known as the party of the first part" and the other one would be "henceforth known as the party of the second part." From that point on, every statement in the contract identified the party to which it referred only by which "part" the party had been assigned. That practice, plus equally flowery and excursive language used in other areas of contract documents, swelled the size of contracts almost as much as it swelled the size of the legal fees incurred in drafting them.

Fortunately, that practice is growing more rare today, and there is gentle pressure on everyone, including the legal profession, to make an effort to write in simple, unambiguous and direct language. Happily, I find more and more lawyers and professors of law who write on the subject urging their professional fellows to follow that principle. So today a contract will usually identify the parties by name or by contractual role—e.g., "contractor" and "client" or "buyer" and "seller."

Whatever language is used, a contract must specify clearly who the contracting parties are (whether they are individuals or organizations), identifying each clearly. Figure 1.4 illustrated a simple, basic format that is generally applicable to agreements between individuals, although it may be used also for agreements between businesses or other organizations. It is, admittedly, relatively informal and lacks many of the legal refinements and safeguards found in major contracts between large organizations, but it illustrates the nature of the information a contract should present in its written form.

TERMS AND CONDITIONS

It is usually necessary to be able to establish when a contract was entered into. A contract must therefore be dated. Many people also like to indicate the date of each signature, although if there is no special dating of signatures, it will be assumed that the contract was signed by all parties on the same date that appears as the contract date.

It also is usually necessary to indicate where a contract was executed and signed and which statutes are to prevail in the event of challenge or dispute. Thus, the contract will normally identify the jurisdiction—the state, in most cases—whose laws shall govern the contract when the parties are from different jurisdictions or whatever is contracted for involves some other jurisdiction.

SIGNATURES, WITNESSES AND NOTARIZATION

Written contracts must be signed by the parties. The signatures of the parties to a contract generally are sufficient acknowledgment of the agreement by the contracting parties to make the contract binding. However, the matter is not always that simple. In many cases the requirement for evidence of agreement and acknowledgment goes beyond the mere inscription of signatures. For one thing, it is deemed prudent in many situations to have the parties' signatures authenticated by witnesses, whose own signatures are intended to certify that the contracting parties' signatures are valid and were inscribed on the document as represented. In some situations even greater certification of the signatures or of the validity of the signatures as competent to validate the contract is required.

Individuals entering into contracts in their own behalf sign their own names, of course, and that is generally, although not always, sufficient. A corporation, although a legal entity, cannot sign. An individual, an officer of the corporation or someone authorized by corporate resolution must acknowledge the corporation's acceptance of the agreement by his or her signature as a qualified representative of the corporation.

In some situations prudence, the law or one of the parties requires that signatures be notarized. For example, when some unknown party gained access to one of my own credit card numbers and managed to charge up several thousand dollars before I learned of it, I was required to sign a legal form certifying that I had not made the purchases. The credit card issuer who had sent me the form required that I sign it before a notary public and have my signature thus witnessed and certified by the notary.

A notary seal provides a neutral witness to signatures to authenticate them. However, a notary acknowledgment can also serve another purpose—that of providing a statement under oath, as in the case of the credit card fraud. I was swearing under oath that the facts were as I represented them in the document I then mailed to the bank.

Notary acknowledgments generally are required for official forms to be filed with government agencies, such as conveyances of real estate and certain other documents, especially those that must be recorded and maintained as public records. The requirement may vary from one jurisdiction to another, and it is wise to check with your own local government or an attorney to be sure that you are in full compliance. In most cases of ordinary contracts, the notary seal is not a necessity or a legal requirement. However, some people use notarization of contracts and other documents to dramatize their importance, despite the fact that the notary acknowledgment does not add legal value to the document.

Figure 2.1 illustrates a contract or agreement with witnessing signatures. Figure 2.2 illustrates the typical notary acknowledgment. Many states require that the notary acknowledgment be authenticated by an embossed seal. The notary will know the state's requirements, of course.

There are certain items required to have a document properly notarized. They are as follows:

- The name of the state where the document is signed
- The name of the county where the document is signed
- The date of the signing
- The name of the signer
- The entity in whose behalf the signer is acting
- The name of the notary public
- The state in which the notary is authorized
- The county in which the notary is registered
- The date on which the notary's commission will expire

Individuals acting for themselves as individuals acknowledge an agreement by a simple signature, witnessed or unwitnessed and notarized or not notarized. Signatures binding corporations, partnerships or any entity other than the signer personally assume special forms, whether notarized or not and whether witnessed or not. Examples of these will be offered in Chapter 11, which is devoted to illustrative samples and models for your guidance.

AGREEMENT

This agreement is entered into this day of _____, 19__ between

_____ of _____

city and state

_____ and _____

of _____.

city and state

     The parties agree as follows:

1.

2. This agreement is the entire agreement, with/without attachments, is the entire agreement between the parties and may be amended or altered only in writing, signed by both parties. This Agreement is governed by the laws of the State of _____.

By_____   By_____

         name   name

_____   _____

      signature   signature

_____   _____

      witness   witness

_____   _____

      address   address

Figure 2.1 Contract Form with Witnessed Signatures   **19**

AGREEMENT

This agreement is entered into this day of _____, 19__ between

_____ of _____
                                              city and state

_____ and _____

of _____.
        city and state

The parties agree as follows:

1.

2.   This agreement is the entire agreement, with/without attachments, is the entire agreement between the parties and may be amended or altered only in writing, signed by both parties. This Agreement is governed by the laws of the State of _____.

By_____   By_____
           name   name

_____   _____
           signature   signature
State of _____ _____, 19__

County of _____

On this date _____ appeared before me and being duly sworn did state that he/she is the person described above and signed the document in my presence.

_____
           signature
Notary Public for the County of _____, State of _____.
My commission expires _____.

PERSPECTIVES AND PERCEPTIONS

It is not unusual that two parties attempting to reach agreement do not succeed instantaneously. Each party wants to give as little and get as much as possible. Both are likely to have a range of positions, starting with the one representing the most desired point and extending to the one representing the last-ditch, won't-give-another-inch point.

Each party may or may not have decided in advance precisely what those two points are. It is likely that each knows how much he or she will yield only in the most general terms and will define his or her bottom line spontaneously as discussions ensue and it becomes clear what are the other party's positions (beginning and final), what he or she appears to want most and what he or she appears to be ready to yield to get it. (This is negotiation, to be discussed more fully in Chapter 9.)

Two perspectives inevitably exist in connection with the agreement and its purposes. Most contracts involve a buyer and a seller, with both common interests and adverse or opposed interests. Both parties want to make the trade—that's the common interest—but the buyer wants to buy at the lowest price, and the seller wants to sell at the highest price. Those are the adverse interests. How are we to be truly objective, hard as we may try, when we have some personal interest at stake? How can we help but color our judgment when we are so conscious of what a word or two may cost us?

In some contracts the parties may not be related exactly as buyer and seller; but whatever they are vis-á-vis each other, they have both common and adverse interests. Each party has or can supply something the other wants: that common interest provides the reason for bargaining and working hard at reaching agreement. But the adverse interests, which also exist, are what make it wise to document an agreement so that it does not depend on human memory and innate honesty. No matter how much each party wants what the other party offers, each will try to protect his and her personal interest. Even when the parties appear to have such a commonality of interest that the likelihood of later disputes seems minimal and agreement is reached quickly, disputes can arise later. (In fact, many negotiators would be uneasy if they reached agreement too quickly and would believe that they had not done much of a job of negotiating.)

For example, consider the case of the author and the literary agent from Chapter 1. Both parties will benefit from each sale made, and both will benefit from getting the best possible terms for each sale. And yet each wants to derive maximum benefit from each sale, which often means benefiting at cost to the other party. For example, until recent years literary agents worked for a 10 percent commission, but many agents have raised their commission rates to 15 percent and tried to persuade clients to agree to the increase, which means amending their contracts. In the author-agent case the agent wants to recover all expenses encountered in making the sale, and some agents want the author to make direct reimbursement of such expenses, in addition to any commissions earned. The agent's client, the author, sees such expenses as ordinary costs of doing business—the agent's normal overhead—and wants the agent to meet all those expenses out of commissions. This is perhaps the most readily visible concern that may scuttle an agreement or lead to problems later if not settled during negotiations. But it is not likely to be the only concern. Many differences not anticipated or envisioned at the outset of the negotiations and contract signings are likely to surface later because we humans cannot anticipate every contingency that may and probably will arise. Suppose, for example, that although the question of typical and ordinary expenses is one that was settled in the original contract, a situation arises in which there are extraordinary expenses. Who is to pay for these expenses? One party may insist that the contract provides for the other to pay them, while the other party may insist that the contract did not provide for this special contingency and thus the situation calls for a separate negotiation to settle the matter. Although there usually are a number of major considerations that every contract should address and make provision for, as far as it is possible to do so in advance, it is more common to discover that the unexpected has happened and there is no provision for it.

There always are ways to provide for the settlement of special problems if we are wise enough to anticipate them. In the previous example, one way to avoid a later problem of agent's expenses is to list the specific kinds of expenses the agent will pay for as normal overhead. Any other expense that surfaces as a necessity later will automatically call for a special and separate negotiation. That is a better approach than providing clauses to define and prescribe procedures to handle special expenses because that leaves open the probability that some special expense will arise that was not provided for specifically.

In any case you should understand that no matter what the commonalities of interests are, the other party has his or her own perceptions. They are almost surely different than yours and adverse to your own interests in some ways at least; this is a basic premise. A major necessity for negotiating a contract successfully is anticipating and understanding the other party's desires and concerns.

THE IMPORTANCE OF LANGUAGE AND MEANING

You don't have to be a Rhodes scholar to understand that contracting parties each try to negotiate the best terms for themselves. What is not obvious is that language is not the clear and precise medium of communication we like to think it is. We haggle, argue, jest, bargain and finally agree on terms, and then we try to document those terms on paper. We draft the paper, and then we again haggle, argue, jest, bargain and finally agree on the words. Then we sign the paper in good faith. We have agreement. Or do we? Do we truly understand the words of the contract precisely as the other party understands them? Did we accept the offer the other party made, or did we accept an offer we *thought* the other party made?

When I contracted to write a training manual, I specified in my original proposal my estimate of 300 pages. (When a proposal is involved, it is considered the offer and is often made part of the contract.) When my client, the U.S. Navy's Bureau of Naval Personnel, asked me to expand the book, I agreed to negotiate an amendment to the contract. But my client did not wish to spend more (or more likely, did not have the funds to do so), and so we went to see the bureau's legal counsel, who was also its contracting official. When he learned that I had made a specific estimate in my proposal, which had been accepted and was therefore part of the specification, the argument was ended. (In my work helping clients with government contracts, I have been amazed at how many contracts and proposals [offers] are written without clear quantification.)

THE POWER OF QUANTIFYING

I personally object quite strongly to using such vague generalizations as *good faith* and *best efforts* or *best commercial practice* in specifying the work or the product contracted for. These are words so open to interpretation that they are almost meaningless and all but ensure later difficulties.

The possibility of future contract disputes can be reduced significantly by the simple expedient of quantifying the offer and the acceptance. All words are abstractions, but numbers are facts. I am not sure what is meant by *best efforts* or *good commercial practice*, but I do know how to count and keep track of the hours worked or the lines of code delivered. To be properly specified, work and products must be *quantified*, as must all costs. You cannot contract for "about $10,000," and no one tries. Yet those who insist—rightly and justifiably—on specifying costs or the basis for the costs down to the fourth decimal place will use such vague terms or even no qualifying terms at all in specifying the work and product.

I refer to quantifying as a "simple expedient," but it is not always simple at all. Many find quantifying a difficult task because estimating is especially difficult or finding a unit by which to estimate or measure is not a simple matter.

Difficulty of Estimating

Most consulting work requires addressing individual problems, usually unique problems in at least some respects, if not in toto. Perhaps you generally work on an hourly or daily rate; thus, with an open-ended contract, you will work as long as the client wishes you to work.

An open-ended contract is apt to be the exception. Even when a client is perfectly willing to pay your hourly or daily fee, he or she is not likely to hand you a blank check unless you have hired on as a temporary, rather than as an independent contractor. Barring that special situation, the client will almost surely want your estimate of how long the job will take and, in many cases, will want your not-to-exceed figure as a guarantee. Some clients will not be willing to contract even on that basis but want a firm fixed price and will negotiate with you only on that basis.

In either case you usually must base your negotiation of a contract on your best estimates. You estimate how much time you will have to devote and what costs you may encounter, and you fix upon a price based on your estimate.

Estimating is always risky, and you will never completely eliminate that risk. Some of us are better than others at the art of estimating, but none of us is infallible. Sometimes we have a much better "feel" for a job than other times, which probably means that we have better or more complete data on which to base our estimates. But we still usually must estimate what will be required to get the job done.

The question is not whether risk is involved but how much risk. What is the greatest possible margin of error in your estimate? What is the worst consequence of that maximum error? Those are the factors to consider in negotiating a contract. You must cover yourself against major error, but you must accept some normal degree of risk in every undertaking.

There are some cases where estimating is especially difficult. This occurs where the definition of the problem or the result required is not completely clear. In these cases you must be especially cautious in making guarantees, such as not-to-exceed or fixed-price figures, unless you can establish some kind of safeguard. That safeguard is quantification of effort or product. Thus, estimate the units of effort or product; price them, based on your experience; and negotiate from that basis. It is far easier to estimate costs and prices realistically when you have first estimated effort on a quantitative basis. This requires translating units of effort or units of product to units of cost, which seems simple enough but rarely is. (This alone can be a subject requiring intensive negotiation.)

Finding Quantifiable Units

One immediate need in estimating is deciding—and agreeing—on the units of measure. The unit appropriate for one contract is not necessarily acceptable for the next contract. For one project you and the client may be able to agree readily on some estimate of days or hours required to get the job done, and you need merely multiply those days or hours by whatever is your standard daily or hourly rate to produce a cost figure.

But is it really that simple? Let's look at a day rate. The first thing we must do is define a day for contract purposes. We can probably agree on a standard day of eight working hours. But my own experience is that in many kinds of consulting work—and certainly in proposal writing, which is almost always done under a pressing schedule—it is almost impossible to simply shut down work at the end of eight hours. "Days" tend to be of interminable length when you work under the gun, and working days sometimes become 24 hours long. Thus, will a 14-hour day be billed at the same rate as an 8-hour day? In pressing circumstances, there also is the need to work on weekends and holidays. Are they to be worked at the same rate as weekdays?

Some consultants charge a high daily rate, and that rate applies to all days, whenever they occur and of whatever length they are. Others charge premiums for anything other than eight hours on a normal business day. A contract must spell out the definition of a day.

The same philosophy applies to hourly rates. Will an evening hour, an hour in excess of eight hours on a given day or an hour worked on a nonbusiness day be at the same rate as an hour on a business day during normal business hours?

However, hours or days of work are not always the most suitable units for estimating, pricing, defining and negotiating a contract. In many cases the units must be such that they describe the product or desired end result, such as pages, illustrations, lines of code, minutes of film or whatever best suits the product. Simply agreeing on the unit of measure may itself often involve extensive negotiation.

DEFINITIONS AND SCHEDULES

Because all the foregoing considerations can become problems and can be the basis for disputes, it is wise to include in many contracts a list of definitions that specify all matters likely to be interpreted differently by different people and under different circumstances.

It is not uncommon for a contract to include a *schedule*—whether it is known by that name or not—which describes what is to be done (if there is a greater list of functions and products than can be described simply in a paragraph). In the case of a purchase order the items would be enumerated on the lines under "description" in Figure 1.1 or as item 1 in Figure 1.4. However, the items may also be described and listed in an attachment to the contract, known as an *exhibit*. When a contract is awarded to someone who has submitted a proposal, it is not unusual to have the proposal serve as the schedule and to include it in the contract by reference.

These matters complicate the negotiations and the agreement, but they are matters that minimize later disputes and attendant difficulties. An excellent example of what can result from a failure to provide the details of a schedule and set of definitions surfaced recently in Washington when the inspector general of the Resolution Trust Corporation (RTC) revealed a scandalous condition resulting from a two-page contract awarded by the RTC to the accounting firm of Price Waterhouse. The contract was awarded directly to Price Waterhouse by the RTC, bypassing normal procedures to speed up the award. It was for photocopying and document management services and was open-ended, setting no limits on the length of the program or the charges for the services. Price Waterhouse subcontracted to another firm for photocopying services that, after being marked up by Price Waterhouse, were reported to cost RTC (i.e., the government) an average of $35 an hour for the workers doing the copying.

Types of Contracts— Practical Distinctions

There are many types of contracts, and they are distinguished from each other in both practical ways and by legal nuances.

MOST COMMERCIAL TRANSACTIONS ARE CONTRACTS

As consultants, we go about our daily business more concerned with finding clients and keeping them satisfied with our services than pondering routine business problems such as contracts. We tend not to recognize that most of the transactions to which we agree and the papers that we sign are contracts—not until we run into difficulties or discover that we shortchanged ourselves by agreeing too readily and without reading thoroughly. There are many legal distinctions among contracts, but I will touch on only the most basic ones. Later we will look more closely at the legal considerations.

One of the most important things to learn is that most of the things to which you agree are contracts, even if they are not titled "Contract" or "Agreement." In the pages that follow you will be presented with many contract models and situations. Nonetheless, it is impracticable to present samples of all possible contracts and contract problems, even if you could commit them to memory. Fortunately, it is not necessary to go quite that far in presenting a comprehensive number of examples. There is a Uniform Commercial Code, referred to casually by lawyers as the UCC or the Code. Understanding the UCC overall and being generally aware of its main provisions will provide you with a powerful tool for understanding and handling most contracts and related situations.

THE UNIFORM COMMERCIAL CODE

The Uniform Commercial Code is a substantial publication, and we shall refer to it and review it here in only a cursory fashion. It was published first in 1952 as a codification of statutory law covering business transactions. The UCC was prepared by the National Conference of Commissioners of Uniform State Laws and the American Law Institute. An official version, with minor changes, was published in 1962 and adopted by 49 of the states, with minor modifications deemed necessary by various states to suit their own needs. (For example, a state with a seaport has a few legal situations that a landlocked state does not have, and an industrial state may have different legal needs than an agricultural state.) Louisiana did not adopt the code overall, although it did adopt certain portions of it. The UCC includes ten articles (11, counting a recent addition not yet accepted by most states) that cover eight areas of commercial law and codify a wide number and variety of statutory and common laws and rules. It collects and creates statutes (specific laws) covering many principles and rules of business law that were previously based only on commercial custom or case law (precedent that is recognized by the courts generally).

In many cases contracts can include clauses that override provisions of the UCC. But the reverse is also true. Aside from creating a much more uniform legal system for the business world (itself no mean achievement), the UCC covers many sins of omission in legal documents. Where a dispute arises because the drafters of a contract have failed to specify something, the UCC provides an immediate remedy by dictating what the missing item must be. You may turn to the code for your state to solve the problem in many cases. More than one legal author strongly recommends that every businessperson have a copy of his or her state's one version of the UCC for reference.

Understand that the UCC does not attempt to dictate how business ought to be conducted. It is instead an effort to cope effectively with the many established business practices and devices, such as contracts, bank deposits and collections, commercial paper and other such matters. (A glossary of special terms used in connection with contracts is at the back of this book.)

The articles or chapters of the UCC cover eight areas of commercial law. None of the articles is restricted to coverage of contracts per se, but most of the articles have some applicability to some kinds of contracts. Thus, most of the UCC is applicable to contracts of one kind or another in one way or another. The main articles of interest follow, with cursory comments on each article. (In most cases there is much more to be said about an article. No attempt is made to offer complete descriptions but only to identify the general nature of the article.)

Article 1: General Provisions. This article explains the basic principles underlying the UCC and presents definitions.

Article 2: Sales. Most of the UCC is relevant to contracts, and a copy of your own state's version of the UCC belongs in your library. However, this article is especially pertinent to this book, with parts 2 and 3 of the article focusing especially on various aspects of contracts. Article 2 alone would provide valuable guidance to any consultant or contractor.

Article 3: Commercial Paper. This article covers negotiable instruments, which are contracts drafted especially to make clear their negotiability (i.e., use as a substitute for money).

Article 4: Bank Deposits and Collections. This article sets minimum standards for simplifying and expediting bank collections.

Article 5: Letters of Credit. This article applies to international and domestic letters of credit.

Article 6: Bulk Transfers. In this article safeguards are set against someone selling a major portion of his or her inventory, equipment, fixtures and other assets in a single transaction and vanishing with the money without paying creditors.

Article 7: Warehouse Receipts, Bills of Lading and Other Documents of Title. This includes the documents that serve as evidence of title or ownership.

Article 8: Investment Securities. This article regulates negotiation of stocks, bonds and other investment securities.

Article 9: Secured Transactions, Sale of Accounts, Contract Rights and Chattel Paper. This article is probably of greatest concern and maximum usefulness to you as a businessperson as it covers transactions that are secured in some manner, such as by chattel mortgages. It was revised in 1972, a compelling reason in itself to have an up-to-date copy of your own state's version of the UCC.

Article 10: List of Statutes Replaced by Code. This article lists the various statutes that are replaced by the UCC provisions and that are repealed by the adoption of the code by a particular state.

Article 2A: Lease Agreements. A new article, Article 2A was added to cover lease agreements, but at this time it appears to have been adopted only by Oklahoma. However, you may wish to check on your own state's status.

A Recommendation

According to many legal authorities, one of the wisest moves you can make is to get a copy of the UCC, as adopted by and used in your own state, and have a general understanding of the code. (Your local legal bookstore may carry copies of your own state's version of the code. If not, check with the secretary of state in your state capital.) Knowledge of the UCC will not make you a legal eagle, but it will give you special insight into legal aspects governing many kinds of business transactions. I must note here that the UCC does not cover all areas or situations—for example, it does not cover real estate transactions—so you must turn to other laws to guide you in those cases. However, the code can guide you in the great majority of all contract questions that arise; it is helpful to you in negotiating, drafting and evaluating any contract. In fact, it illustrates many forms for commercial transactions, and in many cases printed versions of the forms are available from the state offices that administer the contract, usually the offices of the state secretary. Among the forms are the following:

Form 1: Agreement for Sale of Goods, Memo Form

Form 2: Agreement for Sale of Goods, Bill of Sale

Form 3: Agreement for Sale of Goods, General Form

Form 4: Agreement for Sale of Goods, Short Form

Form 5: Promissory Note, by Individual

Form 6: Promissory Note, by Corporation

BASIC CLASSES AND CATEGORIES

There are many types of contracts, with some so standardized that you can buy ready-made contract forms at a stationery store and fill in the blanks to make up valid and legally binding agreements. There are many others that must be custom drafted, almost in their entirety; but even for these contracts, many models are available, along with boilerplate text that may be modified and adapted. But in this book our special interest is addressing the needs of consultants vis-à-vis contracts the independent consultant is apt to encounter. Even with that limitation, the contracts of interest here will be numerous and will fall into the following three classes:

1. General contracts that anyone in any business is likely to encounter
2. Contracts that only consultants are likely to see
3. Contracts that only consultants of a certain specialty will need

The Broad Classes of General Business Contracts

As a consultant, you are a businessperson as well as a professional specialist of some kind. You will therefore engage in many business transactions and sign many general business contracts, such as you would encounter in any business. Perhaps you don't think of most of these documents as agreements or contracts. But if you rent office space, you probably signed a lease. It was an agreement, with an offer, acceptance and consideration, and therefore is a contract. It is just as important to read a lease carefully and understand it before signing as it is with any other contract. Otherwise the day may come when your landlord suddenly says, "Whoa! You can't do that. Read your lease." Leases are negotiable, too, just as is any other contract. But here is a list of just a few of the general business contracts you may encounter routinely as the result of simply being in business:

- Leases for occupancy of business premises
- Leases for furniture, fixtures, or equipment of any kind
- Partnership agreements
- Purchase orders and sales agreements
- Promissory notes
- Letters of acceptance
- Assignments
- Employment contracts
- Agreements not to compete

In these situations you may be on either end—buyer or seller, lessor or lessee, promisor or promisee, employer or employee. For most of them you will be able to use form contracts you can modify to suit the individual situation. In fact, most lawyers keep a store of models that they can adapt easily; this is especially easy to do today, with modern computers in every office. (Samples and models are provided later in Chapters 11 and 12.) There also is software you can buy that will provide you with models and templates to enable you to create most kinds of contracts. (Suggestions on such software are made in "Resources" at the back of this book.) But let's look now at the kinds of contracts that you are most likely to need to support your consulting practice.

Contracts for Independent Consultants

As an independent consultant, you also are an independent contractor, for your typical work assignment or sale to a client usually culminates in a contract, formal or informal, to perform certain specified work or achieve a certain specified result. A consultant is a highly specialized expert in some field, who is called upon to assist others who have a need for someone more highly specialized (e.g., a security specialist will be asked to help a security officer improve a security system). However, the word *consultant* has become a general term, applied to a wide variety of special services that may vary a great deal. This leads to an equally broad variability in consultants' needs for contracts and contractual documents. Your work is typically custom work and varies so much that you may very well need different contract forms for different situations. This may be a significant factor in your need to negotiate the right agreements and the right terms for whatever it is you do for clients. It is thus necessary to have a broad appreciation of a variety of contractual forms available for various kinds of needs.

Some consultants are much more highly specialized than others. If you identify yourself as a *management consultant,* you are probably offering a wide variety of possible services, whereas if you are a *marketing consultant,* you are probably more specialized and if a *computer consultant,* even more so. Even within those categories, you may be specializing further. Many fields, such as computers, have become so diverse that it is almost impossible to be a generalist in those fields.

In some cases the service is so highly specialized that it is almost a commodity rather than a custom service, and the practitioner then tends to develop his or her own set of standard forms that are suitable for virtually all assignments. Only a few blanks need to be filled in. The executive search consultant, for example, usually provides a service that is highly specialized and uniform.

The nature of the specialty or the degree to which your work is specialized may dictate the duration of your average assignment, and this alone may be a factor affecting your contracting needs. If you are a consultant for whom many assignments are only a few hours or a day or two long—a freelance copywriter, for example—you are unlikely to need complex contracts or very formal documentation. A purchase order or simple letter of intent or letter of agreement usually is adequate. You are also likely to be dealing with individuals and very small businesses rather than with large organizations, and this, too, tends toward simple contracts and informal documentation. If you are either this type of consultant or the highly specialized one whose service is so uniformly structured that it barely qualifies as a custom service, negotiations are often almost nonexistent. You probably have or should have standard rates, standard agreements and standard forms that the typical client accepts or does not.

On the other hand, if you are a consultant whose typical assignments run to months of work—even to years, in some cases—you are likely to need fairly complex and detailed agreements with appropriate documentation. If you are a computer consultant who writes software and adapts software to your client's special needs, you may work for months on an assignment. If you are an editorial consultant who helps clients develop newsletters, catalogs, training systems, manuals and other major items, you may also undertake many lengthy assignments. If your work is of that nature, you may be required to write proposals to compete for the work, and they become the basis for contracts that usually are fairly complex, involve negotiation and are documented quite formally.

You may be one of those consultants whose projects tend to fall between these extremes. In that case your assignments usually are on the order of several days to several weeks at most. Proposal-writing projects, for example, usually have that kind of duration and may be awarded after more or less formal negotiations but usually with purchase orders or letters of agreement as documentation.

Consulting practices vary in the nature of the kinds of markets practitioners choose to pursue. I chose to include government agencies as a significant part of my market. (In fact, for a long time it was the major part of my market.) All work with government agencies tends to be fairly formal, although there has been a most distinct trend toward simplification in government agencies over the past several decades. For example, the typical government contract today is no longer the thick recitation of a schedule describing in detail what is to be done. Today's contract may be a simple, single-sheet, standard form that bears all the necessary signatures and includes the supplier's proposal as the schedule of what is to be done—the agreement representing the offer and acceptance. Thus, contract negotiation centers on the proposal, which, as part of the contract by reference, must be revised to reflect the results of the negotiation and agreement reached. The contract also includes the boilerplate of the relevant government statutes and regulations that may be physically enclosed but are usually included by reference, having been first stipulated in the original solicitation.

Thus the majority of consultants tend to work under formal service contracts, or should do so. (Many unfortunately have learned first-hand the hazards of failing to have an agreement on paper.) These contracts will tend to be professional services agreements of various kinds, since there are variants possible. Thus your contract needs as a consultant can run the gamut, depending on the nature of your consulting work. The following are the kinds of contract forms you are likely to encounter and need. They tend to fall into several distinct classes, although each class has variants, with their frequency of use (hence the priority of choice) probably in the following order:

- Purchase orders
- Employment contracts
- Firm fixed-price contracts
- Labor-hour contracts
- Task order contracts
- Cost reimbursement contracts

However, in many cases, especially where the purchase is to be relatively small, simpler contracting forms and formats are chosen (e.g., the purchase order).

Purchase Orders. For contracts of less than $25,000, a federal government agency may elect to use a government purchase order, further simplifying the process. (The contracting officer *may elect* to use a purchase order but is not *required* to do so. He or she may opt, at his or her discretion, to use a more formal contracting procedure and form.)

Ironically, some corporations in the private sector today are more bureaucratic than the government is and will formally negotiate even small contracts and insist on formal contract documents. A formal purchase order form suitable

PURCHASE ORDER   No. 101

HRH Communications, Inc.
P.O. Box 1731   Wheaton, MD 20915-1731
301 649-2499   Fax 301 649-5745

Date:

To:

Attn:

Qty	Unit	Description	Price	Total

Accepted by:_____

Tax:	
TOTAL:	

NOTE: Purchase order number must appear on all
invoices and correspondence.

34   **Figure 3.1 Purchase Order Form for Services**

for service contracts appears in Figure 3.1. Provision is made for entering the unit of measure—hours, days, pages, etc.—the number authorized, the unit prices and the totals. The form can be adapted as necessary for fixed-price projects and to accommodate any notations or special notes. Again, you may be the issuer or the recipient of a purchase order. If you are the recipient and yours is the kind of practice where assignments are frequently in the form of purchase orders, it is important to check the arithmetic in all purchase orders of this type, making sure the extensions, subtotals and total are all correct. Mistakes happen in these matters, and they can cause everyone a great deal of grief later.

In general, purchase orders are used to purchase common commodities and are used for relatively small purchases where the various governments are involved. (State and local governments will have much lower ceilings on purchase orders and small purchases than the federal government does.) There are exceptions, in the case of the federal government. Some agencies may issue an overall contract or a task order contract and then issue a purchase order for each task assigned. In the case of the contracts issued by the Federal Supply Service as "schedules," the purchase orders issued under a given schedule may be much larger than $25,000, even several times that amount.

Private-sector organizations have freedom to do as they wish, and some may use purchase orders for large commitments, especially if the commitment is one for relatively routine services that do not require detailed explanation.

In the case of the federal government and some other organizations, the purchase order may be issued in a number of parts—i.e., copies—and used as an invoice by the recipient. You sign and return all but two copies. One of the copies is for your records; the other is used as an invoice when you have completed the assignment. But this creates a possible disadvantage for you. If the assignment is lengthy and you have not negotiated an agreement for progress payments, you probably will have to wait until you have finished the job before you get paid. That is a potential drawback in using purchase orders for long-term jobs, unless you have made special arrangements. (Ordinarily, you don't negotiate terms for purchase orders.)

Employment Contracts. Due to the nature of some kinds of consulting, the attitude of the IRS and relevant laws in their current form, consultants who accept assignments of a certain kind (usually technical and professional specialists) are often forced to enter into agreements in which they are temporary employees—W-2 workers—rather than independent contractors—Form 1099 workers—which then invokes a need for other kinds of contracts or special clauses in their basic contracts. If you are in a situation of this kind, you may be entering into such a contract with a client or with a broker who hires you as a temporary employee and assigns you to his or her client, to work on the client's premises. In addition to the standard needs of all contracts, these contracts include, but are not restricted to, clauses or separate contracts covering the following matters:

- Working hours
- Compensation
- Term of contract
- Confidentiality/nondisclosure agreement
- Patents and invention agreement
- Noncompete agreement
- Per diem expenses
- Travel expenses
- Termination
- Liquidation clauses for breach of contract

Such contracts typically provide little or no fringe benefits (some have a limited program), termination without notice, per diem and travel expenses only if the job is too far for daily commuting and almost always a prohibition on *poaching*—approaching and trying to do business directly with a client—if you are on a third party's (e.g., a broker's) payroll. That noncompete agreement you are asked to sign is usually for some period after employment, generally about one year, although many consultants try to have it cut to six months and many brokers would like to make it effective for two years. The clause or contract in regard to inventions and patents is intended to reserve rights to the employer or client should you happen to develop a patentable device while employed on the job.

Firm Fixed-Price Contracts. Firm fixed-price or "for the job" contracts are favored by many purchasing agents and contracting officials if their procurement is feasible—i.e., services can be procured via competitive bids, with awards to the lowest bidders. That makes life much simpler for those who must manage and administer purchasing and contract awards. It also is the route to getting the most for the least cost; however, it isn't always a practical method for buying consulting services. Consulting by nature—almost by definition—is custom work, and in most cases it is difficult to estimate the full cost of custom work. If buyers insisted on firm fixed prices (i.e., bids) from competitors for consulting work, the bids would be on the high side, with occasional *low-ball bids*—unrealistically low bids from neophytes—that would create new problems of pressure to award contracts likely to result in project failures. (There are numerous *horror stories* of disastrous projects that resulted from trying to award custom projects by competitive sealed bids.) Firm fixed-price contracts thus tend to be the exception much more than the rule for most kinds of consulting work.

Labor-Hour Contracts. There are many occasions when the client simply wants a specialist to provide a number of hours of specified services, such as writing, computer programming or illustrating. Such a service often is contracted for under an agreement known appropriately enough as a *labor-hour contract*. This kind of contract calls for you to agree to work for a specified hourly rate for some indefinite number of hours, usually within stated bounds.

The reason a firm fixed-price contract is not used in these cases is simply that the client is not sure how many hours are needed. The contract will be based on the client's estimates of hours required in each category or on your own estimates made in response to the client's request, often as part of your proposal. This is one of a class of contracts sometimes known as *indefinite quantity contracts* because the client doesn't know in advance just how many hours of each class of service will be needed. If the client's description of need is detailed enough, you may think that you know enough to come up with a *not-to-exceed* top figure or even a fixed price for the job. The client may very well prefer to leave the total number of hours required open and thus will offer an indefinite quantity contract, usually with some provision in which the client guarantees a minimum number of hours and limits your commitment to some maximum number of hours.

In such contracts, hours generally are the sole chargeable item, with no significant costs for materials anticipated, but there may be travel and per diem costs in some cases. However, note that the billing unit for invoicing a client in this type of contract is the *loaded* labor hour; that is, it is the hourly rate charged to the client, which includes salary, overhead and profit. If you pay yourself $30 an hour, have an overhead rate of 100 percent and demand a pretax profit of 15 percent, you will quote $69 ($30+$30+$9) per hour in negotiating the contract. You need not explain the rate but merely state it as your hourly billing rate.

The term of the contract should be stated, but the difficulty of stipulating the precise number of hours required is an element, too. It is difficult to be sure precisely how long the contract will take, so the end date may be somewhat speculative. However, one way to overcome the problem is to make provision for renewal, if necessary. This usually is quite easy to do by inserting an option clause that may be exercised with a simple written notice.

Task Order Contracts. Task order contracts are also like indefinite quantity contracts, but they do not specify work to be done, except in the most general terms. The task order contract is an agreement (sometimes referred to as a *basic ordering agreement* or *BOA*) to accept tasks assigned by the client as the need arises.

In the usual practice the task order contract provides that the client will call on you to review a description of some task to be performed, and you will respond with an estimate or perhaps a simple letter proposal. The client may accept your estimate and authorize work to proceed (sometimes using purchase orders), or he or she may disagree with your estimate and wish to negotiate.

This contract thus guarantees you the assignments, while it guarantees the client that you will always be available to perform the tasks and that your estimates will be based on hours, with or without other costs (e.g., material) at the agreed to rate(s).

Rate schedules in such contracts need not be based on hourly labor rates but may list rates on some other basis, such as pages of copy, square inches of drawings, lines of code or other units of measure. In practice, many of these contracts list both hours and other units. For example, a publications consultant may be asked to list hourly and/or page rates for writing, editing, typing, illustrating and other functions involved in his or her work. As in the labor-hour contract, you agree to perform all tasks using these rates and you only need to specify billing rates, which should include overhead and profit.

You may have a task order contract exclusively with a client, or you may be one of several contractors. Some clients like to have more than one contractor available on a task order basis to maintain a competitive element in the bids and assignments, or they have tasks arising too frequently to depend on one contractor to handle all their needs. Keep this possibility in mind when negotiating these contracts.

The question of term also must be addressed. Usual practice is to provide for an annual term, often with options for additional years (e.g., a second and third year), with or without renegotiation. However, the purpose of providing option clauses for additional years is to avoid the time, labor and expense of negotiating a new contract every year.

Cost Reimbursement Contracts. Many contracts have been let on a cost reimbursement basis, especially by the government. The reason for this contracting philosophy is that it is all but impossible to make more than wild guesses as to what is required to do the job. The cost reimbursement contract has a few variations, as do others described here, and it is probably best known in the version commonly referred to as the *cost-plus contract.* In any of its versions, it solves the problem of contracting for a difficult-to-define result and an unpredictable cost. You probably will never be offered a cost-plus contract, but you ought to understand the genre.

Cost-plus is an abbreviated form of the *cost-plus-fixed-fee contract.* The typical contract provides a fee to the contractor that generally is in some proportion to the total dollar value of the contract. In the cost-plus contract the client guarantees you some fixed fee, regardless of the total dollar value of the contract, but also promises to reimburse you for all your costs. For example, suppose that you guess that the contract total will be $500,000, and you ask for a fee equal to about 15 percent of that figure or $75,000. You are to get a $75,000 fee whether the total of the contract ultimately proves to be $200,000 or $1,000,000. The client, however, will demand (justifiably) that you reveal your direct and indirect costs and perhaps will demand the right to audit your books and verify the rates you quote. (Many consultants choose to avoid such contracts because they are reluctant to open their books to clients.)

That sounds like an ironclad proposition. How can a contractor lose? In some early versions the contractor's security was absolute: the client would reimburse all direct costs and overhead costs without limit. However, many versions later he or she restricted the amount of overhead and paid only the ceiling value specified by the contract. If the contractor's overhead is greater than the ceiling, the contractor cannot rise above the established ceiling and has to "eat" the difference.

Fees in cost-plus contracts also can vary. Some clients guarantee the contractor only a small fixed fee and award additional fees if and as merited by the contractor's performance in *cost-plus-award-fee* or *cost-plus-incentive-fee* contracts.

Hybrids and Variants. Philosophically, there are only two kinds of contracts: fixed-price and cost reimbursement. All contracts are variations of these contracts, many of them hybrids bearing elements of both. Purchase orders are fixed-price contracts. Task order contracts are fixed-price contracts that are hybridized with both the indefinite-quantity and fixed-price ideas, because they are simply a convenience in negotiating a fixed price for each of the various tasks that arise. Labor-hour contracts are indefinite quantity contracts with cost reimbursement. There are many possible variations, and you may run into many customized versions of these contract forms. It is important to grasp exactly what you are trading off in each case as you try to negotiate wisely and effectively.

4

Legal Distinctions and Remedies

Some of the distinctions among contracts reflect fine legal points, points that help you understand the legal implications and remedies available to resolve disputes.

CLASSES AND CATEGORIES

In Chapter 3 we examined contracts primarily with respect to their applications—e.g., task order, fixed-price and cost reimbursement contracts. However, they can be identified by other kinds of descriptive and distinguishing traits by which the law characterizes them, especially to define their legal status. These categories classify contracts in a different and more subtle, but no less important, way. Understanding these finer distinctions will help you better understand contracts in general. They will also help you understand how lawyers and judges look at contracts when disputes arise and they have to scrutinize the nature and legal status of an agreement, the obligations of each party under the agreement, the law as it applies to the situation, the remedies provided by law and what appears to be a just solution in each case.

Unconscionable Contracts and Exculpatory Clauses

In general the courts do not attempt to judge the fairness or unfairness of any specific contract. But many contracts are of greater benefit to one party than to the other as a consequence of each party's negotiating skills, business judgment and perhaps sheer chance. That is the nature of a free enterprise system, where each party seeks whatever advantages are possible. However, the courts are concerned with unconscionable contracts, as you will see in some of the discussions that follow. Where one party has taken a grossly unfair advantage (as in the case of a high-pressure salesman who sells something at a monstrously inflated price and usually with gross misrepresentations to a poor and only semiliterate victim), the court usually will take appropriate corrective action, using one of the several options discussed later in this chapter. This kind of abuse is found most commonly in sales contracts, but the principle of correcting such abuses is sometimes applied by the courts to other kinds of contracts. Innocently signing away your rights does not necessarily mean that they are not recoverable. The principle applies equally in cases where one party takes advantage of superior knowledge, strength or position to force unfavorable (and sometimes illegal) terms on another.

A similar technique is found in the use of exculpatory clauses, such as those that guarantee to hold the other party harmless, limit or disclaim liability and otherwise attempt to provide escape hatches at the other party's expense. These are not by nature illegal, but they, too, are often questionable and often rejected by the courts, despite the other party's signature agreeing to them.

Understanding the Legal Considerations

In previous chapters I mentioned various classifications of contracts and offered some of the legal/technical terms but did not offer any serious discussion of them. Thus, a few of the special terms you will encounter here may be slightly familiar. In some cases the terms used add little to your understanding, except to make the language of lawyers and courts easier to understand when they discuss legal aspects. In other cases the added information is helpful in understanding the underlying rationales and, more important, what you can and cannot expect if and when you are involved in a contract dispute.

The more you understand of the law and legal reasoning with regard to contracts, the better equipped you will be to negotiate your own contracts and avoid contract problems. It is therefore more than helpful to take a somewhat closer look at contract types and contract law and to cite some examples of the various types now and then later when discussing remedies. Some of the classifications are of only passing interest, for they are contract forms not often encountered by consultants. Others are of much greater interest to consultants, and we will look more closely at these forms and consider some illustrative examples.

There is no particular significance to the order or sequence in which the discussions are presented, and none should be inferred, except where some relationship is obvious or is pointed out. You will find that the distinctions between some contracts are quite subtle, and it may not always be clear why a contract is identified as it is. The definition of a unilateral contract, for example, appears to defy the basic definition of any contract, since it lacks a certain one of the several elements normally required.

After we have laid the groundwork with these discussions, we will examine the various remedies provided by law to resolve disputes as equitably and justly as possible.

Formal and Informal Contracts

Formal contracts belong more to the past than to the present. They ordinarily include a seal as well as the antiquated "wherefores" and "whereases," the ornate definitions of the people involved as "the party of the first part" and "the party of the second part" and the "hereafter known as" phrases to be sure that there can be no doubt as to who is who in the references to follow. In the early times of common law, a contract was not valid or enforceable unless it had a seal. The word *formal* has survived, but in the modern context a formal contract is one that is in conformance with some specified form, with a seal, but not necessarily couched in highly ornate language. Today most contracts do not require a seal, and those without a seal are known as *informal* or *simple* contracts. The trend is decidedly toward informal contracts, except in those few cases where a formal contract, with seal, is required by some specific law.

What is a seal? There is some misunderstanding of that word. A seal originally was a blob of wax, usually colored red, in which an impression of some sort was made, often by a signet ring or similar device. Later (and still in use today) a seal appeared as a raised impression on a sheet of paper, made by a tool designed for the purpose and identifying the organization or signer. However, even that is not necessary today. One's signature and the word *seal* is generally acceptable now when a seal is required.

Bilateral versus Unilateral Contracts

By now you are aware that a contract must include an offer, an acceptance and a consideration, three of the mandatory conditions of a contract. These conditions, however, must sometimes be qualified because they are not always clear-cut. One common variant is the unilateral contract.

The typical contracts we have discussed tend to be bilateral. The idea is simple enough: it is an agreement wherein each party, an offeror and an offeree, makes a firm promise to the other. For example, I promise to pay you a specified sum of money for a specified service, and you promise to provide that service. I may or may not pay you a retainer upon signing; but my promise to pay and your promise to perform are consideration and acceptance, and they are normally sufficient, to make the contract binding.

If you accept my offer by agreeing or promising to provide the specified service, we have a bilateral contract. If, however, I promise to pay you some sum of money *if* you provide a certain service, our contract is unilateral because you have not accepted my offer. Only when and if you provide the service have you accepted my offer.

Unilateral contracts usually exist when there is some question as to whether the offeree can provide what the offeror wants. If I were a collector of rare coins and offered a sum of money to anyone who provided a certain coin, the finder would accept my offer by presenting me the coin and would be entitled to collect what I offered. Therefore, we would have completed a valid contract. You might have agreed to seek the coin, but I would not be obligated to pay you for your effort; I offered to pay you for the coin, not for your effort in finding it. I would thus be required by contract to pay you only for delivering the coin to me. The distinction can become a bit blurred if we are not careful. If I wish to enter into this kind of contract, I must be careful to make it crystal clear that I wish to pay only for an item—some goods or service—delivered to me and for nothing else. If you wish to accept such a contract, you must understand that even if you sign it and declare your intention of delivering what I asked for, you do not have a contract until you make that delivery. It is only when you deliver the item called for that you have accepted my offer and concluded a contract.

Contests are good examples of such contracts. The offeror promises certain rewards to those contestants who can produce the numbers the offeror selects. Games such as Lotto also exemplify these contractual terms; those who have the set of numbers called and come forward to claim the rewards are accepting the unilateral contract originally offered.

You may ask why the term *unilateral contract* is not an oxymoron, since to qualify as a contract, the agreement must include an offer and an acceptance as two of its conditions. Until the offeree delivers what the offeror has asked for, there is no contract. A unilateral contract is thus a contradiction in terms, at least until it has been accepted and so validated.

Later in this chapter we will discuss contracts of adhesion, and you may be struck by some similarities between the unilateral contract and the contract of adhesion. There is a resemblance between the two in one respect, but there is also a most definite difference.

True unilateral contracts are not common in consulting, where the basic item traded is some specialized service. It is therefore unlikely that you will run into them in your everyday business dealings. They are much more common in fields such as real estate, where conditional contracts are commonly offered (e.g., commissions paid upon producing a qualified buyer) or where finder's fees are offered to anyone who can find whatever the offeror is looking for. However, even if you are never in a position where you might enter into a unilateral contract, as a consultant to others in business, you should have a good general knowledge of all contracts.

Express, Implied and Quasi Contracts

The distinction between an express contract and an implied contract is quite simple. An *express contract* is one in which the parties have clearly stated their intentions—verbally or in writing—to constitute an agreement (e.g., an offer to buy or sell goods or services at some stated price and terms, with acceptance and compliance with the other requirements). An *implied contract* (also called *implied in fact*) is one in which the intentions of one or both parties can be inferred, even if not stated clearly, from relevant facts, such as the direct actions of the parties, the history of their relationships, circumstances or other factual indicators.

At Ford Philco some years ago, a consultant, who was highly skilled in solid-state electronics design, spent every Wednesday afternoon at the plant, available to assist employees with relevant design problems. The staff engineers had been advised that this weekly service was available to them. The consultant was therefore present without being summoned each week, and he expected to be paid for his time for each Wednesday afternoon; he didn't need to have a specific agreement for each Wednesday. The client, Ford-Philco, was not entitled to refuse to pay on the grounds that there was no agreement for the most recent Wednesday afternoon. The contract was clearly implied and of long standing. To terminate the arrangement, the client would have to specifically notify the consultant that he was to discontinue his weekly sessions.

If I were working on a client's premises on a proposal that I could complete only by remaining there after hours, I would use my own judgment as to what was implied in our contract, based on the premise that I had promised to deliver the proposal in time to meet the deadline. If no one was there to authorize extra hours, I would still do whatever had to be done to meet the deadline, as I thought implied by our contract.

The court, in a dispute, will try to judge the *intentions* of the parties in deciding whether a contract exists. If I submit a proposal to a client and the client responds with a letter that appears to be an acceptance, a court may uphold my contention that a contract was thus entered into. If the client argues that he or she did not really intend to agree because of his or her reservations about the plan, the court will try to base a decision on what the client's intentions *appeared to be*—i.e., upon the reasonable perception of the two parties' intentions. The apparent intentions will be the ruling criterion because the court recognizes the impossibility of knowing what was actually in the minds of the parties and can therefore only judge and be ruled by the manifestation of the parties' intentions, sometimes referred to as the *meeting of minds*.

A quasi contract falls outside these definitions of express and implied contracts. An implied contract is as much a true contract as is an express contract, once it is confirmed as implied in fact. It may even be a written contract that implies much that is not specifically written there and thus goes well beyond what is written. A quasi contract, however, is not a true contract. It is a contract implied in law, rather than in fact, and imposed by the court as in the interests of justice. For example, it is wrong for someone to profit from what is called *unjust enrichment*.

For example, a classic case illustrating this idea is that of the physician who happens upon an accident or other emergency and renders necessary medical aid to a victim. Of course, the two parties—doctor and patient—had no prior intention of entering into a contract of any kind, express or implied, and did not do so specifically. At the same time, the physician is justified in providing his or her services, under the circumstances, and in billing the patient and collecting a normal fee for services rendered. A court is likely to judge that a quasi contract exists and must be satisfied.

This does not mean that you may not occasionally have a windfall, but you may not do so by taking advantage of another party. Suppose a team of workers came to your house and built a screened porch while you watched calmly, knowing that the men had made a mistake. Because you deliberately permitted that mistake to enrich you unjustly, the provider could take you to court and recover some fair value set by the court as settlement of a quasi contract between you and the porch builders. If you had not been home and the work had been done in your absence, the provider probably could not have recovered, unless you were willing to pay something.

In the end all three types of contracts, once established, result in the binding and enforceable obligations of both parties, as stipulated or as interpreted by a court.

Valid, Void, Voidable and Unenforceable Contracts

A valid contract does not need further definition, except to note that it meets all the conditions cited earlier as required to constitute a contract and is therefore enforceable. On the other hand, contracts in which any of the necessary elements are not met are voidable and can be set aside or made void. The most common reasons for voiding a contract are that one of the parties was not legally competent to contract (e.g., a minor or mentally incompetent person); the contract was an agreement to do something illegal, such as a price-fixing conspiracy; or fraud was used to induce one party to sign (e.g., false representations were made by one of the parties to induce the other to sign). Such a contract is often referred to by the courts as a *void contract,* paradoxical as that term may seem. Even contracts in which one party should be but is not licensed to do whatever the contract calls for may be declared void in some jurisdictions as contracting for an illegal act.

Contracts with usurious elements—interest rates greater than those allowed by law—are void due to illegal elements, although this is a rather complex subject because usury laws vary widely from state to state. There are situations where a contract may be exempt from usury laws, such as may be the case with short-term, high-risk loans.

Many contracts include covenants not to compete. This is common when one sells a business and agrees in writing to refrain from entering into a new, competitive venture for some period of time, such as five years. It is also rather common for brokers who subcontract with others to ask subcontractors to agree in writing to refrain from approaching the broker's client directly for future contracts or other employment. Some of these restrictive covenants are illegal and can render a contract void.

On a par with contracts to commit illegal acts are contracts to commit torts. Defined loosely, a *tort* is a harm done to another that is actionable in a civil action, rather than a criminal one. An agreement to discredit someone's good name or slander someone in some manner, for example, would be a voidable contract.

A void contract is automatically unenforceable, but the term *unenforceable contract* normally is used with reference to a contract that was or appeared to be valid when signed, but circumstances afterward rendered the contract unenforceable. For example, the bankruptcy of one party who owes another money usually makes the contract unenforceable. But a contract that a court holds to be *unconscionable*—excessively and unjustly in favor of one of the parties at the expense of the other—may be made at least unenforceable unless modified to satisfy the court's objection. If, for example, a vendor takes advantage of another's innocence to charge a price far in excess of the fair market value, a court may choose to declare the contract unenforceable.

Compelling another to sign a contract through threats, fear or other pressure—under duress, that is—also renders a contract void, if the duress can be proved. Duress is not easy to prove, and it is well known that individuals trying to have contracts set aside often claim duress as a reason for voiding the contracts.

Contracts of Adhesion

The *contract of adhesion* is one in which one party offers the other a fixed-form agreement on a take-it-or-leave-it basis—i.e., without negotiation of the terms. Most of us sign such agreements frequently (e.g., when we sign standard agreements when checking ourselves or someone else into a hospital or when we leave an automobile for troubleshooting and estimating the type and cost of repairs, as well as on many other occasions). If you contract with federal agencies, you generally sign several of these agreements, in addition to the main contract. They are routine and widely accepted as a necessary procedure for certain kinds of activities. In fact, you may be using some standard contracts of adhesion yourself, such as a subscription to a newsletter or a minimum charge for an estimate.

On the other hand, because contracts of adhesion are those in which one party is in a dominant bargaining position, they are also contracts in which the dominant party can take undue advantage of the other's disadvantaged position to impose unconscionable conditions. Often the other party is not knowledgeable enough to realize that grossly unfair conditions are being imposed or that negotiation is even possible, much less necessary. These are the contracts that may be disputed and taken to court for adjudication of their validity. In fact, some state courts have held these contracts to be inherently unconscionable and have declared them void.

Earlier I mentioned that there is an apparent similarity between the contract of adhesion and the unilateral contract. They are similar in that both are fixed offers by the offeror that the offeree can accept or reject but cannot modify or negotiate. The difference is that in the unilateral contract, the offeree does not accept the contract technically, even if he or she signs it, until he or she delivers what the offeror has called for. Until then, a contract does not exist as such. In the contract of adhesion the offeree accepts the offer immediately, on signing, and a contract then exists immediately.

Executory and Executed Contracts

Once signed, a contract becomes executory; once the performance contracted for is complete, it is an executed contract. The latter term, however, applies to each party, so that if only one party has completed what he or she agreed to do, the contract is executed only with respect to that party.

DISPUTES AND REMEDIES

Contract disputes are inevitable, at least occasionally. They aren't necessarily due to the failure of one party to live up to the terms of the contract (a cynical effort to benefit at the expense of the other party) or other deliberate evasion. They do not always lead to bitterness and legal battles—or to courtrooms. A great many contract disputes result from unanticipated events and simple misunderstandings, and often the parties can resolve the disputes amicably and honorably. Ben Franklin had something to say on the subject of disputes arising out of partnership agreements. His advice is as true in its observations and as sensible today as it was 200 years ago.

> Partnerships often finish in quarrels, but I was quite happy in this, that mine were all carried on and ended quite amicably, owing, I think, a good deal to the precaution of having very explicitly settled in our articles everything to be done by or expected from each partner. So there was nothing to dispute, which precaution I would therefore recommend to all who enter into partnerships.

A good example of a modern dispute settled amicably was offered in Chapter 2, which describes a dispute with the Bureau of Naval Personnel about the number of pages to be included in a manual written for the bureau. A simple discussion among the principals, supervised by the bureau's legal counsel (and contracting officer), who acted as arbitrator, quickly resolved the dispute without rancor. It was clear that there were only two reasonable solutions, since the contractor had fulfilled the contract and delivered what it called for: (1) the bureau's staff could agree to a contract amendment and pay for additional work, as the contractor proposed, or (2) they could withdraw their request for additional pages and accept what had been delivered as satisfactory completion of the contract. Unfortunately, disputes are not always settled that easily, nor is the case for one party or the other always that clear-cut.

As laypersons we tend to think of all action in which lawyers and courts get involved as legal remedies. In fact, remedies for breaches of contracts can be legal or equitable remedies, which are not the same thing. Generally speaking, courts may use their powers *at law* and employ legal remedies—usually the payment of money damages to the injured party. When this is not an appropriate or adequate compensation, the court may use its powers of equity to employ other remedies—equitable remedies.

Legal Remedies

The most common basis for settlement of a contract dispute is the payment of damages as a legal remedy. Where the dispute winds up in a lawsuit, the intent of the law is to determine to what extent the plaintiff has been damaged (if, indeed, the plaintiff prevails) and to attempt to set a fair money value on the damage. However, there are several kinds of damages, including liquidated, compensatory, nominal, consequential and punitive damages.

Liquidated Damages. *Liquidated damages* are damages agreed upon in advance and documented in a contract as the basis for settlement should the contract be breached. This is a well-advised precaution when one or both parties foresee a substantial possibility that the contract will not be completed or perhaps not completed on schedule. Including such an advance agreement helps to avoid or at least minimize the probability of a dispute, since compensation for a breach is all but automatic. It is not a guarantee, however; in any given case, the injured party may decide that the agreed-upon damages are inadequate, or the other party may decide that they are excessive. This will result in a dispute, which will have to be settled in negotiation, arbitration or court.

Compensatory Damages. The award of compensatory damages is the most common remedy for a breach of contract. The court tries to award an amount that will place the injured party in the position he or she would have been in had the contract been completed as scheduled. This is not always easy to determine because in some cases, it may require rather complex calculations to arrive at a reasonable figure.

Nominal Damages. It is possible that a breach of contract will not result in a significant loss or other damage to the injured party. To be more exact, the injured party cannot show a loss. The court may award a trifling sum (even a single dollar) as nominal damages, recognizing that the contract was in fact breached and the plaintiff is an injured party, although only in a technical sense. The defendant, however, may be ordered to pay court costs.

Consequential Damages. In some cases the plaintiff can show that the breach of contract has long-term effects that cause him or her injury beyond the immediate loss, such as the loss of another business opportunity. The court may award consequential damages, although it is relatively rare.

Punitive Damages. Punitive damages are relatively uncommon in breach of contract settlements; courts generally are opposed to imposing them in such cases. They are not, however, unheard of, and there are some statutes permitting punitive damages in breach of contract cases. When they are awarded, it is generally for willful misconduct or to discourage others from such conduct.

Equitable Remedies

The payment of damages is not the only way contract disputes can be settled. Just as there are various legal remedies, there are various equitable remedies that seek to do what is fair, rather than what the law provides. However, the courts do not elect to apply equitable remedies arbitrarily or because one or the other party requests them. Equitable remedies are sought when there is no satisfactory legal remedy. The equitable remedies normally employed include rescission and restitution, specific performance, quasi contract, reformation and injunction.

Rescission and Restitution. *Rescission* is the cancellation of a contract, which may be by mutual agreement of the contracting parties or by a court. The injured party may then seek restitution, so that the net result is that the two parties are placed in the original positions they were in when the contract was signed. Once the contract has been rescinded, quasi contract conditions exist and quasi contract remedies may be pursued—e.g., the injured party may sue for damages rather than seek restitution. (Most jurisdictions do not permit a plaintiff to seek both damages and restitution.)

Specific Performance. When money damages are not a suitable remedy, the injured party may ask the court to order specific performance. This is an order to the breaching party to perform exactly as promised in the contract. It is relatively rare for the court to agree to this because specific performance traditionally is ordered only when the services called for are unique. Real estate usually fulfills that requirement, and specific performance is ordered in cases where a seller reneges in an agreement to sell a real property. The test of uniqueness might also be met in contracts involving the sale of other items that are inherently unique, such as art pieces, specific pieces of jewelry and antiques.

Quasi Contract, Reformation and Injunction. The creation of a quasi contract by the court has already been discussed as one of the equitable remedies. Reformation is another equitable remedy, where the court believes that the contract does not reflect the original intentions of the parties and uses its authority to reform the contract to reflect what the court believes to be the original intent of the parties. Finally, there is the court's power to grant an injunction, in which the breaching party is ordered to do or refrain from doing something necessary to repair the breach.

5

The Potential Hazards—
Both of Them

The hazards inherent in contracting are what compel us to commit our contracts to writing and to lard them heavily with clauses intended to anticipate and provide for every contingency. But therein lies a hazard of quite another kind—a hazard to your marketing.

THE PARADOX OF THE HAZARDS

Some years ago, as editorial director of the company that employed me, I wrote a proposal to the American Red Cross in response to their request. The proposal was in pursuit of a contract to develop certain training materials at an estimated cost of slightly more than $26,000—not a great sum as such things go.

The responsible individual at the Red Cross responded favorably, asked a few questions and made suggestions and requests for some minor changes, which we agreed on and resolved by telephone and a follow-up amendment to our original proposal. The Red Cross then approved our final proposals and invited us to meet with them to negotiate a contract.

Our marketing manager, who was new to the job, unfortunately asked our staff attorney to attend the meeting with him. As soon as he introduced the attorney, a chill descended on the room. The Red Cross representative asked why we thought it necessary to bring a lawyer to what the Red Cross people thought would be a brief, routine negotiation for a small contract.

Failing to take heed of the sudden and foreboding change in atmosphere, the marketing manager next produced what he presented as his standard contract form, a thick document that included certain new protective and defensive boilerplate clauses recently created by our attorney. This was a proposed new standard produced at the request of our marketing executive against the counsel of our production people, who characterized the wording of the new contract as closer to a "threatening letter" than to businesslike contract language and a distinct impediment to the successful marketing of our services as the developers of custom training programs.

Within minutes of examining our proposed contract terms, the Red Cross representatives decided to terminate the meeting and break off further talk. They thought that bringing a lawyer to the table for this routine bit of business was a sign of mistrust on our part and a poor basis on which to begin a business relationship, but the proposed clauses that our marketing manager presented as our standard requirement was too much. They believed it futile to conduct serious negotiations with us.

This can and does happen frequently when you present a prospective client for a small and routine project with a formidable, multipage contract. It suggests that you will be a difficult contractor with whom to do business and one entering into a new business relationship with general mistrust of the other party.

The reverse is also true. If you are a prospective client and ask a prospective contractor to negotiate a small project on the basis of such a forbidding mass of clauses, the contractor may be sufficiently alarmed to withdraw from further discussion. (Many consultants will not even investigate the possibilities of contracts with government agencies because they fear a difficult atmosphere of oppressive government regulations.)

It is ironic because a contract document, even one with an abundance of wherefores and whereases, should protect both parties from future misunderstandings and disagreements. However, many pages of legalistic terms, especially when they are couched in the formal legalese of antiquity and bound in a folder with seals, tends to arouse fears and suspicions, the antithesis of the ideal.

Thus, it is essential that a written contract assume some middle-ground position. There must be a practical accommodation between the extremes, a compromise that states formally what must absolutely be stated formally but that is couched in unassuming modern language and implies that which can be trusted to implication and the good intentions of the parties. (Good intentions must be present to create a workable contract in any case, long or short, formal or informal.) However, there are other measures that enable you to create a simple document that provides a reasonable degree of specific coverage and mutual protection.

THE AGREEMENT MUST COME FIRST

I recently monitored a general discussion among a number of consultants and a lawyer. The lawyer remarked that one of his greatest difficulties is the frequent situation he encounters where he is expected to "write an agreement for people who have not reached an agreement." Some clients seem unable to understand that they must reach verbal agreement before they can create a written agreement between them. The experienced lawyer can, however, guide negotiations, point out needs and warn of hazards—i.e., help the parties reach agreement. In fact, the lawyer pointed out that helping to write an agreement that reflects an effort to foresee and prevent future disputes is one of the most valuable services a lawyer can provide. But even with the best of intentions, the most intense negotiations and the most careful drafting of the agreement, disputes do arise later—and distressingly often.

A Few Major Hazards To Be Countered

The obvious reason for putting any agreement into writing—into what we casually refer to as "the contract"—is to make all conditions of the agreement a matter of record and thus minimize the probability of serious disputes at some future time; provide solutions for disputes in advance (e.g., liquidation clauses), where possible; and have an instrument available to help resolve disputes efficiently, if they do arise and must be arbitrated or settled in court. (However, in the event of a dispute, the overall objective is to avoid the necessity for ever resorting to litigation.)

Minimize is the right word to use in connection with reducing the probability of disputes as the goal of putting an agreement into written form. It is extremely difficult to write a truly bulletproof contract, one that covers every possible contingency. Despite our best efforts, disputes and other contract problems arise, and we must recognize that it is almost impossible to write a truly perfect contract (although we must still try to do so).

You don't expect to have disputes when you enter into a contract. You sign the contract in good faith and with what you believe to be complete understanding of all the terms of the agreement. You have good reason to believe that is equally true of the other party. You did enter into the agreement for your mutual benefit. Each of you wanted what the other party offered. So how can disputes arise later?

There unfortunately are many reasons for disputes or conditions under which disputes arise. Here are a few of the causes of disputes and disagreements:

- *Unexpected contingencies.* You discover only later that you failed to think things through adequately when writing the contract. You did not foresee contingencies that perhaps you should have anticipated. You therefore are now compelled to negotiate resolution of those contingencies with the other party, perhaps now from a disadvantageous position.

- *Murphy's law strikes again.* Despite a well-written and well-thought-out contract, a contingency you could not possibly have anticipated arises unexpectedly, as Murphy predicted.
- *You took certain things for granted.* You expected the other party to be "reasonable" about what you believe to be widely accepted premises that were not necessary to stipulate.
- *Operational project problems arose.* To solve operational project problems, you or the other party found what you thought to be an escape clause or a loophole and decided to try to use it to solve your operational problem.

Failure To Provide for All Possible Situations

There is probably no way that you can anticipate—write a clause to cover—every possible situation that can arise, no matter how many pages or how many clauses are contained in the contract. You must expect the unexpected to happen and be prepared to cope with it as best you can when it happens. However, you can anticipate that the unexpected is likely to happen and that some kind of negotiation will be necessary, and you can try to make provision for amicable discussion and perhaps even arbitration.

At the least, you must try to visualize the various conditions under which you will be working, the various stresses that will be exerted on you and the potential for problems that will lead to disputes. While there is a good reason to refrain from making the written contract unnecessarily formidable by including contract clauses for every possible contingency, it does not mean that you can afford to neglect providing for any contingency you might reasonably expect to arise. Quite the contrary, you should discuss the contingencies and reach verbal agreement or see, at least, how the other party reacts to what you think are reasonable premises that do not require detailed documentation.

Virtual or Unwritten Contract Clauses

It usually is not necessary to cross every *t* and dot every *i* in any given contract. There are many items that do not have to be documented specifically because they already are covered adequately by your state's version of the Universal Commercial Code (UCC), other specific statutes and accepted commercial practices. Thus, not all operable clauses are or must be written into a contract. There are many clauses that exist as part of every contract by reference rather than by being written into the contract. But this is not necessary. It hardly makes good sense to write up pages of copy that simply echo what is already law and directly applicable—what would be, in fact, redundant. The existence of such laws makes them virtual clauses in all contracts that do not specifically exclude or supersede them. For example, it would be redundant and wasteful to write elaborate clauses concerning the cost of delivery when an f.o.b. (free on board) mention covers the matter because the UCC defines f.o.b. clearly enough.

On the other hand, if some warranty greater than that covered by the UCC or other statutory law (e.g., implied warranty) is agreed upon, it should be clearly stated in the contract. In fact, this is stated clearly enough in the code under the definitions provided in part 2 of Article 1, Section 1-201, which gives, among other things, the following definitions of *contract* and *agreement*.

"Contract" means the total legal obligation which results from the parties' agreement as affected by this Act and any other applicable rules of law. (Compare "Agreement.")

"Agreement" means the bargain of the parties in fact as found in their language or by implication from other circumstances including course of dealing or usage of trade or course of performance as provided in this Act (Sections 1-205 and 2-208). Whether an agreement has legal consequences is determined by the provisions of this Act, if applicable; otherwise by the law of contracts (Section 1-103). (Compare "Contract.")

Good Commercial Practice

Note the reference to "usage of trade," which is defined in the section referred to (1-205) as "any practice or method of dealing having such regularity of observance in a place, vocation or trade as to justify an expectation that it will be observed with respect to the transaction in question." In the business world this is sometimes referred to as *good commercial practice.* In practice, conformance with accepted commercial methods relevant to the agreed-upon transaction can itself be as effective an unwritten contract clause as is a formal statute. Therefore, be sure that you are either employing accepted commercial practices or that you have written clauses providing for departures from such standard usages of trade. It can resolve disputes with little or no pain, as in the following example:

Before the relatively recent introduction of desktop computers and modern printers, we used comparatively crude methods for creating reproducible copy for many of our printed and published materials. That was particularly the case with the popular cold type, which largely replaced metal type. Cold type included such original materials as the output of typewriters and pasteups of already printed copy that was considered "camera-ready" for making printing plates. It was a standard commercial practice to make up copy from which printing plates were made by literally cutting and pasting. Even corrections of minor errors were made that way, rather than retyping entire pages. The result was that the pages were far from pristine. By the time they were ready for the camera, they tended to look a bit messy, with many taped and spliced-in corrections. To the eye of one inexperienced in the relevant trades and crafts, they appeared messy no matter how carefully the splicing, taping and pasting had been done.

One client, the project manager for a federal agency for which we had prepared a lengthy training program, was outraged when he saw the copy we were to deliver him as our final product to send to the Government Printing Office. Unfamiliar with the industry, he was repelled and alarmed by the appearance of the patched pages. He threatened to withhold payment and even threatened contract cancellation.

He was not at all mollified or convinced when we told him that what we had done was standard commercial practice and that the printers would have no difficulty using the copy to make printing plates. It was only when we had him show the copy to the production executives at the Government Printing Office and he had their assurances that our camera-ready mechanicals were completely acceptable to them as in good commercial practice that he finally subsided and accepted the delivery. It is therefore important that what you consider to be good commercial practice is widely recognized as such, especially by others whose authority is all but indisputable. It may be necessary to convince a client that you can easily prove that what you are doing is recognized generally in your industry as good practice.

THE POTENTIAL FOR DISPUTES

Anticipating the many possibilities for disputes is not easy for even the most seasoned consulting professionals. The causes for disputes vary according to the nature of the industry or business in which one is working. In the computer field, for example, disputes arise frequently concerning the rights to the software developed under contract by computer consultants. Many arguments rage about who owns the rights to the source code, as well as the copyrights to the finished programs. Even in government contracts under which computer software has been developed, such disputes have forced litigation in federal courts.

Another frequent contract problem arises in situations where consultants are placed in assignments via a broker of some kind. Disputes arise between the consultants and the brokers over such items as noncompete clauses—especially over how long a period is reasonable to maintain the noncompete restriction. In addition, many brokers and job shops insist on contract clauses barring clients from offering permanent jobs to the brokers' subcontractors or to temporaries provided by the job shops. However, there also are other issues that are more general and arise frequently in most consulting specialties, including that of liability.

In one recent case a consultant reported that he accepted a temporary position with an employer who demanded that he sign an agreement saying that he would not accept any other employment while in this individual's employ. The consultant signed the agreement but insisted on having a copy for his own files. He then took it to his own attorney, who examined it and pronounced it absolutely unenforceable as a violation of the 13th Amendment to the Constitution, which bars slavery and involuntary servitude. There is little point in drawing up an unenforceable, and especially an unconstitutional, agreement. Thus, all clauses restricting an individual's freedom to accept a position are somewhat dicey.

Dispute Potential versus Contract Type

Clients tend to be generally consistent in offering a particular type of contract—e.g., firm fixed-price, time and material, task order or other—because they are familiar with only that type of contract or because it seems to them to be proper. Sometimes a client merely suggests a given contract type but invites the prospective consultant/contractor to suggest another type. The consultant may then suggest the one that he is most familiar with or that seems easiest for him to work with. What most clients and consultants probably do not consider in favoring one type of contract over another is the nature of possible hazards and the potential for disputes. That can be a distinct influence in the choice of contract. Some kinds of contracts are easier to administer than others in the face of problems and disputes.

For example, where a large, organized, single project is involved, either a cost reimbursement or firm fixed-price contract is usually most appropriate. Disputes are difficult to resolve in these cases because an unfinished project is usually of zero value to anyone, and a suspension of work may be completely disastrous for both parties. At the least, it usually is difficult to reach a reasonable settlement to terminate this type of contract, if it becomes necessary, and to determine how to liquidate the contract equitably (if that is possible) or set damages if there is no other remedy possible. (How can one set a value on an unfinished project that has no intrinsic value if it is never finished?)

On the other hand, where the work required is a series of tasks or projects that proceeds in successive stages (such as a modernization program), a task order or time and material contract is probably indicated. These contracts are much easier to administer, and disputes are simpler to resolve. This is because a partially completed contract of this nature has a great deal of value, so that it is much easier to set a liquidation value on the contract overall, if necessary to terminate it. In addition, only one task is in dispute, not the contract overall. If necessary, the contract can be liquidated and the remainder taken over by another consultant or contractor.

Estimates and Charges

One of the most common potentials for dispute lies in the charges or costs of your services. If you are employed by a client to do work on the client's premises for an indefinite period and as directed by the client without a specified deliverable item, you are almost surely working as a temporary rather than as a consultant and contractor. (The IRS will almost surely insist on that interpretation of your relationship with the client.) You usually are being paid at an hourly rate, for as long as the client/employer wishes to retain you in that manner. The potential for contract disputes thus is rather small, as the terms are quite simple and the precedents for such work are well established. Your situation is really not much different than that of the office temp, despite the great disparity in hourly rates. In those circumstances you are a W-2 employee.

On the other hand, as a consultant, you are also apt to undertake custom projects with defined requirements that often include deliverable end products. Because you do custom work, each job is unique. You and the client are both faced with estimating the size and cost of the job each time you try to reach an agreement. You both try to remember some previous project that was similar and find some reference for making a reasonable estimate of what you must charge for the projected job. The client tries to do exactly the same thing you are doing to arrive at a maximum estimate of what the job ought to cost and thus to arrive at a budget.

Many consultants—probably most consultants—charge for their services by some time-based rate, usually by the hour or by the day. Thus, the basic cost-estimating problem is determining how many hours or days will be required to produce what the client wants. That can be difficult.

Perhaps both you and the client prefer to establish and contract on the basis of a fixed price for the job. Certainly the administrators—purchasing agents and contracting officers—prefer this method as it involves a relatively uncomplicated transaction with fewer possibilities of disputes arising. However, it is most difficult to use this method unless you get detailed specifications of what is required. Unfortunately, the client is often unable to be completely specific about what is needed, so his or her specifications are general and can hardly do more than point you in the direction of a goal defined in equally general terms. Thus, even if you do attempt to arrive at an agreed-upon fixed price, you are more or less compelled to use hourly or daily rates to arrive at an estimate of the final price.

Few clients will write you a blank check by agreeing to your working at your rate in an open-ended arrangement. Clients want a ceiling on the total cost—or at least control over the charges—with the power to cut them off arbitrarily, although that is not the most satisfactory solution. They usually request a firm estimate of costs that will serve as either a firm fixed price or a not-to-exceed figure for the completed job. That is the basis for most contracts of this type.

Schedule and Cost Overruns

There always is the common concern of the timetable or delivery schedule to be agreed upon in the contract. The client wants a schedule of events, especially a date for final delivery, although in many projects there are important interim dates. As the consultant and contractor, you also need to be working toward a specific date for your own reasons. They include your overall schedule and availability to other clients for other projects and the total number of hours or days of work, since they are the basis for your charges and costs. Thus, you are both concerned with getting the job completed on schedule, and anything that interferes with that may itself be a cause for dispute.

In many contracts, other than the simplest ones, there are interim schedules, perhaps a date or time period in which the client is to review your work (e.g., the draft of a technical manual or the preliminary design of some program) and give you comments or approval so you can proceed further. If the client fails to maintain his or her own schedule, which is not uncommon, your schedules for completing the work are compromised. It may mean wasting many hours waiting for approval so you can get on with the work. That is idle time, and it is costly to you. It may also mean a late delivery, which may be costly to both you and the client. Or it may mean overtime of some sort to meet the deadline, which is costly to you as an overrun unless the client agrees to additional payment. Thus you have cause for a dispute, either now because the client failed to keep up his or her end of the bargain or later because you were put to added expense through no fault of your own, and you now expect the client to pay for that added expense. That is a common and legitimate claim and is the subject of many contract disputes that are rather difficult to settle. Clients do not always see their failure to maintain their own obligations vis-à-vis agreed-upon schedules as a change or contract breach that justifies amendments, although they may protest energetically if you, as the contractor, fail to make deliveries on schedule. The other party, who is so amiable during original contract negotiations, is often not at all amiable if and when a dispute arises later.

Our work as consultants is almost always labor-intensive. The bulk of the costs are labor costs—i.e., they depend on the amount of time we must spend on the job. Thus labor-intensive also means time-intensive. When we must overrun the time schedules, we are normally also overrunning the cost estimates. Therefore, cost overruns usually are in reality time or schedule overruns.

This situation arose in a contract we had with the Bureau of Naval Personnel. Our progress in completing the project was delayed because the bureau's staff failed to complete their interim reviews as scheduled. While waiting for the bureau's review, we were forced into idleness, thus creating for us the added expense of idle time. I protested this to the bureau's contracting officer, who then called us together in a negotiating session to resolve the dispute. The contracting officer eventually ruled that the bureau had to either provide funding to compensate us for extra costs caused by its failure to meet the contracted obligations or to provide some other remedy. The bureau was unable to add funds to the project, but they provided another remedy by modifying the contract so as to bypass other steps of review planned originally, thus enabling us to get the project back on the original schedule. (We insisted, of course, on getting that modification in writing.)

The schedule/cost overrun, due to many possible causes, is a common problem, although I rarely encounter it personally in consulting. That is because I anticipate some unscheduled overtime due to the kind of consulting work I do, which is proposal-writing support. Therefore, I prepare in advance to accommodate schedule and cost overruns.

When I contract with a client to write or help the client write a proposal, I charge a daily rate. I am aware that many consultants prefer to charge an hourly rate, but I think that the daily rate is more appropriate in my work. I prefer this for two reasons. First, I have enough paperwork to contend with normally without adding a requirement to account for each hour of my time—i.e., making continuous notes of when I start, when I take a break and when I finish a task. I simply object to that detailed and meticulous recordkeeping as an additional burden, which itself offers a great potential for disputes. The second and more important reason I prefer this arrangement is that proposal writing is an arduous task, with special problems. For example, there always are absolute deadlines to face, as proposals that miss their deadlines are worthless. And proposal writing is, by nature, rarely completed ahead of schedule or with time to spare; it almost always culminates in frenzied last-minute efforts to wrap it all up. That means more than an occasional overlong day, especially as deadlines near, and the need for all-night efforts in the last day or two becomes apparent. Under these circumstances, it is most difficult to keep meticulous track of hours worked, and there is little time to discuss the matter of necessary overtime with a client when one is racing both the calendar and the clock and working late into the small hours, while the company's executives are in their homes sound asleep. It is a situation tailor-made for disputes about time charges alone. Charging by the day—with a liberal definition of a day—is almost unavoidable as a logical alternative to all other measures.

Therefore, my approach is to charge a substantial day rate, anticipating the certainty of many long days in which I must ignore the clock, as far as my quitting time is concerned. It usually is the only way to get the job done on time while maintaining a reasonably good quality of work. These difficulties are in the very nature of proposal writing, and the approach I use to do this work is the result of my early experiences, evolving as the practical modus operandi. It has meant that I rarely have disputes over my time charges, once the client and I have discussed my daily rate and I have persuaded my client that my rate is a fair one. In fact, I normally assume all the risk of unscheduled and unpaid overtime and usually endure and absorb it as a normal and anticipated cost. By persuading my client to accept my daily rate in exchange for my guarantee of a not-to-exceed ceiling—essentially, a firm fixed price—I can avoid disputes. (I do take some precautions, however, which I will describe in Chapter 6.)

Changes in Scope

In many fields changes in scope are predictable and almost inevitable. Any construction contractor undertaking the construction of a building in a contract running for several years can be sure that there will be at least a few changes in the specification—the *scope of work*—before the job is over. Changes in scope or *changes,* as they are more commonly called by experienced contractors, almost invariably cost the client more money, even if the change eliminates something originally called for, because the change requires a great deal of extra work. Sometimes—but not always—the client acknowledges voluntarily that the change is significant and that adjustments must be made. These are usually in the form of amendments to the contract that call for additional payment to the contractor. However, most often the contractor must dispute the changes immediately as beyond the scope of the contract and requiring negotiation of contract amendment and price.

Changes can come about in any project and for almost any reason. When the U.S. Postal Service was so pleased with the results of a small force of repair technicians I had working on their supply-depot premises in Topeka that they wanted to add two more technicians to the staff, we renegotiated the contract accordingly. When the NASA Goddard Space Flight Center wanted our organization to undertake technical work not called for in our original contract, we renegotiated the contract with them to provide for the services.

Making a change in the specification of whatever was originally contracted for or demanding something not originally specified is technically a breach of contract and should be disputed and settled at the time. That doesn't necessarily mean a hostile action or reaction. It means recognizing the change or request for change as calling for a contract amendment without delay. Delays in disputing contract breaches, even the most amicable ones, can compromise your ability to reach a satisfactory solution. Disputes are best resolved by immediately raising the need for negotiation or renegotiation, for they do normally call for negotiation of a change in the contract and the associated costs. The other party, if he or she benefited from the breach, is not highly motivated to negotiate compensation to you after the contract is completed.

Sometimes an inexperienced contractor accepts the request for change or additional services, with the verbal assurance from someone that any resulting changes in costs "will be taken care of." Too often that proves to be an empty promise and leads to serious disputes later, when it is difficult for the contractor to prove the client's liability for extra costs incurred by the changes. If you accept such a verbal assurance, you may later be forced to fight from the disadvantageous position of having apparently accepted the added or varied requirement as within the contract terms. As the contractor, if the client's program manager asks you to do something beyond the scope of your contract, your most sensible response is to ask for a written amendment. You do not know at the time of the request that the requester has the authority to guarantee you payment for additional services, and you may later run into a stone wall of flat refusal to pay for anything not formally stipulated in your contract. In government contracting there usually is boilerplate copy that provides specific cautions to the contractor against accepting verbal guarantees to provide anything not formally contracted for. That is an admonition well advised for all cases. Even when the client is completely honorable and has no intention of victimizing you, an employee may be less scrupulous.

Changes Are Not Always a Hazard

The probability of changes has been treated here as a contract hazard, which they are, in technical terms and for the client. However, for the well-experienced consultant-contractor in many fields, changes represent opportunity, rather than hazard. The experienced consultant can calculate the likelihood of changes in a prospective project and is afforded a powerful marketing tool where that likelihood is high. He or she may bid the project at breakeven or near that figure because the likelihood of changes that will be negotiable later afford an opportunity to "get well," or recover from a risky low bid used to win the contract. That is because although the consultant is bidding competitively in winning the contract, he or she will *negotiate* the amendment made necessary by changes, without competitive pressure.

The practice of low balling cost estimates in the bidding phase and "getting well" later when negotiating changes is common and entirely legal, sharp business practice though it may be.

WRITING THE CONTRACT SPECIFICATIONS

Requesting proposals has become an increasingly popular method for choosing consultants and other contractors in this technological age. There are several valid reasons for this trend, stemming principally from the same considerations that have inspired the mushroom growth of consultants and consulting specialties, namely, the growing sophistication of modern technology and the resulting need for specialization within so many fields. Clients are less able today to provide detailed specifications of their needs because of both the necessity for extraordinarily specialized knowledge and skills to do so and rapidly changing technology, which makes it difficult for most clients to know what they should specify. Thus, they are almost compelled to rely on consultant specialists to prescribe up-to-date (i.e., state-of-the-art) solutions to their problems.

These days a client can only describe his or her needs in general terms, which are sometimes not much more than a statement of a desired end result or end product, and invite prospective consultants to offer suggested detailed specifications and a proposed program of work. The client then selects the proposal that is most persuasive and awards the contract to its author.

For a small contract the process may very well be just that simple. For a larger project, it is likely that the client will select more than one persuasive proposal and invite the author of each proposal to make a best and final offer. That may involve only an amendment or confirmation of the price quoted originally, but it usually involves at least one meeting with one or more of the proposers to discuss the proposal and review it in some detail, possibly to invite amendment as a result of the discussions.

What is taking place at these meetings is negotiation of what will eventually be the contract requirements because the proposal will become part of the contract by reference. The trend today is that the consultant in effect drafts the contract as a response to the client's RFP (request for proposals), in which the client describes the problem or need as best he or she can. The client needs help in defining the need and specifying the solution, and the consultant must provide that help in his or her proposal. Today it is the proposer who writes the specifications for the project and therefore the contract.

The contract forms requiring signature and mutual agreement thus do not have to be highly complex or voluminous where there has been a detailed technical proposal submitted, negotiated and agreed upon. The technical details that constitute the operative provisions (sometimes presented in a contract as the schedule) have been negotiated and settled earlier in reviewing and, if necessary, amending the technical proposal. Similarly, costs and fees have been settled in negotiating the cost provisions of the proposal (which may in some cases be a separate document).

You must therefore recognize that you are in fact drafting proposed contract terms in writing a proposal. They are the terms to which you will make a commitment—i.e., what you agree to do and what you expect to be paid for doing it. That is why you cannot afford to be vague if you wish to avoid later disputes about what you have agreed to do. You must be as clear as you can be.

The essential element in being highly definitive in your specification lies in quantifying the various elements of performance, especially the deliverable items, as mentioned in Chapter 2. However, one trap that you can fall into easily is being unclear about schedules. A lack of caution in this area can easily lead to idle time and other problems, as described earlier in this chapter in the discussion of schedule overruns. In many projects schedules are as dependent on the client's actions vis-à-vis the project as they are on your own activities. That is, the client may be responsible for difficulties in completing your work according to the original schedule, and you must consider this in your planning.

Interestingly enough, while a client is likely to become alarmed if presented with a thick, bound bundle of pages as a contract calling for his or her signature, the same bundle of pages representing a proposal to be discussed and agreed upon does not engender alarm. Thus, there is a psychological advantage to drafting a proposal as a tentative set of contract terms. Therefore, despite the fact that hardly anyone enjoys writing proposals or wants to do so, there is quite a good reason to encourage clients to request or at least welcome your proposal before even discussing contract terms.

6

Coping Successfully with the Hazards

We often say, "It's just a problem in communication." But just what *is* a "problem in communication"? Do we not speak the same language? Use the same words? Shake hands at the conclusion to signify full agreement? Why is there a problem?

WORDS CAN DECEIVE—AND OFTEN DO

In writing an introductory manual to computer operation some years ago, I used the word *epitome*. I said that the arithmetic unit of the system was the epitome of computer operation. My editor objected rather strenuously to the word as inappropriate, and we debated the issue. Soon we were deadlocked, and it was some time before I finally realized that the editor did not know precisely what the word meant. He had a general idea of its meaning, but he had only a vague and inaccurate idea of its precise definition and true connotation, that fine nuance of meaning that was the very reason I had chosen the word. (He thought the word meant the acme or peak, rather than the essence or embodiment of whatever was referred to in using the word.) I then read him the dictionary definition, after which the editor withdrew his objections rather reluctantly with some embarrassment and agreed that the word was appropriate.

I was unsatisfied and troubled. It disturbed me that an experienced editor would be uncertain about the meaning of what I thought was a common word. I therefore approached several other writers on the staff (it was a large writing project at IBM, under subcontract to the prime contractor of a large U.S. Air Force communications and logistics system) and asked for their definitions of the word. To my dismay, all reflected the same imprecise understanding of the word that had led to the problem in the first place. Evidently, *epitome* is not as commonly used and understood as I had thought. Even more significant was the realization that my judgment of what words to use was far from infallible. It would take more than my personal judgment to be sure that I was using the right words to express my meaning clearly.

At that point I deleted *epitome* from my manuscript and used another word. The new word was not as ideally suited to the point I wished to make, but it was a much more commonly used term and one that my readers were likely to understand without difficulty or added explanation.

Thus, I learned that being "right" is not at all important in such a case as this, where communicating clearly, not entertainment or literary style, is the objective of the writing. Probably no great harm would have occurred if I had used *epitome,* even if most readers did not understand it perfectly; but being clear and specific in helping my readers understand exactly what I mean was and is important to me as a writer. It is even more important to me as a businessman and contractor to be absolutely clear in what I write, as it should be for you when you write—especially when you are writing or participating in writing contracts.

There are relatively few situations in business where communication and clarity are more important than in writing contracts. Dire effects and even tragedy resulting from the lack of clarity are not unknown. The disaster of an early space system (a Gemini capsule), which burned up on the launchpad, was traced to faulty wiring resulting from inexact written instructions, and there have been other instances of serious consequences resulting from carelessness in communication. These flaws normally do not pose life-threatening hazards, but they can threaten your business and your financial well-being.

What Is "Communication"?

One of our more serious problems in communications is a kind of myopia. We usually are so nearsighted about the subject of our writing that we tend to believe it is always the other party's fault if there is a failure to understand us when there is a problem in communication—i.e., when the other misinterprets or is puzzled by what we think we have stated so plainly.

My on-line American Heritage dictionary provides a clue in its definition of *communicate.* Among other meanings, *communicate* means to "impart" or "make known." That makes it an active verb, one that takes an object. It certainly suggests that the burden for communication is on the sender. As a writer, I accept it as my responsibility to ensure that communication takes place—that the reader derives the meaning from my writing that I intended him or her to derive. I must be able to judge what words are appropriate and will be understood. As one of my editors expressed to me a long time ago in a general admonition to all writers, it is not enough to write so that you can be understood; you must write so that you cannot be misunderstood. To minimize later disputes, we ought to pursue that ideal in drafting contract language. Nonetheless, as I demonstrated in the anecdote about the word *epitome,* personal judgment is simply not good enough. We must do more than apply our opinions—and quite possibly, wishful thinking—to the problem of ensuring clear communication. We must employ specific methods to safeguard malcommunication.

How can we accomplish that? How can we control what our readers will and will not understand? There is no absolute method for guaranteeing that accurate and reliable communication will take place, but there are some methods for maximizing the probability. One method is knowing who your intended readers are, and responsible writers take this into consideration and try to get as good a profile as possible on their readers. Another method is choosing language carefully for both denotation and connotation. There is the common problem of connotation, which is the added burden of implication many words carry, especially words that have an emotional content. Thus, it is generally laudable to be "persevering," but to characterize someone as "persistent" or "obstinate" is not usually to lavish praise on that person but to criticize sharply. However, connotations or implied meanings are also attached frequently to certain phrases and even whole paragraphs and sentences that have come into common use and are supposedly well understood, but they can be disastrous traps for those not so familiar with them.

In awarding a major contract to the Educational Science Division of U.S. Industries to operate a job corps center, the government authorized the company to sell $75,000 worth of its own books and manuals to the center it was to create and operate at Fort Custer, Michigan. The company subsequently created $75,000 worth of books and manuals and billed the government accordingly. But the responsible government contracting officer refused to honor the bill on the grounds that the work was not authorized by the contract. The company's position was that the work was clearly authorized by the contract. The matter was deadlocked for some time until company executives finally consulted someone who was familiar with government contracts and contract language. The consultant quickly tracked down the clause and the phrase that defined the problem. The clause that authorized the sale of $75,000 worth of books and manuals employed a familiar phrase, one used quite commonly in government contracts: The company was to supply the books and manuals "at a price not to exceed that offered the most favored customer."

The consultant explained that this meant that the company had to sell its own job corps center books and manuals that it offered generally to anyone who wished to buy them and must offer the maximum discounts—lowest prices—offered anyone else. It meant that the company could not charge R&D money (the cost of developing the books and manuals) as the company's invoice suggested it was doing (and had, in fact, done). Any vigilant government contracting officer would justifiably reject such an invoice as beyond the scope of the contract, as was indeed the case.

Once the problem was identified, it was not difficult to solve. But the problem was that the company officials, unfamiliar with government contracts, did not even notice the qualification of what the company could sell to its own center, much less infer what it meant for billing purposes.

The dispute was settled quite easily, without going to court, once the meaning of the language became clear. But many disputes do wind up in court, and they often revolve around what the language used means—or what it usually is interpreted to mean.

Ambiguity and Other Problems

One of the common faults in communication is ambiguity—i.e., statements that can easily be misinterpreted. Murphy's law is that anything that can go wrong will go wrong. I have paraphrased that in my own law that says that anything that can be misinterpreted will be misinterpreted. Therefore, one practice I have adopted in editing my own drafts is to analyze my writing to see if the words, clauses, phrases and sentences are ambiguous. (Most well-experienced writers do a great deal of self-editing before releasing their drafts to others to review.) Can what I have said be reasonably interpreted to mean something other than that which I intended? Even though I am in a disadvantageous position of editing my own words, I pursue the ideal of unambiguity in my writing generally, and with even greater energy and zeal in drafting contracts. This is the first line of defense against malcommunication. We are all thus well advised to always seek the most unambiguous word or phrase possible—even the most unpoetic one—in the interest of avoiding ambiguity.

We must recognize the fundamental fragility of words as instruments of communication and therefore the inherent weakness of relying solely on words and their definitions. Words are mere symbols; they are not "the thing," as semanticists are fond of pointing out, and as symbols they are easily subject to different interpretations.

One problem is that many words have multiple meanings, depending on the context in which they are used. *Bear,* for example, is such a word. Even my on-line dictionary, a somewhat abridged one, provides 11 definitions of *bear* as a verb and many more as a noun, adjective and adverb, and then still more as used in phrasal verbs and idiomatically. This word clearly needs to be used carefully, if its meaning is to be plain.

Equipment is a word that has no clearly defined meaning, except as qualified in some manner (as in *radar equipment*). This leads to another problem that arises often, namely, deciding what is and what is not included when reference is made to a general term. This problem can become quite involved and can be the pivotal point of a dispute and its remedy. For this reason, adding definitions to a contract can be a wise safeguard, as in the following example:

2.0 DEFINITIONS

1.1 The term "equipment," "product" or "goods" shall mean the "equipment" listed and described in Exhibit I, Specifications, attached hereto.

1.2 The term "specifications" shall mean the documents included here as Exhibit I.

Why Is the Language Your Concern?

You may wonder why this matter of language and clarity are of concern to you, especially if you always use standard (boilerplate) contracts that are well-established already or if you have an attorney draw up or review all your contracts. It may thus appear to you that it is somebody else's responsibility to see to it that the appropriate language is used.

As a first consideration, it is you—not your attorney or the author of that boilerplate, standard contract—who is signing here and agreeing to the terms described. The shortcomings of those other parties are not a defense and will avail you nothing if you get into a contract dispute and have to contest the other party's understanding of the contract language with your own interpretation of what the words say and mean. It is not enough that your lawyer or any other lawyer is satisfied with the language; you have to be satisfied with it, and you have to be aware that your lawyer is not infallible, is not an expert in language generally and is not an expert in the special field of your consulting practice. Your lawyer or the lawyer who drew up those boilerplate contract forms may have been unfamiliar with the uses of or applications for which you entered into a contract. Thus, he or she may not be in the best position to judge how to interpret the words in the relevant industrial or business situations. (In the case of the job corps contract described previously, the company's lawyer was unfamiliar with government contract language and so missed the import of that key phrase.) By the same token, that lawyer would not be likely to be intimately familiar with good commercial practice in your field, another factor that may affect the impact of the contract language. Thus, make it your responsibility to analyze and weigh contract language quite carefully. Even if you have an attorney by your side or you have an attorney review every contract draft before you sign it, both of you must be entirely satisfied with it and accept a large degree of responsibility for it.

There is another hazard here. You may have good reason to believe that you and the other party have discussed your agreement quite thoroughly and in great detail and have a true meeting of the minds. Therefore, you may be lulled into believing that it is not terribly important that the contract language be painstakingly precise. If you have an attorney at your side or reviewing a draft of the contract, he or she will probably urge you to be as cautious and careful in the contract wording as though you and the other party had negotiated fiercely and at great length to reach agreement. It's in the nature of legal practice to be cautious and leave nothing to chance, and I have never met a lawyer who was not of that mind. But that is the mindset you should also have, whether you do or do not have the direct support of a lawyer. You cannot forecast the future, and the most amiable client may be transformed into the most implacable foe when his or her business interests become or appear to have become adverse to and threatened by your own. That perfect meeting of the minds that you thought existed originally can vanish suddenly and completely. You cannot afford to gamble on goodwill and good intentions; they can evaporate as though they had never existed.

PROPOSALS REDUCE THE HAZARDS

I have mentioned proposals several times, especially in Chapter 5, where I pointed out that writing a successful proposal has the effect of writing your own contract specifications. They are then subject to whatever negotiations the client wishes to conduct with you to arrive at final specifications and prices, of course, but they are essentially your creation. Remember that when you and your client have concluded your negotiations and agreed on all final proposal changes, you have written the essence of the contract, which you may now include in the contract by reference. You may make the proposal an actual exhibit in the contract or simply reference it by name: the net effect is the same. You can also add a definitions clause to combat misunderstanding, but if your proposal is written in complete, clear and unambiguous language, you probably will not need to do this.

Thus, it is in the client's interest as much as in your own to write a proposal that presents a set of specifications because it is likely that you are in a better position to do so than the client is. (Consultants, especially in high-tech fields, often keep up on the latest developments more than do their clients.) At the same time, writing a proposal imposes on both of you the opportunity and responsibility for minimizing the hazards and probability of disputes arising later.

The Critical Areas and the Critical Concern

There are certain critical areas, mentioned briefly in earlier references to the use of proposal content to delineate the schedule of events to be contracted for. They primarily concern deliverable end items, schedules and financial matters, although there are some other matters of interest in this context.

The first concern is precision and detail. That is paramount if you are to prevent problems or, at the least, handle them without great difficulty if and when they arise. Everything must be spelled out in detail and in unequivocal terms, even if it is not always possible to predict exactly what will ensue or what you can pledge. (Admittedly, that is sometimes the case.) Nonetheless, there are ways to handle this problem without resorting to vague or evasive language.

Deliverable End-Item Hazards. Most contracts call for a deliverable end item of some sort, even when the contract is for a service. (In many contracts there are also interim deliverables, such as progress reports. When I help a client turn out a proposal, that proposal is the end item. When I conduct a seminar or other training presentation for a client, that is the deliverable item [although I also supply a seminar manual and sometimes other hand-outs].) Even if you work in the client's office doing whatever the client asks you to do, the services and hours of work you put in are the deliverable item. As the consultant, you are frequently expected to produce a detailed report for the client. A marketing consultant might develop a marketing plan, a systems consultant might work on a revision to an existing system or a security consultant might produce a detailed security plan and recommended procedures or even a complete manual. Many, if not most, consulting projects call for a detailed report or manual as an end item.

Whatever the work and end product, it is necessary to describe, define and qualify what is to be done and the end product to be delivered. This area is no place for general statements such as "best efforts" or "good commercial practice." It demands qualitative and quantitative specifications. Although it is often difficult to be scientifically precise in qualitative specification, it is rarely impossible to write a quantitative specification. With a bit of imagination, you usually can devise an objective quantitative measure.

When you are only providing a service, it is easy enough to specify the number of hours or days of your best efforts. If they are to be on-site, that may not be enough. There are questions such as how the hours are to be provided. Is your workday to coincide with the client's regular office hours? Will there be overtime (more than eight hours per day) required at any time? What will be the normal working days of the week? What holidays, if any, will be observed? If situations arise that call for overtime, how will the decision to work overtime be made? For example, will the client determine the need in his or her sole judgment, or will there be some alternative way of judging the need? Will all the hours be on the client's premises, or will some be on your own premises? (You may want to insist on some of the hours spent on your own premises to help combat the IRS's tendency to label consultants as temporary employees rather than independent contractors. If so, it is advisable to get it into the contract as specifically as possible.)

Not every contract will require all these matters to be covered, but you must be alert and try to anticipate all the possible situations you may encounter and provide to accommodate them if and when they do arise.

If there is a physical end item that is the objective of the contract, specifying it quantitatively may become a bit more difficult. In the case of the navy manual referenced in Chapter 2, the fact that the size of the end product was cited as 300 pages made it possible to compel the client to adhere to the contract or negotiate additional payment. In fact, the specification also included 75 line drawings, which were necessary to make the specification complete, and stipulated that they would be included in the 300 pages. Those pages were also specified as manuscript pages in an 8½-by-11-inch format of 10-point, double-spaced typewriter copy, since we had no control over any other kind of printed pages. The typesetting and printing would be done by the Government Printing Office, and the number of printed pages would be quite different, almost surely a smaller number.

That raises another consideration. The qualitative element often needs to be qualified in some way, since words themselves are quite often not precise at all and have more than one meaning or are highly variable in size and kind, as a page is.

The number of pages is one of the commonly used units of measure in publications. Many fields have more or less standardized ways of specifying what is to be done or what has been done. But unfortunately, that is not true for every industry, especially the newer ones. In a computer software project, for example, the end items desired may be a length of tape bearing the software and a manuscript documenting it (providing instructions for its use).

How do you specify the end products of such an effort? The manuscript for the manual is easy enough; these are the pages, illustrations and other accepted measures. But quantitatively specifying the computer program is another matter. The physical size of the medium—tape or disk—may or may not be of any importance. (If the program is to be marketed commercially by the client, the number of disks required might be an important consideration.) You might estimate the number of lines of code as one quantitative index. In any case, it is necessary to find some objective measure to make the specifications precise. If there is no generally accepted unit by which to measure contracted effort or deliverable end product, you must devise one.

Schedule Hazards. Schedules can be particularly troublesome if you are not careful. In many projects the schedule is not simply a start date and a deadline for completion. Instead, it is a lengthy set of events, many of which are interactive and interdependent. That particular complication can create problems.

In many projects, especially those in which a new product is to be developed, there are distinct, successive phases of operation that usually includes demonstration and client-review events. As the contractor, you develop an initial plan, rough model or draft and demonstrate it to the client or simply deliver it for review. The client comments, makes suggestions, calls for changes or otherwise provides the feedback for you to proceed to the next phase.

The phases are ordinarily interdependent. Phase 1 ends with the client's feedback, whereupon Phase 2 begins. The schedule has set a date or a number of days after the starting date on which you will present the draft or rough model, and the client will provide feedback by some specified date or number of days afterward.

There are several problems that can and often do arise with scheduling. One is the use of the word *days* to specify when the various events will take place. *Day,* like *page,* is a variable that must be qualified. If the schedule stipulates an event due 15 days after the prior event, is that three weeks or two weeks—i.e., working days or calendar days? (If working days, is that term defined somewhere in the contract?)

Another pitfall is the use of specific dates when those dates are guesses and therefore inaccurate. For example, the contract was to start on June 1 and event 1 was to be concluded by June 30; but the contract did not actually get started until June 18, and the dates were not amended. That plays havoc with the schedule unless event 1 is scheduled for conclusion 30 calendar days after the start date, whatever that turns out to be.

The same problem occurs when the client does not meet the interim dates for completing reviews. You, the contractor, are left at the altar, waiting helplessly, wasting time and money and hoping to get back to work momentarily. If the schedule clearly establishes the interdependency of events, adjustments probably can be made without resorting to a formal contract dispute. It is inevitable that when schedule slippages begin, your client can easily become your adversary if the terms do not make it clear that he or she is responsible for the slippage and must help you get back on track or pay for your forced idleness. Thus, be cautious in setting calendar dates, preferring specified numbers of days and hours. Define hours and days clearly, either by including them in a general contract section that establishes definitions or by qualification when specifying them in your proposal. (It is preferable to use the latter method to avoid burdening the formal contract document.) Be especially careful that complex schedules show clearly that your actions are dependent on the client's actions, which, remember, are part of the client's contractual obligation.

Costs and Pricing Hazards. After completing a contract to provide a major can-manufacturing client with a training program, the marketing manager of the firm in which I was the editorial director forwarded a customer's request to me. The training director of the can company had called him to ask for an additional 150 copies of the training manual that we had developed for his company.

I called the gentleman and reminded him, as gently as I could, that we had already shipped 60 copies of the manual, although the contract called for only 50 copies. He agreed that he had received these but found that he needed 150 more copies. I agreed that I could and would supply these but observed that while I might supply a few more copies on a complimentary basis, I would have to charge him for 150 copies. His response was that he wanted to do the right thing for his company. I complimented him and said, "Yes, Pat, indeed you should do the right thing for your company, but please allow me to do the same for my company." He had little recourse but to agree to pay for the additional copies, since it was clear in our contract, and we thus settled the matter amicably. Once again, a possible dispute was avoided by being quite specific about quantities in our contract.

Costs and pricing are not completely separate issues, as this example illustrates, although it is useful for purposes of explanation to discuss the subject separately here. In reality, almost everything connected with contract items and disputes is connected also with costs and prices.

Take the matter of specifying hours of work, for example. When the subject of hours comes up, the question of hourly rates comes up. If there is to be overtime or working on weekends and holidays, will it be at the standard rates or will the client agree to pay overtime premiums? If so, just what are the premium rates? (Presumably, they will be some multiple of the standard rates, but they must be specified in the agreement.)

Changes in the scope or nature of the work contracted for may appear at first to have no effect on your costs. This was the case in a contract with NASA for technical writing support. *Technical writing* is far from a definitive term, for it includes writing and illustrating across an almost limitless range of equipment and activities. Technical publications specialists thus handle many tasks that are not exactly writing tasks by nature, but they do fall under that broader class of material known as *documentation,* which includes engineering drawings, tabulated parts lists and other specialized documents that are referred to functionally as *provisioning.* There is also something called *reverse engineering,* which is the practice of creating or revising and updating engineering drawings to match the physical equipment, for which accurate drawings do not exist (for reasons not germane to this discussion). Many of these activities require ultraspecialized experience and skills. When NASA began to assign a support contractor with a general task order contract for these types of specialized jobs, the contractor soon found that the original staff could not do many of the functions called for and also found that the specialists needed were available only at higher rates than the contract authorized for billing NASA.

Getting relief meant either refusing the work, which NASA might have interpreted as a contract violation invoking a dispute, or inducing NASA to view this work as beyond the original scope and intent of the contract, and thus meriting renegotiation of rates as a change.

The argument was a bit dicey. Because the work proposed originally by the contractor did not specifically limit the kinds of documentation to be covered under the contract, NASA did not agree immediately to recognize their new requirements as representing a change in scope. A lengthy negotiation ensued before agreement was reached. Fortunately, NASA finally agreed that the contractor's request was not unreasonable.

This again illustrates the hazards of failing to be completely specific and the almost inevitable effect on costs. It also illustrates the double-edged nature of changes. They often help a contractor in trouble "get well," but they may also get the contractor into the original trouble and lead to the quest for some desperately needed remedy. Most of all, this points up sharply the near impossibility of anticipating every possible contingency when writing a contract. Therefore, we should consider some general safeguards that may not prevent oversights and shortcomings in how our contracts are written but that will provide remedies to resolve differences before they turn into dogfights. They are, in fact, prior agreements as to how differences and disputes may be settled quickly.

PRIOR AGREEMENTS AND PROTECTIVE CLAUSES

The best way to settle disputes is to avoid or prevent them by the use of wisdom in negotiating agreements and foreseeing problems downstream. The next best way to settle disputes is by agreeing in advance to methods and measures to resolve them if and when some unanticipated event creates or threatens a dispute. This is done by entering into prior agreements, inserted as clauses in contracts, for the handling of any problem that arises. For example, the parties to a contract may agree to arbitration to settle any disputes.

Arbitration is not widely used in all contracts, although it is a fairly popular way to settle disputes in certain types of contracts as an alternative to lengthy and expensive legal battles in the courts. The American Arbitration Association provides arbitrators and rules (and they are generally the agreed-upon medium of arbitration) when the parties agree to submit any disputes that arise between them to arbitration, inserting a formal clause to that effect.

Another measure used to prevent or settle future disputes is providing penalty clauses. This is fairly common in many kinds of contracts, such as leases, mortgages and construction projects. Tenants who do not pay rent or mortgage payments on time are billed penalties, which were stated in the original contract. Construction firms who fail to complete projects on time are often penalized, again as a result of a clause inserted in the contract. (These are good reasons to be sure that your contract spells out what the client must do, so that you do not pay penalties for delays that are not your fault.)

METHODS OF DISCHARGE

As a rule, penalty clauses are in the interests of both parties. They help avoid the delay and cost of lawsuits, as a first benefit, but there are other considerations. Sometimes the problems or disagreements that arise between parties are such that the best solution is to terminate the contract. That is sometimes difficult because one or both parties believe their interests would be sacrificed, and they would be seriously damaged unless compensated by the other party for agreeing to a contract discharge by other than performance of all original contract provisions. This is the seedbed for a dispute, of course. Thus, there is great potential benefit in agreeing in advance to some method to discharge the contract—to conclude it in some fashion—even if all the obligations it calls for are not satisfied fully as originally intended.

There are a number of ways in which a contract can be discharged. One way is by the mutual agreement of the parties. However, that may come about prematurely—before the contracted obligations are fully satisfied—as the result of a dispute, with both parties claiming financial loss and great difficulty in reaching agreement on terms for terminating the contract legally. The liquidated damages clause provides an agreement in advance for settling the matter of money damages in case of termination so the contract may be properly discharged.

Most contracts are discharged by performance—i.e., by both parties completing all obligations contracted for. However, many contracts are terminated before they are completed, but they must still be discharged in one way or another. There can be many reasons for wishing to discharge a contract before all activity originally contracted for is completed. It is possible, however, to terminate a contract before all original obligations are met and yet discharge it by performance. The following case illustrates this point.

Discharge by Both Mutual Agreement and Performance

One independent consultant in Washington, D.C. signed a contract with the Federal Aviation Administration (FAA) to prepare a report for Congress describing the year's accomplishments by the 21 engineering divisions of the FAA. The work went well until the time came for client review of the manuscript draft. The draft was reviewed by the FAA staff. Unfortunately, there were 21 engineering specialists doing the review, and they had great difficulty reaching agreement on all points. Changes made by one reviewer were rejected by others. The deadlock continued for weeks.

In time, the contracting officer concluded that agreement was impossible, and the contract had to be terminated. He conferred with the contractor, who agreed that it was probably wise to stop work and reach a settlement. However, there was still a bureaucratic/legal problem: It is not a simple matter to terminate a government contract in any way but completing it.

Together, the contractor and the government's contracting officer found a solution. They amended the description of what was to be done in such a manner that all work required of the contractor was now complete, and they agreed upon a price that was appropriate for the situation. Thus, the contract was discharged by performance—both parties' contracted obligations had now been met. (In the private sector, there would be no obligation to find a legal device to discharge the contract by performance. The two parties' agreement to discharge the contract and reaching terms are sufficient to satisfy the legal requirement.)

Other Methods for Discharge

The other methods for discharge fall into three classes: (1) discharge by performance, (2) discharge by agreement of the parties and (3) discharge by nonperformance. Each class has a subclass, explained briefly here. Some of these ideas may help you get out of an awkward or otherwise undesirable situation without getting singed too badly or involved in litigation. It may or may not be wise to provide methods for discharge by including clauses in your contracts to cover such contingencies, but it is helpful to be aware of the alternatives to continuing with a bad contract and, especially, litigating one.

Discharge by Performance. Complete performance is one way to discharge a contract. But another way is *substantial performance*. This results from an agreement to discharge a contract in which there have been some relatively minor deviations of original provisions. There may have to be some adjustment—damages paid—and that might be the result of negotiation, arbitration or lawsuit.

Discharge by Agreement. A contract may always be discharged by agreement of the parties, and that agreement can take one of several forms. One is a *release,* which should be in writing, include a consideration and relinquish rights otherwise remaining under the contract terms.

Another method of reaching agreement is by *rescission,* in which both parties voluntarily relinquish further rights and thus rescind the contract. This may be verbal but is better in writing.

Still another method is *accord and satisfaction,* in which the parties agree to accept performance differing somewhat from the original terms of the contract.

Finally, there is *novation,* a somewhat complex method that creates a new agreement, including someone not a party to the original agreement that was discharged.

Discharge by Nonperformance. Sometimes an unforeseen event—perhaps a natural disaster or a sudden death—makes contract performance impossible. That is justification for discharging a contract by *impossibility*. (Impossibility is a concept taken rather literally by the courts, and it is not easily accepted, as a rule.)

The doctrine of *commercial frustration* is a variant of impossibility as a method of discharge. Under this doctrine a condition that would not be acceptable as an impossibility may be accepted as a condition that nullifies the value of the contract, making it questionable that the parties will be served by fulfillment of the contract.

Actual breach of contract—i.e., the failure of one of the parties to meet his or her obligations as specified—is a reason for discharge. But there are degrees of breach, and this is a true failure to live up to the terms.

Anticipatory breach of contract is another condition—one in which neither party has actually breached the contract, but one declares or somehow indicates that he or she is not going to live up to the terms.

Finally, there is the concept of *conditions* imposed in a contract, such as a provision that makes performance dependent on whether some future event takes place.

The Typical Contractual
Needs of Consultants

As in any field, we consultants are interested most in those contracts that bear directly on duties to and relationships with our clients. However, we are likely to encounter many other kinds of contracts—many having a bearing on our work, direct and indirect, that is not immediately apparent.

CONSULTING *IS* A BUSINESS

As an independent consultant, you are not only a professional practitioner; you are also the operator of an independent business. Whether that is a sole proprietorship or a corporation, it has all the typical duties and problems of any business, small or large. You therefore have to enter into a variety of agreements with banks, suppliers, vendors and others as well as with clients. (The word *agreement* is, technically, synonymous with *contract.*) Of course, consulting contracts normally provide for services to clients, which is what your business is all about. These agreements are thus directly related to the success of your practice and are consequently your first and major concern, as far as contracts are concerned.

This chapter will therefore focus primarily on the kinds of contracts that most directly relate to the work you do. A number of typical consulting contracts and related service agreements will be presented and discussed. Beware of the word *typical,* however; there are distinct limits to just how typical any consulting contract can be, since consulting is a custom business in which most, if not all, situations are unique. Beware also of the term *directly related* because contracts covering matters only indirectly related to your work and relationships with clients can be as important as the contracts that address your direct interests as a consultant.

The type of contract you are most likely to encounter directly in working with clients is the agreement to provide professional services. This kind of agreement can appear in many forms, and we will consider the most common ones. There also are confidentiality agreements, although these may and often do appear as specific clauses within a general services contract. If you happen to be a computer consultant, you may encounter a need for agreements covering software licensing and other considerations connected with computer software. If you are an engineer, your contracts may include clauses covering rights to patentable devices you develop while under contract (referred to sometimes as *shop rights*). But there also are other corollary matters that may be clauses in a general contract or separate contracts covering the conveyance or retention of certain rights in products developed while under contract or used in the performance of a contract. And then there are agreements for teaming, paying finder's fees, retainers, employment agreements, subcontracts, system maintenance, turnkey operations, noncompete commitments and many other contract alternatives.

However, before we turn to discussions of sample consulting contracts, let's discuss a problem many independent consultants have today. It is relative to their legal status as independent contractors, for this has a direct bearing on the subject of consulting contracts and what clauses and language should and should not be included in them.

INDEPENDENT CONSULTANT VERSUS INDEPENDENT CONTRACTOR

By the nature of what we do, those of us who call ourselves independent consultants must think of ourselves also as independent contractors. Unfortunately, there is a controversy today about the status of independent consultants as independent contractors. One factor that has brought the controversy about is an enormous increase in the number of independent consultants that has resulted from the introduction and swift spontaneous growth of personal computers and other high-tech equipment in forms affordable by and useful to even the smallest businesses. The work of many independent consultants today consists of many relatively short projects and assignments that are counted in days or, at most, weeks. By the nature of the work required, however, much of the work of computer consultants and other kinds of specialists in technical fields consists of long-term, on-site assignments. Thus, it is not at all uncommon for an independent consultant in these fields to have only one or two clients per year and to work entirely on the clients' premises. (In practice, many projects conducted entirely on the clients' premises have continued over several years.) That has raised some questions as to the validity of the consultants' representation of themselves as independent contractors and some ill-advised legislation that has hurt many consultants. It has never been easy to define an independent contractor with any great precision, but the following is generally regarded as a broad definition:

> An independent contractor is one who contracts with another, a client, to do something for him or her, but is not under the client's direct control of his or her physical activities in carrying out the undertaking. The client can control the contractor only with respect to the product or end result contracted for, and not with regard to how the contractor goes about producing that end result.

Admittedly, that is so broad as to be a somewhat vague definition, but it does identify the underpinnings of the IRS's argument in disallowing many consultants' tax returns as independent contractors. The IRS insists that the consultant is a temporary employee of the client and not a contractor at all.

Many consultants in computers and other technological fields sign contracts with brokers (business people who contract with a client to provide certain numbers and types of specialists to work on the client's premises) and then, as the prime contractor, sign the consultants to individual subcontracts. In that situation you, the consultant/subcontractor, work on the premises of the broker/prime contractor's client. However, it is the broker, not his or her client, who is *your* client.

This once appeared to be a great asset for the consultant. It meant that you had a greatly simplified marketing need, confined largely to being registered with enough brokers to have a steady stream of available subcontracts. You could devote yourself to billable hours almost 100 percent of your time, since you relied on the broker for 100 percent of your marketing. The smaller hourly rate at which you worked was more than compensated for by the ability to devote all or nearly all of your hours to billable work. Unfortunately, there arose serious problems in this classic prime and subcontractor arrangement when it came to individual consultants acting as subcontractors.

The problem began with the enactment of the Tax Reform Act of 1986, with its now famous (or infamous, if you prefer) Section 1706 and its 20 questions. Prior to this time, the tax statutes included a "safe harbor" provision. That provision stipulated that in certain named occupations in which working on a client's premises for long periods was commonplace, the consultants were automatically accepted as bona fide independent contractors. However, the now well-known Section 1706 changed that. It provided the basis for the IRS's rejection of the independent contractor status claimed by many consultants. The most significant of the questions are closely related to the general definition of an independent contractor just offered. In general, the major arguments tending to prove or disprove independent contractor status include the following key points:

- You do (or do not) work hours of your own choosing.
- You do (or do not) work exclusively on the client's premises.
- You are (or are not) contracted to produce some specific result or product (or you work only as directed spontaneously).
- You have a number of clients (or only one or two during the year).
- You can (or cannot) suffer a loss, as well as a profit, in doing the work.
- You do (or do not) have to do all the work personally.
- You can (or cannot) be terminated suddenly at the client's sole option.

The choices among these alternatives tend to "prove" to the IRS whether you are an independent contractor or temporary employee, at least in the judgment of the IRS. The alternatives appearing in parentheses are those suggesting to the IRS that you are not an independent contractor. Thus, if you do not meet their standards as an independent contractor and were placed in a project by a broker, you are the broker's employee. If there was no middle-person and you work directly for the end user rather than for a broker, you are the end user's employee. It is a Catch 22 situation.

(Interestingly enough, long before the Section 1706 clause was legislated in the tax legislation, the federal government followed analogous principles with regard to contractor employees working on government premises. They were by regulation permitted to work there only if the agency could demonstrate that the work had to be done on-site [e.g., operating government facilities or requiring continuing access to government property that had to remain on-site]. Thus, the basis for distinction between contractor and employee was not completely arbitrary or without guiding precedents.)

At this time, the IRS appears to be pursuing only those cases involving the third-party relationship (i.e., cases in which a broker places a number of consultants on a client's premises). So far, there have been few reports of individual consultants who contract directly with clients having confrontations with the IRS related to Section 1706 and the 20 questions. However, the IRS can pursue the individual cases under present law (although it probably lacks enough manpower to do so on any all-inclusive scale at present). Thus, the hazard exists potentially, at least; any independent consultant or broker can be threatened by it. Many brokers, in fact, have been induced to change their modus operandi and operate as job shops, placing consultants on their own payrolls rather than subcontracting with them. Clients—end users of consultants' services—may also feel threatened. As they have become aware of the problem, they have decided that they don't care to be in the middle of such disputes, since the IRS will probably insist that the broker or client, whichever holds the contract with the consultant, withhold taxes and pay penalties for having failed to do so.

The problem appears to be spreading to other types of self-employed individuals as well. A national magazine recently refused to accept contributions from freelance writers as independent contractors. It insists that they become temporary employees of a company that has been set up as a broker and will withhold taxes and issue W-2 forms to the writers! This has given rise to the *statutory W-2*, a fiction assigned to independent, self-employed individuals who are forced to accept this status or lose sales. (Even the IRS apparently feels compelled to recognize the fiction of a contractor forced to accept a quasi-employee status by providing a checkoff box for "statutory employee.") As a statutory employee, you still report your income on a Schedule C, but the client pays withholding taxes on your fee as though it were salary. It still is an injustice and an affront to the consultant and implies that the IRS does not trust the consultant to pay his or her own taxes. However, the precedent is the frightening aspect, since it denies the independent consultant the right to conduct a completely independent business as anyone else does, even if it is better than being denied that right totally and being forced to be an employee.

Thus, signing a contract does not automatically make you an independent contractor, as far as the IRS and legal technicalities are concerned. Nonetheless, you can take certain steps, with regard to any contract you sign, to strengthen your claim to the status of independent contractor, without restrictions or exceptions should it be challenged. One important step is to specify in the contract some specific end product or end result required as the objective of the agreement. Another is to incorporate a statement that affirms your position and agreement between you and your client that you are an independent consultant. The statement should be along the following lines:

> The parties to this agreement intend that their relationship be client and independent contractor, as identified herein. Neither the contractor nor any agent or employee of the contractor can be deemed to be the employee of the client. The client is interested only in the end results stipulated in the statement of work included in this agreement; the manner and means of producing that end result are entirely under the control and at the discretion of the contractor. None of the benefits provided by the client to his [or her] employees, including compensation insurance, unemployment insurance, hospital insurance and other fringe benefits, are available to the contractor or the contractor's agents, employees or subcontractors during the performance of this contract.

This statement is not bulletproof, but it will reinforce your argument if you have a dispute with the IRS about your status. Always make sure you are identified as "contractor" and your client is identified as such.

There are other considerations that can help you establish and confirm your position as an independent contractor. One of these is defining the place of work. One of the linchpins of the IRS arguments for disallowing independent contractor status is working solely on the client's premises. Therefore, do not stipulate the other party's premises as the sole or main place of work. If a place of work is to be stipulated at all, do so with a general statement that implies otherwise, such as, "The client agrees to make work space on the client's premises available for any portions of the work that must be done on the client's premises, if such necessity arises." When drafting a contract with a client, always check the list of questions to verify that your contract avoids those conditions that the IRS might use to support an argument against your right to be treated and taxed as an independent contractor. The more items you can include in your written contract to combat the implications of those questions specifically, the stronger will be your position if you must one day go head to head with the IRS over your status and right to conduct your practice as an independent business.

Some consultants make the mistake of agreeing to clauses that enable clients to insist on converting the independent consultant/contractor to temporary employee (i.e., from a 1099 status to a W-2 status). (See the discussion of escape clauses later in this chapter.) Such clauses may sometimes be used by the other party to exercise special leverage in disputes.

CONTRACTING AS A CORPORATION

The major problem you face with the IRS and their contesting your claimed status as an independent contractor is the inherent weakness of your position as a one-person venture operating as a sole proprietor. That is the least complex and most direct kind of business organization, which may suggest that you have not made a serious investment and fully intend to be permanently employed as an independent contractor, an issue that one of the 20 questions addresses.

In that connection, you may wish to consider incorporation. Some consultants incorporate their practices and make themselves employees of their own corporations. Contracts for their services are written between their corporations and their clients, rather than between themselves personally and their clients. This does not guarantee that the IRS will not dispute your claim to status as an independent contractor, but it does make you a W-2 employee (of your own corporation) and provides some defense against IRS efforts to deny you the status you seek.

STANDARD OR BOILERPLATE CONSULTING CONTRACTS

Those who do not know better may believe that one consultant service is pretty much the same as another, except for the difference in the field of expertise in which the services are offered and performed. That is, of course, not at all true.

Consultants exist for, in and of just about every trade, craft and profession known; and the more complex the trade, craft or profession, the greater the number and variety of consultants. The mechanical engineer who offers consulting services in bridge design is in quite a different specialty than the mechanical engineer who is a specialist in stress analysis or the mechanical engineer-consultant who solves problems in highway design. The differences extend well beyond the field of expertise because each field has its own peculiar problems, needs and considerations. In some fields where the consultant produces an end product he or she has developed for the client, the question of rights in and to the product design are not always apparent or obvious but may have to be the subject of contractual agreement. This is a fairly common problem with computer consultants, and we shall have more to say about that later in this chapter.

The diversity of specialization applies in almost all fields today. But it is not the only reason that one size does not fit all when it comes to consulting contracts. There is also the diversity of problems and projects, which is inherent in consulting because consulting is custom work. You probably will never have two projects that are exactly the same, and you may not even have two projects that resemble each other more than superficially. I have written many proposals for clients, and not only was the subject of the proposal a variable, but there were many other variables in the working conditions, the definitions of what I was to deliver and the definitions of what the client was to provide.

For those reasons, standard consulting contracts are useful only as bare skeletons that have to be clothed to suit the needs of the individual requirement. Certain types of clauses may be standardized or typical—e.g., confidentiality and noncompete clauses—but even they must be tailored to the occasion. Thus, it is somewhat dangerous to assume that the boilerplate contracts you can buy at your office supplies emporium can be simply plugged in by inscribing the relevant names and dates in the blank places. At best, they can be only a rough fit and will be of limited value if you have contract problems, such as a dispute of any kind.

Unfortunately, even those who should know better often do not know better. If you deal with small companies (especially those with little or no experience in using consulting services), the client is likely to leave it to you to produce some kind of agreement, assuming that you know best about what is usual and appropriate. In fact, I have found many small companies perfectly willing to contract on the basis of an informal conversation and verbal agreement, although I do not recommend proceeding without at least a purchase order or a letter of agreement. Anything in writing is generally better than a handshake contract when and if there is a dispute. Moreover, the existence of something in writing itself discourages and may prevent disputes. That idea argues for a formal contract with all bases covered.

On the other hand, your client may be a large and bureaucratic corporation. (Are there large corporations that are not bureaucratic?) As such, the corporation's purchasing agent is apt to present you with a standard consulting agreement. It may be a well-used and well-worn form the corporation has long used, or it may be one the purchasing agent has quickly written up on a form borrowed from somewhere. However, whenever a standard form is offered, examine it carefully and defensively. Unless what you are contracting to do is quite simple and straightforward, you probably should add whatever safeguards you believe you need. You must study a contract offered to you as carefully as you would one you were yourself drafting.

Consulting Contracts and Special Clauses

As discussed earlier, consulting contracts must meet the basic legal requirements of all contracts. Inherent in many kinds of consulting assignments, however, are conditions that impose a need for certain special requirements, and they are therefore found commonly in consulting agreements. The typical consulting contract is likely to include clauses covering some or all of the following items, depending on the nature of the work:

- Identification of the parties
- What the consultant is to do, when, specifications and delivery schedule
- Terms of payment and nature of contracts (e.g., fixed-price or time and material)
- Warranties by consultant, if any
- Confidentiality and nondisclosure agreements
- Assignments of patent rights, copyrights and other rights to products developed by consultant during course of contract
- Noncompete agreements
- Liability assumptions or related provisions, if any

Confidentiality and nondisclosure agreements are not peculiar to consulting contracts because consulting, by its nature, often makes it necessary to work with information your client holds to be confidential and proprietary. And the reverse may be true as well (i.e., you must reveal to clients information that you hold to be confidential and proprietary). For that reason, the confidential and nondisclosure agreements are usually bilateral, binding on both parties.

Warranty and liability concerns are also common to consulting work because often the client must entrust a great deal to your judgment as a consultant. Thus, the client's fate is in your hands to some extent—and sometimes to a rather large extent.

Because you may be working in connection with development of something your client sells or proposes to sell, concerns about rights in data and patents often arise.

Thus, these clauses and others (e.g., noncompete clauses) are often found in consulting contracts and should be anticipated. While they may seem to reflect your client's concerns mostly, they also reflect your own and are probably as much in your own interest as in the client's.

Specimen Clauses and Contracts

Specimen contracts vary widely in their complexity of language, formality and level of detail. This is the consequence of the philosophy of the authors of these contracts. The models recommended by some are simple, while others are at the opposite extreme. Thus, the popular notion that all lawyers insist on ornate and pompous language in multipage documentation of even simple agreements is false. Many of today's lawyers recommend simple forms and simple language. Lawyer-author John Cotton Howell exemplifies simple language and simple formats in the examples he uses in *The Guide to Business Contracts,* mentioned in Chapter 1. Figure 7.1 illustrates some of the kinds of clauses covering basic items in simple terms.

Confidentiality Clauses

Consulting work often invokes the question of confidentiality because as a consultant you are often placed in a position of access to the client's most sensitive proprietary data. The client therefore has an understandable concern. At the same time, you may have a similar concern that your own service requires the revelation of some of your own proprietary information. Thus, it is common to find relevant clauses in consulting contracts. Figure 7.2 illustrates such clauses from one of the contracts in the QuickForm Contracts program (by Invisible Hand Software of Annandale, Virginia).

SERVICE CONTRACTS

A complete service agreement between a client and a computer consultant is offered as Figure 7.3. The language in this agreement is somewhat more formal but is still simple English. Note that it makes provision in advance for liquidated damages in the event that the contract is breached with respect to the confidentiality and nondisclosure agreement. Provision is also made for possible default and termination.

A separate statement of work is incorporated in Exhibits A through D. The statement of work includes a proposal or the key elements of a proposal, as recommended in earlier chapters. There are a number of other clauses that are more or less typical, however.

Note that the term *contractor* applies to anyone you have brought into the project, whether as an employee, subcontractor or some kind of associate. This is made clear in the clause labeled "Parties defined." It would probably be the case even if not specifically defined because you are the other party to the

SERVICE AGREEMENT

This Agreement is between HRH Communications, Inc., Client, and Peter Jones, Contractor, under the terms and conditions following:

1. Term and Termination. HRH Communications, Inc. hereby retains Peter Jones to perform professional services described in the attached Exhibit, titled "Statement of Work." This Agreement shall exist from the latest date signed below and be concluded when the work described in the Exhibit is completed.

2. Prices. All services shall be performed on a time and materials basis at rates listed in the Exhibit. The Contractor shall maintain daily time records for all periods billed.

3. Travel and Per Diem Costs. Client shall reimburse Contractor for preauthorized cost of travel by coach class air fare, economy car rental, and lodging.

4. Invoices and Payment. All services rendered shall be invoiced monthly. Invoices shall be paid within fifteen (15) days after date of submission.

Figure 7.1 The Basic Clauses of a Service Agreement

CONFIDENTIALITY AND NONDISCLOSURE CLAUSES

(a) Acknowledgment of Confidentiality. Each party hereby acknowledges that it may be exposed to confidential and proprietary information of the other party including, without limitation, Custom Work Product, Embedded Software and other technical information (including functional and technical specifications, designs, drawings, analysis, research, processes, computer programs, methods, ideas, "know how" and the like), business information (sales and marketing research, materials, plans, accounting and financial information, personnel records and the like) and other information designated as confidential expressly or by the circumstances in which it is provided ("Confidential Information"). Confidential Information does not include (i) information already known or independently developed by the recipient; (ii) information in the public domain through no wrongful act of the recipient; or (iii) information received by the recipient from a third party who was free to disclose it.

(b) Covenant Not to Disclose. With respect to the other party's Confidential Information, the recipient hereby agrees that during the Term and at all times thereafter it shall not use, commercialize or disclose such Confidential Information to any person or entity, except to its own employees having a "need to know" (and who are themselves bound by similar nondisclosure restrictions), and to such other recipients as the other party may approve in writing; provided, that all such recipients shall have first executed a confidentiality agreement in a form acceptable to the owner of such information. Neither party nor any recipient may alter or remove from any software or associated documentation owned or provided by the other party any proprietary, copyright, trademark or trade secret legend. Each party shall use at least the same degree of care in safeguarding the other party's Confidential Information as it uses in safeguarding its own confidential information.

Courtesy QuickForm Contracts, Invisible Hand Software

Figure 7.2 Confidentiality and Nondisclosure Clauses 91

SERVICE AGREEMENT

STATE OF

COUNTY OF

THIS AGREEMENT IS entered into on _____, 19___
between _____, Client, of _____
_____ (address), and _____, Contractor, of
_____ (address).

STATEMENT OF PURPOSE

Contractor provides professional services in computer programming,
systems analysis, computer design, project analysis, project management and facilities management. The Client wishes to retain the Contractor to perform certain of such services, and Contractor agrees
to accept such engagement, under terms and conditions set forth
here. The parties hereto mutually consent, covenant, represent, warrant and agree as follows:

Services to be Provided. During the term of this Agreement, Contractor shall perform the services specified in Exhibit A, attached
hereto. Client agrees to make available to Contractor, at Client's
expense, any and all materials and facilities reasonably necessary
for Contractor to perform such services, including without limitation, the materials and facilities specified in Exhibit A.

Term. The period during which Contractor shall perform the services for Client hereunder is set forth in Exhibit B, which is attached hereto and is hereby made a part hereof.

Fees. In consideration for the services to be performed for Client
by Contractor, Client agrees to pay, promptly and fully, the fees described in Exhibit C, attached hereto and made a part hereof, in accordance with the provisions set forth therein. Client agrees to pay
15% of the total fees set forth on Exhibit C on the date hereof as a
down payment to be applied against the final bill for the services.

Expenses. In addition to the expense of required materials and facilities as provided for in Paragraph 1 and Exhibit A, Client agrees
on demand to pay to Contractor, or reimburse Contractor for, the expenses set forth in Exhibit D, attached hereto and is hereby made a
part hereof.

Liability. Contractor agrees to perform the services in a professional manner and as otherwise set forth in this agreement. Contractor warrants that custom software written for Client will perform as

specified by the agreement of the parties. If Contractor is unable to cause custom software to perform as agreed, Client shall be limited in its damages to a refund of the money paid for these services. Client expressly agrees that neither Contractor nor the Personnel shall be liable to the Client for any loss, liability, damage, cost or expense of Client (including lost profit or any other direct, indirect or consequential damages) resulting from, or attributable to, performance of the Services. Except as provided herein, Contractor neither makes nor intends any express or implied warranties of any description including merchantability and/or fitness with respect to the services or any product thereof.

Solicitation of Personnel or Employees. Contractor agrees that during the term of this Agreement and for a period of 180 days after the expiration or termination date of this Agreement, it will not, without the prior written consent of Client solicit, hire, contract with, nor engage the services of, any employee of Client with whom Contractor or the Personnel have worked directly in conjunction with performance of the Services.

Nondisclosure by Contractor. All knowledge and information which Contractor may acquire from Client, or from its employees or consultants, or on its premises respecting its inventions, designs, methods, systems, improvements, and other private matters shall for all time and for all purposes be regarded as strictly confidential and shall not be directly or indirectly disclosed by Contractor to any person other than to the company without Client's written permission.

It is further expressly agreed that Contractor will not intercept any data transmitted through Contractor facilities and that all such data shall be regarded as strictly confidential as described above. However, that Contractor may disclose as part of its sales presentations to third parties the following:

The identity of the company and its employee responsible for computer operations,

Size and nature of the network: what type of machines are connected with what type of network operating system,

The general type of application run on the network, e.g., MRP, word processing, spreadsheets.

Nondisclosure by Client. Client agrees that the method by which Contractor has networked its computers is a trade secret of Contractor. Client agrees that the method used shall be for all time and for all purposes regarded as strictly confidential and shall not be directly or indirectly disclosed by company to any person without the prior written permission of Contractor.

Default. In the event that Client is in default with respect to any of the provisions of the Agreement, Contractor shall give notice to Client of its intention to terminate this agreement if such de-

Figure 7.3 Service Agreement with a Computer Consultant   93

fault is not cured to Contractor's satisfaction within said seven-(7) day period. Contractor shall have the right to terminate this Agreement on the first business day following the end of the seven-(7) day period. In the event of any such termination, Contractor shall be entitled to such damages and remedies as are available to it in law or in equity.

Liquidated damages. The parties agree that the damages resulting from a disclosure of confidential information are difficult to establish. They agree that in the event of a breach that portion of this agreement, the damages awarded to the nondisclosing party, shall equal three times the amount of the underlying contract(s) for service, together with reasonable attorney's fees. This provision is the exclusive remedy for a breach of the nondisclosure provision, and is in addition to the other remedies that may be available at law or equity for the breach of the other provisions of this agreement.

Parties defined. References to Contractor and Client include the parties' officers, employees, agents, and independent contractors and subcontractors.

Assignment. Neither party to this Agreement shall assign or transfer the rights, duties and obligations hereunder unless the other party hereto consents to such assignment in writing prior to any such assignment. Provided, however, that Contractor may assign, without restriction, its right to payment to a third party as a part of hypothecation of its accounts or otherwise.

Notices. All notices and other communications hereunder must be in writing and shall be deemed to have been duly given when personally delivered or when placed in the United States mail, first class, postage prepaid, addressed to the party to whom such notice is being given at the address set forth in this Agreement. A party may change the address to which such notices shall be given by notifying the other party in accordance with this Paragraph of such change of address.

Severability. Should any provision of this Agreement or part thereof be held under any circumstances in any jurisdiction to be invalid or unenforceable, such invalidity or unenforceability shall not affect the validity or enforceability of any other provision of this Agreement or other part of such provision.

Governing Law. This Agreement shall be deemed to have been made and entered into in the State of _____, and the construction, validity and enforceability of this Agreement shall be governed by the laws of the State of _____.

Entire Agreement. This Agreement constitutes the entire Agreement between the parties hereto with respect to the subject matter hereof. All prior contemporaneous or other oral or written statements, representations or agreements by or between the parties with respect to the subject matter hereof are merged herein.

Miscellaneous. This Agreement shall inure to the benefit of the parties hereto and their respective permitted successors and assigns. This Agreement shall not be changed or modified orally but only by an instrument in writing signed by the parties which states that it is an amendment to this Agreement.

In Witness Whereof, Contractor and Client have caused this Agreement to be signed by their respective duly authorized officers as of the day and year above written.

For _____, Contractor For _____,
Client

By _____   By _____

_____   _____
        (date)   (date)

ATTEST:

By: _____ Secretary

Figure 7.3 Service Agreement with a Computer Consultant   95

EXHIBIT A
SERVICES TO BE PERFORMED

The Services to be performed by Contractor pursuant to the Agreement to which this Exhibit A is attached are as follows:

MATERIALS AND FACILITIES TO BE PROVIDED BY CLIENT

During the term of the Agreement to which this Exhibit A is attached, the Client shall provide to Contractor and the Personnel, at Client's expense, safe and adequate working space and facilities, clerical, typing and technical publication services, machine time and related services and supplies in addition to the following:

Business hour access to at least one personal computer (IBM AT compatible) with a hard drive, along with the following software:

EXHIBIT B
TERM

The Services to be performed pursuant to the Agreement to which this Exhibit B is attached shall commence on _____, 1994 and shall continue until _____, 1994 and, except in the instance of default, shall be extended and continued under the same terms and conditions until written notice of termination of this Agreement is given by either party to the other party at least fourteen (14) days prior to the effective date of such notice.

EXHIBIT C
FEES AND PAYMENT

Fees due and payable to Contractor by the Client pursuant to the Agreement to which this Exhibit C is attached shall be equal to the gross number of hours worked by the Contractor in performing the Services multiplied by a rate of $_____.00 per hour. Client agrees to pay all sales, use, service or other tax imposed on Contractor with respect to rendering the Services. Additional fee provisions follow:

At the end of each week during the term of the Agreement beginning with the first week of services provided, Contractor will submit to Client a statement for Services rendered during that week. Statements shall list the number of hours worked during that period by the Contractor, and the total fee due and payable to Contractor for those services. Payment in full of the fees specified in such statements shall be due and payable within seven (7) days of the date of the statement. If charges are not paid at the end of the seven (7) days, Client shall pay to Contractor a late fee equal to 4% of the unpaid balance of any such statement and, in addition, shall pay to Contractor interest on the unpaid balance computed on a daily basis from the date of the statement at a rate equal to 1.5% per month, which late fee and interest shall be immediately due and payable.

EXHIBIT D
EXPENSES

Pursuant to the Agreement to which Exhibit D is attached, the Client agrees to pay on demand to or reimburse Contractor for the following costs and expenses:

1. Any and all reasonable expenses incurred by Contractor in training the Client's personnel to perform the procedures with respect to the Services:

2. All reasonable travel and living expenses incurred by Contractor necessary to perform the services, including, but not limited to, airfare, ground transportation, lodging, meals, phone, parking, and incidentals.

Figure 7.3 Service Agreement with a Computer Consultant 97

contract, as will be confirmed shortly, but many lawyers prefer to have it stated explicitly in a separate clause. This means that you, as contractor, are solely responsible for anything and everything you have agreed to. (See the clause labeled "Assignment.")

Assignments

An *assignment* is a contract, generally a simple one (as the examples illustrate), transferring a right, title or almost any other asset or interest (e.g., copyright, trademark, patent, damage claim, income, debt, insurance policy, lease or even a contract in toto) to someone else. As a contract, an assignment has the normal requirements of any contract. It can therefore be used to transfer contractual rights to a third party. In fact, you can generally assign even your contractual duties or an entire contract to a third party, but there are exceptions to this rule. The contract in Figure 7.3 is an exception because it specifically bars assigning or delegating contractual duties. (A specific clause in a contract supersedes the priority of rights obtaining in the absence of any agreement to the contrary.) The only assignment either party can make without the permission of the other, under the terms of this contract, is the assignment of payments. You may borrow on your accounts receivable by assigning to a bank or other party the right to collect the fees otherwise due you. In reality you are not borrowing, however; you are selling your receivable to the bank through an assignment. Often referred to as *discounting your paper,* it means you can sell your receivable to a bank or other source of finance in return for a payment of less than the value of your receivable. This is a common practice in the business world. (You actually sell your right to collect the money to a bank or other factor, discounting it by some percentage, as automobile dealers, mortgage companies, department stores and many others do to finance their operations.)

Figure 7.4 offers two examples of a simple assignment of the right to collect money due. Figure 7.5 offers two examples of a simple notice advising the client of the assignment, which of course, is a necessary step. (The notice may be sent by either party to the assignment.)

The point of the assignment clause is to make it clear that you can assign your right to collect money due you from the other party to the contract, but you cannot assign your contractual duties. This does not prevent you from utilizing help by bringing an employee, subcontractor or associate into the project to do some of the work, but you cannot assign responsibility to others. You are contractually obligated to get the work done, as agreed, regardless of the possibility that an employee or even a subcontractor or associate may fall down on the job and fail to get it done. You will still be responsible to perform under your contractual duty, and you cannot escape that responsibility through an assignment without the consent of the other party.

The contract in Figure 7.3 is a relatively simple one of only five pages, plus the attached exhibits, which describe specific provisions of work to be done and

ASSIGNMENT OF RECEIVABLE

FOR VALUE RECEIVED, the undersigned hereby conveys, transfers, and assigns to _____ all right, title and interest in all moneys due or that may become due from _____ upon the attached statement of account.

The undersigned warrants that no payment on the attached statement of account has been made to the undersigned, by _____; that the amount set forth in the annexed account is due and owing from _____; and that _____ is not entitled to claim an offset, defense, or counterclaim, and that no valid deduction may be made by _____ other than that which is set out in the attached statement of account, if any.

Signed under seal this _____ day of _____, 19___.

_____   _____
                        Witness

_____

I, John Doe, of Maximillian Road, Mountaintop, North Carolina, for and in consideration of the sum of twenty-two thousand dollars ($22,000), hereby acknowledged, have sold and hereby do sell, assign, and transfer to the Mountaintop National Bank of Mountaintop, North Carolina a debt due me from the Hardwood Furniture Company of Hipoint, North Carolina in the sum of twenty five thousand dollars ($25,000) for services rendered, with full power to collect, discharge, sell, or reassign same.

I certify that the sum of $25,000 is justly due as represented here.

Dated August 12, 1997

_____
Signed
John Doe

Figure 7.4 Assignments of Receivables 99

NOTICE OF ASSIGNMENT

Date:

To:

RE: Assignment of Debt

   You are hereby notified that _____, Creditor, has
sold and assigned to the undersigned all rights to its claim against
you in the amount of $_____.
   All payments should be sent to the undersigned at its address.
   A copy of said assignment is enclosed herewith.

                    _____
                    NAME

                    _____
                    ADDRESS

To: Hardwood Furniture Co.

Subject: Notice of Assignment

   I hereby give you notice that John Doe, of Maximillian Road, Mountaintop, North Carolina, has assigned to use all his right, title,
and interest in and to the sum of twenty-five thousand dollars
($25,000) due him from you for services rendered, per the copy of
his assignment and statement of account attached here.
   In accordance with the assignment, I demand payment of the sum of
twenty-five thousand dollars ($25,000) to us at the address listed
herein.

Sincerely,

_____

results pledged, relevant responsibilities of the client, scheduled start and finish dates, fees, payment and expenses. Exhibit A, which describes the work to be performed, might occupy a great deal more than part of one page, depending on the scope and nature of the work. The other exhibits are brief enough that they can easily be included in the main body of the contract as individual clauses.

Assigning a receivable is quite simple. Other assignments may be just a bit more complex, although not excessively so. For example, Figure 7.6 illustrates the assignment of a copyright. This form, although somewhat more complex, is still quite simple and straightforward.

Practices vary widely from one case to another. Some lawyers favor a formal contract format, even for assignments, complete with seal and notary signatures to complement the formal language; others use the simplest possible form and simple language. As long as the intent is plain, there is agreement between the parties and the normal contract requirements are met, all that matters is that the assignment is written clearly and documents the agreement accurately.

VARIATIONS ON A THEME

The term *service contract* is a rather general one. In fact, there are a number of common variants of the service contract. Figure 7.3 is an example of a contract for a fixed-price, single project. The following are brief discussions of other kinds of service contracts you may encounter and be asked to agree to.

Time and Material or Task Order Contracts

The service contract in Figure 7.1 is a skeleton, perhaps the simplest possible form for a formal agreement. It is a paraphrase of a service contract because it does not include the many details needed to make it a useful instrument that will cover most contingencies. The exhibit referred to in clause 2 will illuminate what is to be done, along with suitable specifications and qualifications, although this is not certain without seeing the exhibit (which may be a proposal, as discussed in Chapters 5 and 6).

One variant of the general service agreement in Figure 7.3 is the general contract that provides the basis for ordering a variety of tasks as the need arises. There are several terms used to identify this type of contract:

- Time and material or T&M contract
- Task order contract
- Basic ordering agreement
- Indefinite quantity contract
- Term contract

ASSIGNMENT OF COPYRIGHT

John Doe (Owner) owns the copyright identified herein and wishes to assign those rights to Jane Roe (Buyer).

In consideration for the payment described in the following section of this agreement, Owner hereby transfers and assigns all rights to said copyright and all other rights in (title of property) to Buyer. Buyer shall have the right to register the copyright in Buyer's own name and shall have the exclusive right to dispose of the copyright in any way Buyer sees fit. Owner retains no rights whatsoever.

The assignment of this section shall take effect on (date).

In consideration of the Assignment described above, Buyer shall pay Owner the sum of $_____ on (date). This shall be the only amount paid to Owner.

Owner warrants that Owner has the legal right to grant Buyer the assignment set out in this agreement and that such assignment does not infringe on any third parties' rights.

Owner warrants that there are no pending lawsuits concerning any aspect of the copyright and that the copyright has not been published in such a way as to lose any of its copyright protection.

This Agreement is freely assignable by both parties.

This Agreement is binding upon and shall inure to the benefit of the legal successors and assigns of the parties.

_____   _____
Signed (Owner)   Signed (Witness or Notary)

Date: Date:

In essence they are the same kind of contract. Typically, there is a master contract in which are the hourly rates to be charged; material costs, if any; and other expenses, if any. The schedule or other exhibit detailing the nature of the services and the rates usually includes a "laundry list" of labor categories, such as the one shown in Figure 7.7. This might be a request for staffing a computer consulting contract that would include writing manuals. The publications work might be listed by staff positions or by units of production, as suggested. (This does not preclude one individual doing more than one job, however. The senior person might do the system analysis, the programming and the writing.)

The client will issue task descriptions, as his or her needs arise, and the contractor will estimate the cost, based on the labor rates and other applicable costs that are established in the master contract. The client may accept this estimate of costs and schedule or negotiate with the contractor to reach agreement. The agreement then becomes a fixed price for the task.

Such a contract must provide some method for handling disagreements (i.e., failure to reach agreement when the client contests the contractor's estimate) on costs and schedules. There are several options available for settling situations where client and contractor cannot reach agreement.

- The client is free to seek another contractor for that single task.
- The task is performed at the midpoint between the contractor's and the client's estimates of a fair price and reasonable schedule requirement.
- The contractor will perform the task at the most accelerated schedule possible and submit the disagreement to arbitration later, via some prescribed method.

Difficulties rarely reach the stage of impasse in such contracts. The client wants the task performed, and the contractor wants to perform it. With the desires mutual, the parties generally can work out their differences. The provision of remedies to pursue, however, lessens the probability of deadlock.

In effect, such a contract guarantees the client fixed rates for the term of the contract, along with a simplified method for purchasing the necessary services when the need arises. It assures the contractor of a certain amount of work, at least of a preferential position for each task. Other than that, this type of contract may include any or all clauses covering confidentiality and other matters. In fact, each task is a contract in itself, one that automatically invokes all conditions of the master contract. One might write this master contract for an extended period (e.g., for one or more years) or for an indefinite period to continue until terminated by either party, if such a clause is included, or by mutual consent.

Governments often offer these contracts. They are almost always indefinite quantity contracts because the client cannot know in advance what requirements will arise during the term of the contract. In many cases, when the client has had such contracts in earlier years, they can and usually will supply

RATE LIST FOR TASK ORDER CONTRACT

Specialist Class	Rate per Hour	Rate per Page
Programmer, junior	$	
Systems analyst	$	
Trainer	$	
Writer	$	
Editor		$
Typist		$
Proofreader		$

Figure 7.7 Rate "Laundry List" for Task Order Contract

estimates of total dollar volume and amount of work, based on the history of earlier contracts, so you don't need to fly blind when pursuing such a contract. And the client will usually offer a contract similar to that in use with prior contractors, possibly with modifications based on experience.

In cases where the amount of material required is insignificant, the contract may not specify reimbursement of material costs but may expect them to be covered as part of the contractor's normal overhead. In cases where the contractor will actually be buying some item for the client's account, the client may ask for the cost to be placed *beneath the line,* meaning that the contractor will be reimbursed at cost but will not be permitted a profit. (*Cost,* in such a case, should include G&A—general and administrative indirect costs.)

Similar contracts are let for supplies and equipment as annual supply contracts and may be included as part of (i.e., clauses in) an annual contract for services if the client wishes the consultant to also do buying for the program.

CONDITIONS

Many contracts include clauses that stipulate certain conditions. In contract law, a condition technically is an express or implied provision in a contract that will terminate, create or suspend the rights and duties of one party or the other if a certain event takes place. That is, duties or rights are conditional on some event. I might agree, for example, to sell you a property if the city zones the property for commercial use before some date. Thus, my promise to sell you the stock is conditional, and I may be relieved of that promise. That is called a *condition precedent;* my obligation to keep my promise depends on a preceding event. There may also be a *condition subsequent,* wherein my obligation changes after a certain event, such as in the event that you did not make payment by a certain date after the sale. Or you can have a *condition concurrent,* where two conditions must coexist—for example, you must present a certified check and I a clear deed on a certain date at a certain place.

The distinctions may be important in litigation. But for general purposes, the important thing is to know that you can and should protect yourself in advance against these contingencies by stipulating in your contract the conditions that must be met. For example, sometimes a client is intolerably slow in making progress payments due a consultant working on a long-term project. There have been numerous debates on whether it is advisable and, indeed, whether it is a contract violation to suspend work until the account is no longer delinquent. You can avoid the problem of contractual liability by simply making work continuance dependent on prompt payment of your invoices through stipulating relevant conditions.

ESCAPE CLAUSES AND CONDITIONS OR QUALIFICATIONS

Many contracts include what some people refer to as *escape clauses*. Those are clauses that permit one party or the other to terminate the contract by the individual's simple option. When an escape clause is agreed to, the clause usually applies equally to both parties. Either party may opt to end the contract, usually with some stipulated notice (e.g., 30 days written notice to the other party).

For some types of contracts, exercising escape clauses usually causes no great damage to either party; for others, if one party arbitrarily exercises an escape clause, it causes great hardship to the other party. For example, a simple agency contract, such as that between a professional public speaker and a speaker's bureau, normally includes an escape clause, with 30, 60 or 90 days notice required, thereby enabling the parties to adjust their affairs so as to suffer no damage from the termination. On the other hand, if a contractor abandons a project abruptly, it may cause great damage to a client; and the reverse is also true. In one case a computer consultant reported that he agreed to an escape clause in a contract, and at some later date, the client decided to ask the consultant to convert from contractor to employee status. The consultant declined, whereupon the client threatened to simply exercise the clause and terminate the contract abruptly. This was leverage enough because such a premature termination would have had great disadvantages for him. It caused the consultant to feel compelled to bow to the client's wishes.

The hazard in an escape clause that can be exercised arbitrarily and spontaneously is not the existence of the clause itself but the fact that it has no conditions or qualifications. The requirement of a written notice, for example, is one condition that often accompanies an escape clause, and it may be sufficient in some cases, as noted. However, in those cases where that is not sufficient to protect the interests of each party, other considerations must be stipulated as conditions of arbitrarily terminating the contract. One such approach is that of stipulating in advance, as part of the clause, the amount of liquidated damages or a method for assessing them. (See Chapters 4 and 6 for more discussion of liquidated damages.) Conditions may be agreed upon in connection with any requirement of a contract, but you should be especially watchful for conditions to be met to exercise any arbitrary right under the contract. In the next chapter we will discuss this subject at some length in connection with contract negotiations.

GENERAL OR ENABLING CONTRACTS

Figures 7.8 and 7.9 are enabling agreements. That is, neither calls out a single specific project as the purpose of the agreement but simply establishes a set of terms under which the consultant will provide services as needed. In fact, Figure 7.8 is a model of a typical task order contract, somewhat along the lines of the GSA Schedules awarded by the federal government, which also use purchase orders to contract for each task individually. Figure 7.9 is yet another example of such an arrangement, although it makes no direct reference to tasks and purchase orders.

TASK ORDER CONSULTING AGREEMENT

This Basic Agreement is between U.S. Technology Corporation (UST), with principal offices at Technology Plaza in Backwoods, Pennsylvania, and Harry Hazleton (Consultant), of Rosemary Lane, Pennsylvania.

In consideration of the mutual obligations specified in this Agreement, and any compensation paid to Consultant for his services, the parties agree to the following:

I. PURCHASE ORDERS:

UST will issue Task Orders which will include a statement of work to be performed by Consultant, Consultant's rate of payment for work, expenses to be paid in connection with such work, the maximum UST shall be obligated to pay under each Task Order, the UST facilities and work areas which shall be made accessible to Consultant, and other terms and conditions as shall be deemed appropriate or necessary for completion of the Task Order.

UST is not obligated to issue any Task Orders under this Agreement. Consultant will not commence work in any area without an approved Task Order.

II. NONDISCLOSURE AND TRADE SECRETS:

Consultant shall not disclose to any person, company, or corporation any trade secret or other confidential information of UST.

III. OWNERSHIP OF WORK PRODUCT:

Consultant shall specifically describe and identify in Exhibit A to this Agreement all technology (1) which Consultant intends to use in performing under this Agreement, (2) which is either owned solely by Consultant or licensed to Consultant with a right to sublicense, and (3) which is in existence in the form of a writing or working prototype prior to the effective date of this Agreement. ("Background Technology")

Consultant agrees that any and all ideas, improvements and inventions conceived, created or first reduced to practice in the performance of work under this Agreement shall be the sole and exclusive property of UST.

Consultant further agrees that except for Consultant's rights in Background Technology, UST is and shall be vested with all rights, title, and interests including patent, copyright, trade secret and trademark rights in Consultant's work product under this Agreement.

Consultant agrees to grant and hereby grants to UST a non-exclusive royalty-free and worldwide right to use and sublicense the use of Background Technology for the purpose of developing and marketing UST products, but not for the purpose of marketing Background Technology separate from UST products.

Consultant shall execute all papers including patent applications, research assignments, development assignments, and writing assignments, and otherwise shall assist UST at UST's expense and as reasonably shall be required to perfect in UST the rights, title and other interests in Consultant's work product expressly granted to UST under this Agreement. This Section shall survive the termination of this Agreement for any reason including expiration of term.

IV. INDEMNIFICATION/RELEASE:

Consultant agrees to take all necessary precautions to prevent injury to any persons (including employees of UST) or damage to property (including UST'S property) during the term of this Agreement and shall indemnify and hold UST and its officers, agents, directors, and employees harmless against all claims, losses, expenses (including reasonable attorney's fees) and injuries to person or property (including death) resulting in any way, from any act, omission or negligence on the part of Consultant in the performance or failure to perform the Scope of Work under this Agreement, excepting only those losses which are due solely and directly to UST's negligence.

Consultant warrants that it has good and marketable title to all of the Inventions, Information, Material, work or product made, created, conceived, written, invented or provided by Consultant pursuant to the provisions of this Agreement ("Product"). Consultant further warrants that the Product shall be free and clear of all liens, encumbrances, or demands of third parties, including any claims by any such third parties of any right, title or interest in or to the Product arising out of any trade secret, copyright, or patent.

Consultant shall indemnify, defend, and hold harmless UST and its customers from any and all liability, loss, costs, damage, judgment or expense (including reasonable attorney's fees) resulting from or arising in any way out of such claims by any third parties and/or which are based upon, or are the result of any breach of the warranties contained in Subsection IV. In the event of a breach, Consultant shall, at no additional cost to UST, replace or modify the Product with a functionally equivalent and conforming Product, obtain for UST the right to continue using the Product and in all other respects use its best efforts to remedy the breach. Consultant

Figure 7.8 Task Order Contract 109

shall have no liability under this Subsection IV for any Product created in accordance with details and specific design instructions created by UST.

Should UST permit Consultant to use any of UST's equipment, tools or facilities during the term of this Agreement, such permission will be gratuitous and Consultant shall indemnify and hold harmless UST and its officers, directors, agents and employees, from and against any claim, loss, expense, or judgment for injury to person or property (including death) arising out of the use of any such equipment, tools or facilities, whether or not such claim is based upon its condition or on alleged negligence of UST in permitting its use.

Consultant shall maintain appropriate insurance with the following minimum coverage: i. Employer's liability - $100,000 per employee. ii. Blanket General Liability, including Contractual Liability, Contractor's Protective Liability and Personal Injury/Property Damage Coverage in a combined single limit of $1,000,000.

A Certificate of Insurance indicating such Coverage shall be delivered to UST upon request. That Certificate shall indicate that the policies will not be changed or terminated without at least ten (10) days' prior notice to UST, and shall also indicate that the insurer has waived its subrogation rights against UST.

V. TERMINATION:

Either UST or Consultant may terminate this agreement in the event of a material breach of the Agreement which is not cured within thirty (30) days of written notice to the other of such breach. Material breaches include but are not limited to the filing of bankruptcy papers on other similar arrangements due to insolvency, the assignment of Consultant's obligations to perform to third parties or acceptance of employment or consulting arrangements with third parties which are or may be detrimental to UST's business interests.

UST may terminate this Agreement for convenience with thirty (30) days' written notice. In such event, Consultant shall cease work immediately after receiving notice from UST or sending notice to UST unless otherwise advised by UST and shall notify UST of cost incurred up to the termination date.

VI. COMPLIANCE WITH APPLICABLE LAWS:

Consultant warrants that the Material supplied and work performed under this Agreement complies with or will comply with all applicable United States and foreign laws and regulations.

VII. INDEPENDENT CONTRACTOR:

Consultant is an Independent Contractor, is not an agent or employee of UST, and is not authorized to act on behalf of UST.

VIII. GENERAL:

This agreement may not be changed unless mutually agreed upon in writing by both parties.

In the event any provision of this Agreement is found to be legally unenforceable, such unenforceability shall not prevent enforcement of any other provision of the Agreement.

Consultant is responsible to ensure that all of its workers adhere to the terms and conditions of this Agreement, and have signed the appropriate non-disclosure Agreement prior to commencing services.

This Agreement shall be governed by the Laws of the Commonwealth of Pennsylvania.

IN WITNESS WHEREOF, the parties hereto have executed this Agreement.

UST CORPORATION   CONSULTANT

_____   _____
Purchasing Representative   Authorized Agent of Consultant

Date: Date:

Figure 7.8 Task Order Contract   111

GENERAL CONSULTING AGREEMENT

This is an agreement, effective this date, _____,
19___, between Henry Warden, of 3134 Marigold Lane, Columbus, Ohio
(Consultant) and Ohio Technology Corporation (OTC), a Delaware Corporation.

Background

Under the terms set forth below, OTC retains the services of Consultant to advise and consult with it with respect to its business, and
Consultant agrees to render such services.

Terms

1. Consultant agrees that for a period of one (1) year, commencing
with the effective date of this Agreement, he will, consistent with
his other obligations, render OTC such consulting services as OTC
may request relating to the field set forth in Exhibit A, attached
(the "Field"). All such services shall be rendered by Consultant or
by Consultant's associates or employees, as approved by OTC. All
such personnel, if any, shall be directly supervised by Consultant
who shall be present with such personnel at such times as he deems
reasonably necessary. Consultant shall not be required at any time
to render services that would conflict with obligations of Consultant undertaken prior to the request for such services by Consultant.

2. OTC agrees to reimburse Consultant for such consulting services
at the hourly rates shown in Exhibit B, attached. Consultant shall
invoice OTC each month for services rendered and such invoices shall
be payable upon receipt. Invoices shall include the hours worked,
the hourly rate, and a brief description of the services rendered.
Upon adequate substantiation, OTC will reimburse Consultant for all
travel and related living expenses incurred by Consultant in connection with any travel requested by OTC. Prior written approval by
OTC shall be required for all travel outside the United States and
Canada in connection with this Agreement.

3. Consultant shall act as an independent contractor and not as an
agent of OTC and Consultant shall make no representation as an agent
of OTC. Consultant shall have no authority to bind OTC or incur
other obligations on behalf of OTC.

4. Consultant will promptly disclose to OTC each discovery which he reasonably believes may be new or patentable, conceived by him in carrying out the consulting services under this Agreement. OTC shall have the right to file a patent application, at its own expense, on each such discovery and Consultant agrees to cooperate with OTC and to execute all proper documents, at the expense of OTC, to enable OTC to obtain patent protection in the United States and other countries. Consultant agrees to assign all rights to each such patent application and patent to OTC, but Consultant shall have a free, non-exclusive, irrevocable license, with the right to sublicense, in all areas except the Field. In the event OTC fails to file a patent application on any such discovery within six (6) months after written disclosure thereof to OTC, Consultant shall have the right to file such application, at his own expense, in the United States and foreign countries. On each patent issuing from such application, OTC shall have a free, non-exclusive, irrevocable license, with the right to sublicense, in the Field.

5. In the event OTC discloses information to Consultant that it considers to be OTC's proprietary (Proprietary Information), Consultant agrees to maintain the Proprietary Information in confidence and to treat the Proprietary Information with at least the same degree of care and safeguards that he takes with his own proprietary information. Proprietary Information shall be used by Consultant only in connection with services rendered under this Agreement. Proprietary Information shall not be deemed to include information that:

(a) is in or becomes in the public domain without violation of this Agreement by Consultant; or

(b) is already in the possession of Consultant, as evidenced by written documents, prior to the disclosure thereof by OTC; or

(c) is rightfully received from a third entity having no obligation to OTC and without violation of this Agreement by Consultant.

6. Consultant warrants that he is under no obligation to any other entity that is in any way in conflict with this Agreement, that he is free to enter into this Agreement, and is under no obligation to consult for others in this Field.

Consultant shall not, during the term of this Agreement, perform consulting services for others in the Field, but shall have the right to perform consulting or other services for others, outside the Field.

Figure 7.9 General Consulting Agreement 113

7. This Agreement may be terminated by OTC at any time on sixty (60) days advance written notice. In the event consulting services requested by OTC hereunder, for immediate performance, shall in any calendar month total less than $2,000.00, then Consultant shall have the right to terminate this Agreement by thirty (30) days advance written notice, provided, in the event OTC shall within such thirty day period place sufficient requests with Consultant to bring the total for the previous and current months to the minimum amounts set forth above, such notice shall be of no effect.

8. The secrecy provisions of Section 5 hereof shall survive any termination of this Agreement for a period of three (3) years after such termination.

9. This Agreement is not assignable by either party without the consent of the other.

Henry Warden, Consultant

_____ (Signed)

Date:

Ohio Technology Corporation

By_____(name)

_____(signed)
Director of Engineering

8

Writing and Reading Contracts Defensively

Unfortunately, it's a predatory world. We hope and expect that others are honorable and mean to do business in an ethical manner for mutual benefit. Nevertheless, we must never forget that we live and do business yet in a *caveat emptor* society despite the existence of many statutes having some of the opposite philosophy and effect.

THE OLD CAVEAT IN MODERN DRESS

The doctrine of *caveat emptor* originated in a day when buyers were very much at the mercy of sellers. It was a time of *laissez faire:* the government did not interfere with business, and business kept its hands off government. Thus, businesses were free to do much as they wished. There was little recourse from unwise buying decisions, even when those decisions were prompted or influenced by misrepresentations and other trickery by unscrupulous merchants. Perhaps it was assumed that the buyer was an adult, sophisticated in knowledge of the world, who entered into sales contracts—formal, informal and implied—with full knowledge and responsibility and with bargaining power equal to that of the seller. Or perhaps merchants and other businesspeople were simply predators who did not give much thought to the morality of what they did, or they thought it perfectly reasonable to use their wits in any way that benefited them. In any case society (i.e., government) had not yet decided that some buyers were in need of special protection from fellow humans who were slyer and less scrupulous or that we needed laws to help further the goal of achieving fairness and justice in commerce. Courts also tended strongly to shy away from what they interpreted as interference in the traditional "freedom to contract."

As a society in general, we have progressed. We no longer base our rules of behavior entirely on that ancient assumption that all's fair in business, as in love and war. In time, with the growth of merchants and brokers selling the goods produced by others and consumerism growing steadily as a major economic factor, changes began to come about. Large business organizations began to develop, and it became more and more evident that consumers, as a class, did not have bargaining powers equal to those of the merchant class. Soon government began to create statutory protection for consumers. (In fact, as some legal scholars have observed, our laws today have something of the effect of *caveat venditor*—let the seller beware.) We now profess the belief that the naive, ingenuous and unsophisticated among us need a degree of protection from deceit and trickery in business transactions, and so we have quite an enormous array of statutes that we hope will help level the playing field somewhat and deter the strong from taking advantage of the weak. There is, for example, statutory voiding of contracts for illegal activity or contracting with one who is not of age or is otherwise incompetent to be a signatory to a contract. Our courts are clogged with civil actions arising out of and justified by myriad statutes enacted under this and related philosophies. Thus, one may enter into a contract, duly sign all forms and commitments thereto and yet find or at least seek to find legal justification for contesting the agreement or the other party's interpretation of it and be justified in breaching or voiding the agreement—and even in seeking to recover money for damages suffered.

The fact is that the caveat is no longer served on the buyer alone but applies equally to the seller, especially in the case of selling goods, where warranties of several kinds are prescribed by law. (These provisions of law will apply to you, presumably, if you sell books, tapes, discs, newsletters, equipment or other goods as part of your practice or as an end product of your work for clients.) Aside from that, under modern law, with its many safeguards or legal remedies available to buyers, either party, (buyer or seller) can and often does sue the other for alleged breach of contract even when the contract does not involve a sale of goods. (The contest that ensues between the parties is sometimes referred to sardonically—and not without some justification—as a contest to determine which side has the best lawyer, rather than as a contest for the victory of justice.) That does not and should not mean that you must depend entirely on your lawyer to achieve a measure of justice. Instead, you should understand and participate as much as possible in all proceedings in re contracts you sign. But you should also have some understanding of the most common remedies available. That knowledge—the law of sales—will help you understand contract law and, more to the point, will help you write and read contracts more effectively—and more defensively. Even if you do not sell any kind of goods or produce any kind of physical end product, but deal totally and exclusively in services per se, it is helpful to understand the philosophy of the law of sales as it applies to warranties and especially as it applies to the concept of statements and misstatements of fact versus statements and misstatements of opinion, predictions and other things that are not facts within the meaning of the law.

The word *defensively* is easily misunderstood and therefore merits some explanation as to how it is used here. But let us first have a look at some of the regular remedies generally available under the law to contracting parties. We will begin with those contracting relationships where the sale of goods is involved.

WARRANTIES

Every sale of goods by a merchant who deals in those goods involves warranties of one sort or another. A *warranty* is a promise that something represented is true, more freely interpreted as a guarantee that what is sold will perform and be as represented or reasonably inferred. As a promise, the warranty becomes a part of the contract. There are, however, several kinds of warranties, and you should be familiar with each one.

The Express Warranty

The *express warranty* is a warranty made expressly by the seller in specific language, which may or may not be in writing. (Of course, as buyers, we ought to insist that any express warranty be in writing.)

An express warranty may be created in several ways:

- An affirmation of a fact or promise that the goods will be as described or promised.
- The description of the goods creates an express warranty.
- Any sample or model of the goods creates an express warranty that the goods will be as represented by the sample.

The rationale is that the statement or characterization must be the basis of the agreement—the basis on which the agreement was reached—for the statement to become an express warranty. The creation of the express warranty depends on facts, such as those cited. For you as the seller to state that what you sell is of the highest quality or that you will provide goods of the highest quality is not an express warranty, for you are expressing a general opinion, not a verifiable fact. Typical commercial puffery is not itself an express warranty. However, if you say that what you will provide has a half-dozen characteristics that you describe in your proposal, that becomes an express warranty. If you say that all delivery and installation will be completed within 30 days, that is also an express warranty.

In general, quantified statements are taken as statements of fact and thus are express warranties. Statements promising specific and verifiable results or characteristics tend to be regarded as express warranties. Statements of relative qualities (i.e., "the most advanced," "the latest developments," "peerless" and other such characterizations) are not usually regarded as promises or statements of fact that can be interpreted as express warranties. If you did make such a statement and wished to defend against the claim that the statement or representation you made was not an express warranty, you would have to prove somehow that the statement or representation was not the basis for the sale. In short, you must be quite careful what you promise. Do not state as a fact something you are not absolutely sure is a fact. You might believe that you are merely expressing an opinion, but the law may say something quite different!

The Implied Warranty

Whereas an express warranty does not exist unless the seller creates it, an *implied warranty* is imposed by law (under the UCC) unless the buyer voluntarily surrenders or foregoes it. However, there is more than one type of implied warranty:

- *Warranty of merchantability.* The goods must be suitable for the purpose for which they are sold, and the seller must be a merchant who deals in this kind of goods. It thus does not apply to the individual who sells his used lawn mower to a neighbor.
- *Warranty of title.* As the seller, you are conveying a clear title to goods you have the right to sell, and the goods are free of encumbrances of any sort.

The Statutory Warranty

For any goods manufactured since January 3, 1975, the manufacturer must provide the consumer with the terms of whatever warranty applies before the sale is made. (Prior to that time, it was often only after the sale, when the package was opened, that the buyer had an opportunity to read the manufacturer's warranty provisions.)

FRAUD

The very word *fraud* conjures up visions of sensational criminal activity—Ponzi schemes, confidence games and sundry other white-collar crimes. Fraud is easy to recognize in such dramatic circumstances. In actuality, however, it is often easier to define generally and morally than by firm legal definition. In fact, it is difficult to pin the legal definition down. There are numerous uncertainties and borderline situations, even more so than in the case of warranties.

Definition

In its essence *fraud* involves a deliberate misrepresentation or misstatement of fact designed to induce another to enter into a contract based on that misstatement. The difficulty in definition lies in that four-letter word *fact*. Understanding is probably best accomplished by the following examples of what is and what is not a misstatement of fact:

> "I reduced the operating costs of Jones & Company's production department by 27 percent." (That is a statement, or misstatement, of fact.)

> "I will reduce the operating costs of your production department by 27 percent." (That is a promise, and it states an opinion or prediction, not a fact.)

It is difficult to hold anyone to account for such general promises or predictions as the second statement makes. Under the law they do not constitute fraud. As in the case of warranties, the dividing line is often a fine and almost undetectable one, but it is a dividing line, nevertheless. The law addresses the entire matter rather gingerly in making distinctions.

Difficulties

Even with numerous guidelines, there are many exceptions. For example, the rule that applies to a layperson may not apply to an expert. That is, a jeweler might be held to have committed fraud by grossly overstating or understating the value of a gemstone to a prospective buyer or seller, while you or I would not be expected to be able to make a fair assessment of such an item. As a consultant, you are deemed to be an expert in certain matters, and perhaps a misstatement that would be an opinion and an innocent misstatement when expressed by someone else will be taken to be a statement of fact and deliberately made to deceive when made by you. Thus, you must be especially careful in making statements about those areas where you are a professional and an expert.

Unfortunately, there are further complications. One of them is the factor of silence, or the failure to inform the buyer of some significant fact that might have caused the other party to change his or her mind about entering into a contract. In most circumstances silence is not fraud. You normally have no legal "duty to speak" or to discuss the downside of what a client wants and you propose to do for him or her. But there are exceptions to this general rule, circumstances in which you do have an obligation to make full disclosure of facts, such as when you know of a hidden defect that would have had a decisive effect on the other party's decision had he or she known of it.

Materiality

That brings up the factor of *materiality* or the role of the seller's statement or failure to make a statement about a material fact, one that might have been decisive in the other party's decision. The fact in question must be one that influences the other party to enter into a contract. On the other hand, if a misrepresentation or silence is such that the other party is indifferent to the fact it addresses and is unaffected by it in making a decision, the misrepresentation is not fraud.

Thus, to constitute fraud, the misrepresentation must be false, concern a fact, be material and be relied upon by the other party as a principal factor in the decision to contract. It is innocent misrepresentation, however, if it is made with the reasonable belief that it is true. It is fraud only if it is stated with knowledge that it is false and is intended to deceive the other party. If it is an innocent misrepresentation, the remedy is rescission; if fraud, the remedy is rescission and possibly recovery of damages.

In terms of writing and reading contracts defensively, the main objective is not remedies or recovery of damages; the objective is avoidance of bad contracts and problems that might arise as a result of entering into them. Even if you make a misrepresentation in all innocence and are not guilty of fraud or deliberate intent to deceive and mislead, you have lost control and may have lost a contract and a client as well. Your clients want bad contracts no more than you do, and they may tend to blame bad contracts on you, whether justified or not.

CLAUSES AND OPTIONS

The foregoing discussions have covered many general considerations that are negative in the sense that they represent possible pitfalls or hazards to be avoided in writing and reading contracts defensively through knowledge of the law in general. An entirely different aspect of writing and reading contracts lies in examining and understanding the various options available to you and choosing those most in your interest. Bear in mind that everything is negotiable, in theory at least, and fighting up front for what you want now may very well mean not having to fight later to complete the job and get paid. That may mean not having to fight in a court, where winning is often almost indistinguishable from losing. In any case you must study the contract on a clause-by-clause basis to be sure that you have covered all pertinent matters. The following are a few of the clauses most typically affecting areas of concern.

Term and Termination

A service agreement normally is entered into for some term, which may be specified in a clause dedicated to the purpose or prescribed in a proposal or statement of work attached as an exhibit and referred to in the contract. Or it may be for an indefinite term, with provision made for termination at the option of either party or by mutual agreement of the parties. (The discussions of task order contracts and basic ordering agreements in Chapter 3 refer to this arrangement of an ongoing contract for general support services, as the needs arise.) Bear in mind that any right granted must be granted to you as well as to the other party. For example, if the other party can opt to cancel the contract arbitrarily on some specified notice, you must have the same right and on equal terms.

There are many options, and presumably all are negotiable. The client may have stipulated these matters in advance, in a request for proposals, in preliminary discussions or in a written contract offered to you for signature. In some cases the question of term is settled automatically by the nature of the work, such as when I was retained to help clients write proposals. The proposals normally had due dates, and my task ended when they were ready for delivery on or before those dates. On the other hand, many consulting contracts are for general support and can go on indefinitely. (The federal government often writes these types of proposals for three years, generally with annual options that either party can exercise.)

You must decide whether there is some marked advantage to you in opting for a fixed term or variable one, and what that term should be. If the other party's wishes conflict with yours, you will have to negotiate an agreement.

The following are among the many other kinds of clauses and conditions that are commonly included and may have to be negotiated:

- *Fees and fee basis (hourly, daily, for the job, etc.).* There may be one fixed fee basis, or fees may be variable, according to the type of tasks required.
- *Expenses.* These may be included in the price or they may be billable separately and as the need arises. Definitions of allowable costs may be prescribed in advance in the contract, or they may be negotiated in each instance.
- *Progress payments.* If these are agreed upon, as in the case of long-term contracts, you must agree on the frequency with which you may bill the client and the basis for billing (e.g., estimated percentage of work accomplished, hours expended, etc.).
- *Payment of invoices.* Specify how soon the client must pay invoices after being billed and penalties for late payments.
- *Custom product(s)* (if they are the result of your work). Specify who owns the products and under what terms. (This may call for a separate agreement.)

- *Warranties.* Express warranties, if any, by consultant, should be specified clearly.
- *Consequential damages (if you subcontract).* Determine whether to assert or forego your right to seek consequential damages. Your client may wish to have a clause to this effect, and you may have to negotiate this also.
- *Disputes.* How will you handle disputes? Will you litigate or arbitrate, and if both, which will be litigated and arbitrated?
- *Forum.* Specify the state where litigation/arbitration is to occur. This is a consideration if your client is in another state.
- *Law.* Specify the state whose laws will govern if you and your client are in different states.
- *Right to stop work in event other party fails to carry out agreement.* Even if this is an implied right, it is best specified clearly by a clause.

You may use this list as the basis for a master checklist to keep with you in writing, reading or evaluating contracts. There are so many matters to consider that it is easy to overlook one or two, and those will inevitably be the ones to cause you problems later.

THE BATTLES OF OBFUSCATION

The conflicts that often accompany contract negotiations and performances under contracts do not necessarily mean that one party is deliberately and cynically seeking to take advantage of the other by employing deceit and other trickery (although that is admittedly sometimes the case). They are not even always the result of one party being a superior negotiator or more experienced in making deals. Conflicts can arise from many causes, even rather innocent ones.

Contracts are agreements that are usually reached through compromises, and compromises are the typical means for settling differences in opposing positions. It is in the nature of business that you and your prospective client will have opposing positions. The fact that some contractors have less than pure motives doesn't mean that it is dishonorable for you to negotiate the best terms you can get for yourself. Honesty and honor do not demand that you give the store away. Even the most noble quality standards stop short of insisting that you yield to the other party more than he or she demands, ought to have or can persuade you to cede. The most honorable clients will still try to get the best possible terms—i.e., the best prices, quickest delivery, greatest amount of service, most extensive guarantees and any other legitimate advantages they can get through respectable negotiating. Being the best negotiator you can be is perfectly honorable. Most of us even take great pride in being superior negotiators and we are regarded with respect as good negotiators, when we bargain well within the acceptable codes. There is nothing dishonorable in out-negotiating opponents and gaining more than we give up. It is in the finest American traditions of honorable "horse trading."

At the same time, many disputes arise out of honest misunderstandings and misinterpretations by well-intentioned contractors and clients. That makes it all the more imperative that you know exactly what you are and are not agreeing to before you sign a contract. It is sad but true that you must read, write and negotiate defensively if you wish to minimize problems. Legal battles are best avoided altogether. One side must lose in these battles, and more often than not, both sides lose more than they could have gained. The best litigation usually is the litigation prevented or, at least, avoided.

The Meaning of *Defensively*

The injunction to write, read and negotiate contracts defensively may easily be misinterpreted. It probably is true that some people entering into contracts with others read, write and negotiate them with deliberate intent to find and exploit advantages, using such tactics as fabrications and chicanery to deceive and outwit the other parties. The best defense against this is to refuse to enter into the contract. There is no contract language that is completely foolproof against a dishonest or unscrupulous other party. Only a contract in which the two parties are sincere in their desire to reach agreement fairly and abide by their agreements is a good contract. Thus, the intended meaning of *defensively* is not that of defending yourself against an opponent trying to take advantage of you. Instead, it means learning to negotiate well by legal standards, by commonly accepted standards of ethical conduct in business and by defending yourself against badly written contracts that have the seeds of disputes inherent in their failure to specify clearly, accurately and completely the entire agreement. The opponent of a good contract is poor documentation as much as any other factor. As a hazard to the interest of you and the other party, it is the equal opponent of each of you. It is as much in your client's or subcontractor's interest to have crystal-clear documentation as it is in your own interest.

Obtaining a clear understanding of the legal principles of contract law is itself an ample justification for the existence of this book. The more you know about contracts and the legal provisions connected with them, the more likely it is that you will read, write, negotiate and enter into contracts written wisely and with minimal probabilities of difficulties. But that is not all that is necessary. You must also ascertain that the agreement is properly documented in the clear and precise language that ensures understanding. You should also have some knowledge of negotiating tactics and methodology.

Bear in mind at all times that the sheaf of pages is not itself the contract, despite the fact that we refer to it as "the contract." It is a *statement* of the contract or agreement. (Remember that the words *statement* and *contract* are synonymous and interchangeable.) Remember what you are trying to do in writing up the agreement. You are committing to paper a clear and complete statement of your agreement—or as E. Thorpe Barrett says in *Write Your Own*

Business Contracts, the *evidence* of the agreement. The paper recording of the agreement thus has no merit of its own but has only the merit of the agreement it is intended to document and record for any later reference necessary. Because later reference may become necessary to avoid a bitter dispute, and possibly even litigation, it is very important to make the writing as unambiguous, unequivocal, accurate and complete as possible. (It is in the sincere, dedicated efforts of lawyers to ensure this that the contracts they draw up are so often redundant and overly verbose.)

The words *clearly, accurately* and *completely* connote not only that specific language be used to define the agreement in all its clauses but that all terms of the agreement be covered and no important right or duty be overlooked. What is not stated (i.e., the failure to even mention a right, duty or condition) may prove to be as serious a problem as the failure to be clear and specific in what is stated. It, too, must be guarded against as part of defensiveness regarding contract matters.

A General Principle for Minimizing Problems

E. Thorpe Barrett also observes that lawyers have elevated redundancy to a high state of art and write long contracts rather than short ones because the fees are higher for long contracts. Whether or not his observations are meant to be sardonic jests is not clear, but I accept them as serious and significant comments and join with many others in advocating the shortest contract in the simplest language that will get the job done properly. I am reminded of the government contracting officer who once described to me his responsibility in these words: "My job is to get the best job done, in the shortest amount of time, for the least amount of money." I am sure he would have agreed with the philosophy of the shortest contract writing that does the job. (When I did business with a contracting official at the Bureau of Naval Personnel, he often said that he would regard with favor my making my proposals as brief as possible.) It is true enough that lengthy contracts—i.e., lengthy in relation to the amount of information they present—are characteristically redundant, as though stating the same thing in several different ways adds something to the effectiveness of the writing.

The two characteristics—brevity and simplicity—are not unrelated. You may have discovered by now that lengthy documents tend to be written in verbose, dense, obfuscatory language that impedes and even prevents understanding, whereas short, to-the-point documents tend to be direct and crystal clear. In fact, over-long prose is often indicative of fuzzy thinking and is used, probably unconsciously, to mask the lack of clear ideas that can be stated briefly and unequivocally. These documents often are heavily larded with "whereas," "party of the first part" and similar locutions that add neither meaning nor effectiveness to a contract. Such expressions tend to obscure meaning and introduce equivocations. They also focus attention on the language instead of the intent of the parties and thus should be shunned when possible, despite the fact that they appear in some of the models shown in this book.

Examine the contracts in Figures 8.1 and 8.2, which are simple contracts for similar commitments, and compare them for brevity and clarity. Each contract includes the same provisions and is equally binding on the two parties. The second version has simplified the language. Fortunately, in this case the original version was not particularly dense or verbose and thus required relatively little simplification. The original referred to one party as "The Company." That is somewhat better than "the hoary Party of the First Part" or "Party of the Second Part," but changing "The Company" to "Seller" in Figure 8.2 both simplified and clarified the language, making the contractual role of the company clear as the seller of the goods.

There are multiple hazards in a contract with lengthy and overblown language. On the one hand, the fact that the written instrument is less clear than it should be may itself lead directly to dispute as to what are the intended duties and rights of each party. Moreover, the lack of adequate clarity—a misunderstanding of what the language said—may be responsible for one or both parties agreeing to clauses they would never have agreed to if they had understood them more clearly. Thus, the evidence of the written document is misleading and does not record the agreement—i.e., what the parties meant to agree on—accurately. Furthermore, if a dispute arises and becomes the subject of a contest in court or even in arbitration, the court or arbitrators may also have great difficulty in deciding what the intention was, since the language used is the most direct evidence. Finally, the longer the contract language is, the greater the deliberations required to settle a dispute. Wrangling over a single paragraph (which may have been itself totally unnecessary) can easily consume many hours or even an entire day in court or in arbitration. We can be easily trapped into arguing over the absolute meaning of the language, rather than the meaning we intended to explain and document for future reference as the complete agreement between the parties.

It can thus be inferred that the written contract should be as brief as possible, consistent with covering every point that must be covered (a first consideration, of course). By compelling ourselves to make documents as brief as practicable, we also eliminate redundant and otherwise extraneous distractors.

How To Achieve Brevity and Clarity

Most of us, even professional writers, do not write succinctly in our first drafts, especially when we are concerned about including all pertinent details. Pithy and terse writing is rarely created that way. Instead, such writing is the result of careful and unrelenting editing and revision, often through many drafts. (It is something of a cliché accepted by many professional writers that all good writing is rewriting.) For most of us, the key to the ideal of concise text that includes all the necessary details is writing it all out in a first draft and then

STATE OF

COUNTY OF

    This Agreement is entered into this _____ day of _____, 19___ between _____(Company), whose business address is _____, and _____ (Buyer), whose business address is _____.

    Sale. The Buyer agrees to purchase and The Company agrees to sell, on the terms and conditions following, the machines and equipment listed in Schedule A attached hereto and more fully described in the attached Specification Sheets.

    Price. The prices listed in Schedule A are for machines and products delivered to and set up at the place of business of The Buyer. An additional charge shall be made for State sales tax where applicable. Any personal property taxes assessable on the machines and equipment after delivery shall be borne by the Buyer.

    Terms of payment. A deposit equal to 35% of the total listed on Schedule A is due upon contract signing. An invoice for the balance of machines and products will be issued as of the date of installation. Payment for the machines and products shall be made in full within 10 days of delivery.

    Late charges. A late charge of one and one-half percent (eighteen percent per annum) shall be added to the outstanding charges when an account becomes thirty days past due, and for each month thereafter.

    Installation. Machines and products purchased under this agreement will be installed and placed in good working order by The Company. The Buyer shall make available a suitable place of installation with all facilities required. The date on which the Company notifies The Buyer verbally or in writing that a machine/product has been placed in good working order and is ready for use shall be considered the date of installation for all purposes of this Agreement.

    Restocking fee. In the event that The Buyer refuses to accept any machine or product, or in the event that The Company must repossess any machine, The Buyer shall pay to The Company a restocking fee equal to twenty percent of the invoice amount. This restocking fee is in addition to any damages that may be available for any breach of contract.

    Warranty. Machine and Products shall be covered by a manufacturer's warranty. In the event that a machine or product fails within the period of the manufacturer's warranty, The Buyer may deliver the machine or product to The Company's place of business to obtain warranty repair. The Company will ship the machine or product to the manufacturer for repair. The Buyer expressly agrees that The Company shall not be liable to The Buyer for any loss, liability, damage, cost or expense of The Buyer (including lost profit or any other direct, indirect or consequential damages) resulting from, or attributable to the failure of a machine or product to operate. The Company neither makes nor intends any express or implied warranties of any type or description including merchantability and/or fitness with respect to any product thereof. The terms of this paragraph may be modified by a separate extended warranty.

Title. Title to each of the machines and products is to remain in The Company until the full purchase price is paid. Failure to pay the balance of the purchase price of a machine or product when due shall give The Company the right, without liability, to repossess that machine or product, with or without notice, and to avail itself of any legal remedy.

Governing Law. This Agreement shall be deemed to have been made and entered into in the State of _____, and the construction, validity and enforceability of this Agreement shall be governed by the laws of the State of _____.

Entire Agreement. This constitutes the entire agreement between the parties hereto with respect to the subject matter hereof. All prior contemporaneous or other oral or written statements, representations or agreements by or between the parties with respect to the subject matter hereof are merged herein.

Assignment. A party to this Agreement shall not assign or transfer the rights, duties and obligations hereunder unless the other party hereto consents to such assignment in writing prior to any such assignment. Provided, however, that The Company may assign, without restriction, its right to payment to a third party as a part of hypothecation of its accounts or otherwise.

Miscellaneous. This Agreement shall inure to the benefit of the parties hereto and their respective permitted successors and assigns. This Agreement shall not be changed or modified orally but only by an instrument in writing signed by the parties which states that it is an amendment to this Agreement.

In witness whereof, The Company and The Buyer have caused this Agreement to be signed by their respective duly authorized officers and their respective corporate seals to be hereunto affixed, all as of the day and year first above written.

Figure 8.1 Formal Purchase Agreement   127

```
_____
The Company

By:_____

Title:_____
        (CORPORATE SEAL)

ATTEST:

By:_____
     Secretary


_____
The Buyer

By:_____

Title:_____
        (CORPORATE SEAL)

ATTEST:

By:_____
     Secretary
```

SCHEDULE A

LIST OF GOODS SOLD AND PRICING

TOTAL PRICE $

PURCHASE AGREEMENT

STATE OF

COUNTY OF

Date:

_____, Buyer, agrees to purchase from _____, Seller, the machines and equipment described in the Exhibit attached, at the prices listed in the Exhibit, which include the State sales tax only. Other taxes and assessments, if any, shall be paid by Buyer. Seller will deliver and install the equipment on the Buyer's premises.

Thirty-five percent of the price listed shall be paid on signing this agreement. The remainder shall be invoiced on date of installation and paid within 10 days of issuance. A late charge of one and one-half percent (eighteen percent per annum) shall be added to the outstanding charges when an account becomes thirty days past due, and for each month thereafter.

If Buyer refuses to accept any machine or product or Seller must repossess any machine, Buyer shall pay Seller a restocking fee of twenty percent of the purchase price, plus any damages due as a result of the breach of contract.

Warranty. Machine and Products are covered by manufacturers' standard warranties. If a machine or product fails during the warranty period, Buyer may deliver the machine or product to the Seller's place of business for repair. Buyer agrees that Seller shall not be liable for any loss, liability, damage, cost or expense of Buyer (including lost profit or any other direct, indirect or consequential damages) resulting from, or attributable to the failure of a machine or product to operate. Seller neither makes nor intends any express or implied warranties of any type or description including merchantability and/or fitness with respect to any product thereof.

Title. Title to machines and equipment remains with Seller until the full purchase price is paid. Failure to pay the balance of price when due shall give Seller the right, without liability, to repossess that machine or product, with or without notice, and to avail itself of any legal remedy.

Figure 8.2 Purchase Agreement Simplified 129

Governing Law. This Agreement shall be deemed to have been made and entered into in the State of _____, and the construction, validity and enforceability of this Agreement shall be governed by the laws of the State of _____.

Entire Agreement. This is the entire agreement between the parties with respect to the subject matter hereof. All prior contemporaneous or other oral or written statements, representations or agreements by or between the parties with respect to the subject matter hereof are merged herein.

Assignment. A party to this Agreement shall not assign or transfer the rights, duties and obligations hereunder unless the other party hereto consents to such assignment in writing prior to any such assignment. Provided, however, that Seller may assign, without restriction, its right to payment to a third party as a part of hypothecation of its accounts or otherwise.

Miscellaneous. This Agreement shall inure to the benefit of the parties hereto and their respective permitted successors and assigns. This Agreement shall not be changed or modified orally but only by an instrument in writing signed by the parties which states that it is an amendment to this Agreement.

In witness whereof, Seller and Buyer have caused this Agreement to be signed by their respective duly authorized officers and their respective corporate seals to be hereunto affixed, all as of the day and year first above written.

_____, Seller

By:_____

Title: _____

ATTEST:

By:_____, Secretary

_____, Buyer

By:_____

Title:_____
        (CORPORATE SEAL)

```
ATTEST:

By:_____, Secretary




                 SCHEDULE A

      LIST OF GOODS SOLD AND PRICING



                 TOTAL PRICE $
```

Figure 8.2 Purchase Agreement Simplified 131

editing and rewriting until the goal is reached. The process should generally follow these six steps:

1. Write the first draft.
2. Go over the draft and verify that all bases are covered.
3. Start editing out all verbose and unnecessary text.
4. Replace all obscure, multisyllabic words and terms with simpler ones.
5. If technical jargon is necessary, make the meaning clear by whatever means necessary (e.g., a definitions clause).
6. Rewrite and polish until there is no doubt as to the necessity for and the meaning of every word.

Note that all these steps apply to all the parts and elements of the contract, such as exhibits, attachments and other documents included by reference or a separate set of specifications or proposal. These are a part of the contract, even if they are separate attachments, and it is equally important that they be clear and precise.

What If You Do Not Draft the Contract?

This guidance in writing activity is suitable if you yourself are drafting a contract. And that does not necessarily mean drafting the contract from scratch; you may be working with a standard contract form or model, marking it up for your application. But you will not always be in that position, and may instead be handed a contract by the client, with the request to review and sign it. What do you do then?

The steps laid out in the previous list are as suitable a guide for studying and reviewing a contract already written as they are for writing one. Even if you never draft a contract yourself, the education of learning to draft one is suitable to qualify you to read, understand and evaluate a contract that is handed to you. It is essential that you be able to do this if you are to negotiate successfully—and you should always assume that a contract must be negotiated. Even if you cannot find any faults in a contract offered to you, you must read it and verify that it is acceptable. But many businesspeople will try, as a matter of course, to negotiate better terms in any contract offered them. That is a perfectly respectable and acceptable thing to do and probably is a wise standard practice.

The contract handed you to sign might be one of those preprinted models that you can buy in a stationers or office supplies emporium. It may be a model from a book such as this or one generated by a computer program. It may have been drafted by the client's lawyer (in which case it is almost surely based on one of the lawyer's own models), or it may be a client's long-standing standard form.

When the other party offers you a contract for signature, you cannot begin editing and marking it up; however, neither should you simply sign it. Your first action is to read the document carefully. Never sign anything, and especially not a contract document, without reading it carefully. The immediate purpose is to make sure you understand precisely what it says and what it provides as the rights and duties of both parties.

Those are the key elements, and they are found in every contract. They are involved with the *terms* of the contract, and they are what negotiations are all about, for each party is endowed by a contract with certain rights and duties defined in that contract. Now you are at the point where negotiation begins. First you must understand what the contract says and what it means, not approximately but precisely. You must know all the terms and conditions.

Clarifying the Language

Most standard forms are replete with such words as "whereas," "party of the second part," "warrants" and other terms that add to the fog surrounding bad writing. They don't do any direct harm because they are almost meaningless, and so it is not in your interest to worry about them or make an issue of them. That only leads to fighting the wrong battles. The chief hazard is that these words are often distractors, clouding clear communication and presenting barriers to complete understanding. You can shun them when you are drafting a contract, but you must usually suffer them when you are working with a client's contract. On the other hand, be wary of imprecise language affecting contractual rights and duties, both yours and those of the other party. That is where potential hazards of both commission and omission lurk—especially of omission, or the failure to specify or define something that should have been specified or defined. (One common problem many consultants complain of, for example, is clients' slowness in paying invoices.)

Thus, be watchful in reading a proffered contract for all vague language. In some cases you may be compelled to accept such general terms as "best efforts" and "good commercial practice," as noted earlier (e.g., Chapter 5), but accept these terms reluctantly and only when you find it impossible or impracticable to substitute more precise language.

Some terms are vague because although they refer to something concrete, they do not specify just what that is. If a clause refers to "fiscal year," it is rather meaningless unless you know to whose fiscal year the reference is made (e.g., yours, the other party's or the government's). The following list presents some of the many terms you may encounter that are useful only if they are properly qualified:

- Value
- Property
- Company
- Revenues
- Board
- Arbitration

- All reasonable efforts
- Promptly
- Without delay
- Proper compensation

One way to clarify language is to insert a definitions clause, as shown in Chapter 6. In practice, that is usually a reasonable measure when a contract is replete with special terms. Otherwise, it is usually more practicable and more effective to clarify each term directly, when and where it is first used in the text. "Prompt payment" of invoices, for example, should be stipulated as some maximum number of days, and the penalties to be exacted for late payments should also be stipulated in precise and measurable terms.

THE SINS OF OMISSION

The underlying problem that so many consultants have in getting their invoices paid promptly is further complicated as the result of an omission. Most contracts simply do not stipulate payment terms at all, except in rather general terms, under an assumption that it is not necessary to do more than that. Unfortunately, in a great many cases that is an unwarranted assumption. If you have a slow-paying client, what are your remedies, other than dunning? Even though interest rates have declined somewhat from the highs of recent years, many business owners are still pursuing cash flow management rather aggressively, and one of their major tactics is aging their payables as much as possible. That is a hardship many independent consultants are unable to tolerate.

Many consultants say they no longer offer discounts for prompt payment because it isn't often effective in inducing clients to pay promptly. Many clients take the discount but still do not pay promptly. Some consultants have tried penalizing clients for slowness in paying by demanding interest or penalty payments, although many others are fearful of alienating and losing clients as a result of making such demands. Some bold consultants simply suspend work until the client has brought the account up to date. A bitter dispute sometimes arises as to whether the consultant has a right to do so or is in breach of contract in suspending work. As long as the contract does not address the matter specifically, the latter is probably a moot point and could wind up in litigation, which a contract is designed to avoid.

These are proper matters to incorporate contractually by specific clauses, but the language must itself be specific. A clause that says the client under-takes to "make payments promptly" is meaningless because the client's notion of promptness may be quite different from yours. The language should specifi-cally state that the client will pay your invoices within 15 days or whatever is the period of time to which you can both agree. But that is not enough because it does not stipulate your remedy if the other party fails to meet the contractual duty or obligation specified (unless you want to void the contract as having been breached). The client's failure to perform a duty must result in your right to do something remedial. That condition can suspend your obligation to perform a duty or can confer on you a right, such as that of suspending work or exacting a penalty of some sort until the client has paid your invoice. But to make this effective and bar it from leading to a dispute as in breach of contract, it should be clearly specified in the contract. *Specified* means stated in precise and, where appropriate, measurable terms, not in some generality that covers maximum time for paying your invoices, penalties and/or your right to suspend work until payment is made when payment is delinquent.

It is difficult for clients to object to a specific clause in which they promise to pay bills when due, even if they object to the implications of such a clause. Any client who objects flatly to this kind of clause is sending you a signal that should make you hesitate to do business with that client. Some may complain that such a clause is insulting, but that too is a signal that does not bode well. You should never be criticized for being businesslike in a business relationship. This is not to say that clients should not have the right to attempt to negotiate the language and substance of clauses. It is far better to thrash out any differences over what "prompt payment" means before it becomes an issue. You must not permit the fear of possibly offending a client deter you from being businesslike. In fact, one of the benefits of asking for such clauses is to gauge the nature of a client who is new to you. If you can't reach agreement on a contract, it does not bode well for working together later. You should never have a disagreement over being businesslike in your transactions, and a contract negotiation is a good time to get a firm handle on how businesslike and ethical a new client is likely to be.

9

Negotiating Contracts Defensively

Negotiation is not just "one of the things we do" in the business world. For some, it is *the* thing, the raison d'etre of their existence in the world of commerce, politics and the other businesses of our many organizations. For negotiation is fundamental to all societal relationships, and we could not survive as societies without it.

THE ART OF NEGOTIATION

Negotiation is not something new and strange to any of us—not as individuals, members of organizations of various kinds or members of society at large. We negotiate all our lives, whether we are conscious or unconscious that what we are doing is negotiating. We negotiate every day, often many times a day. When we are children, we negotiate with our friends for positions on a team or participation in a game. We negotiate in trading baseball cards. We try to negotiate with Dad for an increase in allowance or permission to use the family car. And as we get older, we continue to negotiate, whether it is with a prospective employer for a job or with a spouse to decide who will do the dishes and mow the lawn. But we also negotiate with strangers, such as the automobile salesperson and the house painter. The need to negotiate never ends for any of us; but for some of us, it is a serious element or duty of our careers and business lives.

In some parts of the world—the Middle East, for example—negotiating is integral to the culture. You never pay the merchant's asking price in those societies. If so, the merchant knows that you are naive, stupid, American or perhaps all three. He or she might even feel cheated out of the opportunity to haggle and bargain, which is perhaps a merchant's greatest talent, greatest joy and the secret of his or her success.

In our Western culture we believe in standard pricing and fixed prices, even when we are talking about discount pricing, an increasing practice today. But that represents the other element: competitive pricing. We normally tend to pay the fixed price if we want the item, haggling only in certain circumstances, such as in buying an automobile or a house. Even then, a great many Americans are hesitant to haggle, as they think it's demeaning and are conditioned by society to believe that you pay the listed price or you go on your way. We simply don't consider the possibility of negotiating. Negotiating is an honorable and honored business practice; haggling is not. Negotiating is for the boardroom; haggling is for the fish market. Even when we buy an automobile or house, most of us make rather feeble attempts to negotiate better terms or special concessions of any kind, if we try to bargain at all.

Most of us feel unempowered as buyers. But as the party with the power to make choices—to buy or not to buy and to pay or not to pay the asking price—we have the greater power. Unfortunately, most of us tend not to recognize that. We surrender negotiating power to the seller. The seller, who has the greater negotiating experience and skill, has power of another kind. Negotiating skill—the ability to bargain well—is its own power base; and for really good negotiators, it is a remarkably powerful tool.

The notion that one has little choice but to pay the price or not to pay (i.e., to make the purchase or not to make it) is faulty thinking. As writers on the subject have often said, everything is negotiable. (Well, nearly everything. You can encounter situations where your opponent will flatly refuse to yield a micron on some issue. That is when negotiating wisdom is most useful. In these cases, you should accept that position of the other party, at least for the moment, and try to trade something else in compensation or shelve the item for the moment and move on to something else.) One best-selling book was titled *You Can Negotiate Anything,* by Herb Cohen, who is reputed on the book's cover to be "the world's best negotiator."

This chapter is not a complete course in negotiating; that is not an objective of this book. Entire books have been written on the subject by negotiators who are far more expert than I, and some of them are listed in the "Resources" section if you want to acquire more wisdom on the subject.

GOOD AND BAD CONTRACTS

It has been my privilege to negotiate many small contracts and occasional larger ones with the executives of a variety of government agencies, associations, corporations of several kinds and a few other odd and assorted organizations. Many were routine, easily concluded negotiations. Others were lengthy, hard-fought contests to reach complete agreement, and some even resulted in later disputes that had to be settled by further negotiations. Among the many negotiating experiences, some of the most memorable were those I conducted or participated in with the then contracting officer for the Office of Economic Opportunity, Milton Fogelman.

The thing I most remember about the soft-spoken but self-possessed and erudite Fogelman was his never-failing query after we had concluded negotiations and were preparing to sign a contract. He always asked if I or others of my team (when we were a team of negotiators for a large contract) had any remaining doubts, misgivings, uncertainties or points of discontent. If so, he wished to discuss them before we signed anything because the contract was not a good one unless both parties were satisfied. (I have found most government contracting officials to be wary of taking advantage of a supplier's naiveté or negotiating weakness because it is not in the interests of the government to enter into a contract that the other party may not be able to perform satisfactorily, which is always a hazard in bad contracts.)

That is not an unusual idea. It is a concept echoed by many who teach the art, strategies and tactics of negotiating. A good contract is one in which both parties get what they want and believe the agreement was fair. A bad contract is one in which the trade is definitely not fair, one in which one of the parties has been exploited somehow, even if that party does not yet know it. It is even worse if there is resentment or a feeling by either party of having been bludgeoned into submission or otherwise exploited unfairly. For a onetime contract relationship (as in selling a house), a bad contract is likely to have unpleasant consequences that will make the sale no bargain at all for either party.

Bad contracts are bad for both parties. If you allow yourself to be coerced into accepting a contract that imposes harsh terms, you may have trouble performing properly—i.e., doing what you contracted to do. You may find yourself forced to seek shortcuts and cutting corners even if they mean compromising the quality of the work. That is not in the client's interest, but it is not in yours either. And if you subcontract to others, the same argument prevails, but you are the client in that case.

It is especially undesirable for you, as a consultant, to enter into bad contracts where you may not be able to do the job as it should be done. It is especially important for your purposes to conduct negotiations that end in good contracts, based on the assumption that you will wish to sign many contracts with each client and thus will want each contract to be as satisfactory to the client as it is to you. In the long term it will be better for you to walk away from any contract in which the terms imposed make it difficult for you to do the job without cutting a few corners and probably foreclosing the possibility of doing business with that client again. In any case negotiating in good faith to achieve a contract both parties can live with will be the underlying concept in this chapter. As boxers are instructed before the bell, protect yourself at all times, but don't cause low blows or other fouls.

Expert negotiators have many ruses, ploys and other artifices that help them win in their negotiating sessions, often at the expense of their opponents. In this chapter, I will neither advocate nor explain ruses that are intended to deceive or mislead the other party. I think they are unscrupulous and unethical methods of negotiating; but even worse, they only lay the groundwork for future problems. Admittedly, there is such a fine line between what is and is not ethical in negotiating contracts.

Why Negotiate at All?

As a seller of services in a highly competitive field, you may wonder why a prospective client is willing to negotiate with you at all, rather than offering you a contract on a take-it-or-leave-it basis (i.e., entirely on his or her terms). Your own reason for a willingness to negotiate is obvious enough: you want the contract as a sale, and you probably have already invested a great deal of time, effort and money in reaching the point of discussing the terms under which you will be doing business together. (That would be true even if the contract was a verbal one.) On the other hand, the client presumably can turn to any other consultant to get what he or she wants, possibly on whatever terms he or she wishes to dictate. So why should the client be willing to bargain with you for your services?

The willingness to negotiate and often settle for less than he or she would prefer to settle for must be due to some specific factor. That factor is a characteristic desire for gain or fear of loss. The client may especially want your services, as he or she is motivated by a belief that you are more competent than others because you have been highly recommended, have furnished the most convincing and persuasive proposal, made some outstanding other presentation or otherwise struck a responsive note. The client may fear to place trust in anyone of lesser apparent competence and dependability than you. On the other hand, the client may be led to believe that you are hungry for work and thus will be especially pliable and perhaps willing to work for less than your competitors. Whatever the reality, the client has some motivation for negotiating, and it is something you should try to understand for at least the following reasons:

1. You need to enter into negotiations with some confidence that the other party wants to do business with you enough to be willing to negotiate and make whatever compromises are necessary to reach agreement and settle on terms. That self-confidence and feeling of having some leverage—i.e., negotiating power—is essential to your mental set for negotiating successfully. You certainly cannot negotiate from a feeling of weakness; you must feel some strength.

2. You need to formulate some sort of negotiating strategy, basing it on a the theory that your negotiating strength lies principally in what the client wants or fears—wants to avoid or prevent. You may use both motivators in your arguments, offers and promises during negotiations; but overall your strategy should to be based principally on one or the other, and your success in negotiations will depend, in part at least, on how accurately you have gauged the client's principal motivation.

Just What Are You Negotiating?

I am reminded of two sardonic platitudes that seem appropriate.

1. When you are up to your navel in alligators, it is difficult to remember that your original goal was to drain the swamp.
2. Having lost sight of our goal, we are doubling our efforts.

It is dismayingly easy to be diverted from your goal and to forget what it was you originally wanted or needed to document in your contract. That amnesia sometimes shows up in negotiations, and you find yourself fighting hard for something that is of no importance, while you are neglecting to fight for something that is most important. That can be the result of forgetting to listen carefully—to *hear*.

Negotiation as an Art

The principle that both parties should be satisfied with the bargain resulting from negotiations does not mean that negotiation is not a battle of wits, an exercise of skills and a contest, for it is all of those. When you ask for $20,000 and the other party offers you $15,000, it doesn't necessarily mean that he or she thinks $20,000 is excessive and unwarranted. The other party may be quite willing to pay what you ask, but as a matter of principle will try to get the price down if possible. His or her assumption may be that you are asking for more than you expect to get, as part of your negotiating strategy. Your opponent will probe in an effort to find out what you really expect and demand. The counteroffer is not usually an ultimatum; it is a probe to gauge your reaction, your true position. That is, will you accept less? If so, how much less? What might persuade you to accept less? In the meanwhile you ask yourself related questions: *Can* you accept less? Will accepting less win the contract for you? If so, how much less will do the trick? Will insisting stubbornly on the price you want cost you the job? How determined is the other party to pay less than $20,000?

You normally have no easy way to learn the answers to these questions or others that may arise in your mind. You can and should do whatever advance research is possible with regard to getting a slant on your client; but otherwise, you must depend on your knowledge of the industry, your own expert judgment and those clues you can gain during the negotiations. That is why negotiating is an art and not a science. Your success depends primarily on your skill in drawing the other out, reading signs of the other's intentions, persuading him or her to your views, solving problems, finding reasonable compromises and perhaps exercising your abilities as an actor and skilled bluffer. Your opponent will try to mask his or her feelings and intentions as much as possible, but you can gain some notion from subtle clues. Some believe that an opponent's reactions and intentions are signaled by body language, but I have some doubts. For example, folding one's arms doesn't necessarily mean defiance: it may be an unconscious habit that has no significance at all. I am more inclined to try to judge an opponent's intentions by expressed positions and what I happen to know or think I know of the industry, the market and what is practicable or impracticable.

You can't depend on your opponent voluntarily or inadvertently giving away his or her position. If you are a good negotiator, you ask certain questions and make certain statements with the deliberate intent of evoking a response that will furnish clues to judge your opponent's intentions and your own best next move. It is wise to assume that your opponent is a competent negotiator, at least as good as you.

Characteristics of a Good Negotiator

There are many good and not-so-good negotiators. Some people happen to be good negotiators naturally—almost by instinct—just as others have inherent talent for certain activities. There are many characteristics and practices that are common to most successful negotiators. Some of the outstanding traits are as follows:

- Advance preparation
- Setting negotiating goals
- Persuasiveness
- Patience
- Perseverance
- Poker face
- Listening carefully
- The art of silence
- Likeable persona
- Ability to "betray" emotions when desirable
- Willingness to understand the other's position
- Ability to play the rube
- Asking questions
- Problem-solving talent

These are just a few of the abilities and traits that mark the successful negotiator. The ability to persuade—to sell—is rather obvious, but it can be learned, as can all the others. (If you study the matter, you will find many similarities between the principles of selling and negotiating.) Good negotiators plan and prepare for each negotiation in some proportion to the importance of the contract at stake. But let's discuss a few of the most important traits and abilities.

Advance Preparation. Negotiating success depends in large part on advance preparation. You should prepare carefully for each negotiation. Otherwise, you are likely to encounter surprises you will not know how to handle well, especially if the other party has prepared properly for the negotiation. You should do these things in advance:

- Make up a list of your negotiating goals—what you want.
- Set the negotiating range—what you want and the minimum you will accept.
- Estimate what the other party is likely to want and will accept as the minimum.
- Decide or estimate what your trade-offs might be.
- Learn as much as you can about the other party as a trader.
- Decide what are your strengths and weaknesses as a negotiator.
- Estimate the other party's strengths and weaknesses.
- Consider what your alternatives are if the negotiation is unsuccessful—i.e., if you are unable to reach agreement.

The last item is an especially important one and perhaps should be the first item in the list. If you enter negotiations feeling that you absolutely must have this contract and so *must* reach agreement, you may be conditioning yourself to accept a bad deal if it is the only one you can get. That mental set almost ensures that you will get a bad deal because it will make you timid in seeking to achieve your own goals in negotiations. A competent opponent won't have great difficulty detecting that timidity and taking full advantage of it. To be strong and confident, as you must be to negotiate anything effectively, you must be prepared to walk away from the table. You must have some alternative to this contract planned, some course of action you will follow if your negotiation does not succeed in reaching terms acceptable to you. The knowledge that you are prepared to exercise an alternative to reaching agreement is a source of strength. Your opponent can sense that strength and confidence as easily as he or she can sense timidity and weakness. Accept the reality of some minimums to your requirements and the possibility that you will not be able to come to terms with the client. That will increase the probability that you will succeed at the table.

One of several problems I inherited when I became editorial director of the former Educational Systems Division of U.S. Industries was an uncompleted contract with a writer to write a programmed-instruction book in transistor technology, then the hottest subject in electronics. The author had received one-half of his advance on signing the contract and had written about one-half of the book but had not done more in many months, and the contracted-for completion date had long since passed into history. I had a conversation with the author that went something like this, beginning with my opening query after introducing myself and the project I wished to discuss:

"I need to know your plans for completing this project and satisfying your contract with us."

"I need money."

"That seems to me a good reason for finishing the book and collecting the rest of your advance fee."

"But I need money now."

"I am prepared to make progress payments. I will pay you a prorated amount of the balance each time I get an acceptable new section of the manuscript."

"No, I need the money in advance, now."

"Sorry, but I can't do that. I am stretching a point, as it is. Your contract did not call for progress payments, and you have long since breached your contract by nonperformance."

"I guess you are not going to get the book then."

"If you refuse to consider my offer, I will be forced to send you a formal notice that your contract has been voided by your failure to perform."

"Then you will never get the book."

"Well, if necessary, we will finish the book ourselves. In fact, I will personally do it."

"It's pretty technical. How will you manage that?"

"That is not your problem; it's mine. But for your information, I can easily find another author to complete it, if I have to. However, I will probably write the rest of it myself."

"Oh. Do you know enough about transistors?"

"Enough to write this book from scratch, if I have to, and certainly enough to finish it. You aren't the only writer around who has had an electronic education."

"You won't be able to use my name."

"That is not a problem. The success of this book does not depend on the author's reputation, and you don't have one that would help, in any case."

This author's resistance and arguments collapsed when he found that we were ready to accept the alternative and were not dependent on him to finish the job. He went on to accept my offer and completed the book, chapter by chapter. My knowledge that I could finish that book myself and my willingness to do that if necessary gave me a position of strength from which to negotiate, and I took advantage of that, although I gave the other party more than a fair deal under the circumstances, despite his defiant attitude and the arrogance of his position. It was in our best interest to have him finish the book and satisfy the contract, and I made concessions to that end.

This anecdote illustrates negotiating from strength, from being more or less independent of the other party and his or her role in the principal matter under negotiation—i.e., of having a viable alternative to agreement. But it illustrates also the occasional fallacy of believing that you are negotiating from strength or that the other party has no strength, so that you can impose harsh terms. In this situation the other party was negotiating from what appeared to be a weak position, and yet he "won" too because he did have a certain strength in our desire to have him complete the book as the best way for us to satisfy the project and resolve the problem. To at least some degree, the strength of your position depends on the desires and objectives of the other party, and you must consider that when you assess your own position. But the anecdote also illustrates that contract negotiations are not necessarily complete when the contract is signed; there may be additional negotiations later. Don't ever overlook that possibility. Even when one party to a contract may be in default in some manner, the other party may not find it in his or her own interest to void or cancel the contract but may be willing to renegotiate the terms of the contract to enable its completion in some satisfactory way.

Setting Negotiating Goals. For some consultants, the list for negotiations rarely changes much from one contract or assignment to the next because they are so highly specialized in what they do that their requirements or demands rarely change much. For others, those who undertake a wide variety of projects and offer a diverse array of services, each project represents a new and fresh challenge. If your requirements rarely change, you may have a set hourly rate or range within which you will work and your own standard contract that you offer clients. Clients may or may not accept your contract, but even if you find it necessary to negotiate on the basis of a contract the client offers, you know in advance what you want, the minimums you will accept and the trade-offs you will consider. It helps greatly to go into a negotiation with these limits already established in your mind and with a certain knowledge of how much you can compromise your objectives without impairing your ability to perform on the contract.

Persuasiveness. There has always been the notion of the "born salesman," a talent some people think is on the order of acrobatic or singing ability. It may be true that some men and women have inherent instincts for persuading others to buy, but persuasiveness can be learned, as Frank Bettger found. He was a baseball player whose playing career ended with a knee injury, which forced him to turn to selling insurance for a living. He was a dismal failure as an insurance salesman—for a time. But he persevered and learned from his daily experience, eventually becoming the original member of the million dollar roundtable, a group of insurance sellers who have sold $1 million or more insurance in a year. His book, *How I Raised Myself from Failure to Success in Selling,* quickly became a classic and has been in print continuously in many editions since 1949 and is still reprinted today.

Bettger isn't the only man or woman who learned how to be persuasive and became supersellers. However, this is not the place to teach the fundamentals of selling itself but to focus on the benefits to the other party of closing the deal. The art of selling successfully lies in managing to learn or judge accurately what the other party wants most or fears most and finding a way to appeal to that prime motivator. That principle also applies to the art of negotiating successfully.

Patience and Perseverance. Patience, or the appearance of patience, is an indispensable requirement for a negotiator. If you are not naturally a patient person, try to conceal your impatience. If you have a deadline, by all means don't reveal it. For example, don't glance nervously at your watch every few minutes or appear to be rushing the other party, for knowing you have a deadline can easily become a negotiating weapon for your opponent. There are occasions when you may wish to use a deadline, real or imagined, as a negotiating tactic to force the other's hand. Unless that is the case, never appear to be under the pressure of a deadline. Appear calm and unhurried. But if you learn the other party's deadline, you may be able to use it to exert pressure on him or her to settle.

Perseverance is equally important. Negotiation is not a game for those who are too quick to quit, impatient to persevere or hasty to come to a conclusion. You must not only *appear* to be patient; you must actually *be* patient.

Be a good listener, too; that is a large part of being patient. Always be willing to hear the other party out at length.

Listening—and *Hearing*. Listening is not as passive a function as it may seem. Nor is *listening* necessarily synonymous with *hearing*. You may appear to be listening but do not hear what the other is saying. You may be mulling what the other party said previously, what you think about it, how you will respond or what your next argument will be and not hearing what the other is saying at all. Or perhaps you are just bored with the whole process of negotiating in general and are thinking about totally unrelated matters.

That's a hazard because it is difficult to respond intelligently to something you did not hear, and it may well have been something of special importance. If only for defensive reasons, it is essential that you both listen and hear what the other is saying.

The Art of Silence. Silence is a secret weapon and a powerful one, used far too little by salespeople and negotiators. Some master salespeople say that once the salesperson completes the presentation, he or she should fall silent and wait for the prospect to speak. Some even say that it becomes a contest between the seller and the prospective buyer, and the first one to speak loses. That is, if the seller says another word, the sale is probably lost; whereas the seller wins by waiting for the prospective buyer to speak, no matter how long and awkward the silence.

It is easy to overemphasize the importance of silence as a negotiating tactic and to overuse it as well. It is a tool to be used sparingly and judiciously, when the occasion is right. When the other party pauses or has completed a statement (e.g., "I need this project completed in 90 days without spending premium time on it"), he or she expects you to respond with agreement to the demand, opposition or comment.

If you sit silently and look thoughtful, the other may think you are mulling the demand over for acceptability, agreeing to it or preparing to rebut and reject it. Whatever the case, if you remain silent long enough, the other will resume talking, probably a bit nervously and iterating and reiterating the demand with explanations of why it is necessary, the consequences of not achieving the schedule and other expansion. This is the time to listen and hear with special awareness, for the other is now likely to provide a clue as to how you can best respond. You may find that the 90 days is not as rigid a demand as it seems or that the rejection of charging for premium time to meet the schedule is not as firm as first stated. In any case, silence at a well-chosen stage of the negotiation usually will put the other party in a slightly nervous and probably defensive state, which is a good time for you to make a counteroffer or demand.

Poker Face. There are times when you want the other party to read your emotions, such as concern, regret and fear, but only when you can see some advantage in revealing or appearing to reveal them. Otherwise, you must hold your cards close and maintain a bland expression. Whatever one party reads in the face of the other may become a useful weapon. Try to reveal by expression or other indirect method only that which you wish to reveal as part of your own strategy and tactical method.

Playing the Rube. Even if your opponent knows you are putting on an act, it is helpful in many negotiating situations to seem like the totally naive and ingenuous amateur who asks dumb questions. Your opponent cannot help but be at least partly disarmed or amused, and he or she can never be sure how much of your trusting innocence is real and how much is a clever and probably ingratiating act!

Likeable Persona. It is much easier to reach terms with someone who finds you likeable than with someone who dislikes the personality you display. People want to believe and trust a likeable person. Smile freely and be as pleasant as possible, even when disagreeing with your opponent and fighting for what you want. Use "yes, but" rather than "no" arguments as much as possible. Express your regret that you cannot be more accommodating.

Understanding the Other's Position. It is a sound negotiating tactic and part of that likeable personality to feel and to indicate complete understanding and empathy when your opponent explains his or her problems and concerns. Try to sincerely consider the other's needs and wishes and to find accommodations that will enable both of you to be satisfied. Finding the acceptable compromise is the real art of negotiation.

Asking Questions. Asking questions to get the information you need is a negotiating tactic not used enough. There are ways to ask questions that help you, and there are ways to ask questions that hurt you. Don't, for example, ask questions that imply contempt or ridicule for your opponent or his or her position. Try to frame questions that require information to be revealed, rather than simple yes or no questions. If you have a really tough question to ask, don't spring it suddenly but try to make it part of a series of questions that start with soft ones and progress to tougher ones. Ask questions with an objective or neutral tone of voice and facial expression. Try to frame questions to elicit positive rather than negative responses. For example, "How many of your proposals have been winners in the past year?" rather than "How many of your proposals didn't quite make it last year?" Embarrassing your opponent is generally not to your advantage in a negotiation.

Your opponent will not always furnish the answers you want to hear. He or she may automatically put up a barrier to even innocent questions, fearful of giving something away. However, it is often almost as helpful to get an evasion as it is to get a direct answer. You can usually infer something useful from an opponent's refusal to answer a question or evasive response. Skilled negotiators often get information or verify suspicions by asking questions they know will probably not be answered.

Problem Solving. Nothing is more valuable in negotiations than problem-solving ability. (As a consultant, problem solving ought to be one of your principal skills.) Every impasse—when the immovable object and the irresistible force meet each other—is a challenge to the negotiators' problem-solving skills. (Note how closely related this is to finding acceptable compromises.) Failure to solve the problem that results in an impasse means the negotiations break down and fail. *Both* parties then fail. You must believe that there is a solution and that it can be found. When a solution cannot be found immediately, it is often helpful to shelve the item temporarily and go on to the next item. If you manage to find agreement on all other items, there is greatly increased motivation to solve the problem when you return to it. Deadlock-breaking compromise then becomes much more likely. In fact, the solution to an earlier deadlock may evolve from agreements reached after temporarily shelving the sticky problem. Problem solving is an often critically important element of contract negotiation and is useful in most negotiating situations. But it is especially appropriate in what are often called "win-win" negotiations, as you will read shortly.

STRATEGIES AND STYLES

As in most things, there are standard strategies in negotiating; there are also strategies of improvisation and expediency. The clever negotiator will often invent a new strategy or a new model of a strategy already used because it is necessary or because he or she sees a sudden opportunity.

Most negotiators have some specific strategy or approach to negotiations, although they may not use the same approach in each case but may opt for the approach that seems most appropriate to the occasion.

Most experienced negotiators know all the standard negotiating strategies, and you need to know them too, at least well enough to know when they are being used against you. But even without perceiving a particular strategy your opponent is pursuing, his or her general style and approach should be apparent to you long before you get very far into the discussions.

Adversarial or Win-Lose Strategies

The layperson probably believes that all negotiating is stubbornly adversarial, with each side trying earnestly to outwit, outmaneuver and outbargain the other side or, that failing, to bludgeon the other into submission, perhaps with a take-it-or-leave-it ultimatum. Unfortunately, there are negotiators who reason similarly. Anyone with whom they must negotiate even inconsequential matters, such as who will go and get coffee for the two of them, is an adversary to be bested. A young man who worked for me once in a large organization rarely did the job I assigned him. I discovered that he always worked immediately at persuading someone else to do the job. He had an overpowering desire to feel the satisfaction of outbargaining or outwitting another person, and never missed an opportunity to try.

Such negotiators usually begin from extreme positions, making demands that they know are far in excess of anything they can expect to get. They are stubborn in defending their positions, and they are limited in their authority to make concessions and reach compromises, or they claim to be. They may argue all day over a minor point. And yet it is a mistake to concede victories to them too easily, for it does nothing to assuage their appetites for winning but only sharpens those appetites. They probably will regard you as "easy" and naive if you let them win even the minor points too easily. To this kind of negotiator, making concessions without a bitter struggle is weakness. In fact, they soon decide that it is their right to get quick and easy concessions from you.

Such negotiators may or may not always be successful. They frequently think they have been successful, but what they won was not worth much and they could have had it much more easily. They would not have appreciated it earlier, however; it would not have represented being smarter or better than someone else in "winning."

In many cases it is easy to best such a negotiator by letting him or her win many points while you win only one or two, but you win the one or two most important points. If you let this kind of opponent win enough small victories, you will get relatively little opposition on the larger victories. In one case when our sizable team was negotiating for a multi-million-dollar contract, we found ourselves struck down on point after point. Although they were relatively minor points, it stung us that the client was entirely arbitrary and simply rejected our arguments without hesitation. The head of our team, who happened to be the president of our company, finally blurted out, half in jest but showing a bit of annoyance, too, "You've been taking and taking and taking. How about giving a little, too?" The head of the client's negotiating team was startled and looked slightly embarrassed. Then the atmosphere in the room changed sharply, and negotiations went on in much more of a win-win philosophy with less adversarial tone.

Win-Win Strategy

The strategic approach to negotiating known as *win-win* is one in which the adversarial condition that is inherent in all negotiations is tempered by an approach designed to work together to find problem solutions satisfactory to both parties (i.e., both sides "win").

This sounds like a wonderful way to negotiate, a situation in which nobody loses. What could be better? It's not quite that simple, however. There are problems here, too. And the first problem is persuading your opponent to bargain in a win-win style rather than in the competitive mode we tend to think is required and inevitable in negotiating agreements. Win-win negotiating requires that both parties agree that the objective is not to outwit, outbargain and outlast each other but to find the point at which they can agree that their needs have been met by the final terms and they are satisfied with the agreement.

This does not mean that there is a basic conflict of interest. If there were not, there would be no need for a contract, much less a negotiation. Each party wants something from the other party, and the two wants appear to be in serious conflict. Each party thinks that to get what he or she wants, the other must give up what he or she wants. Wants, however, are not always the same thing as needs, and that is often the heart of the problem. Each party fails to see that the felt want is a premise (not always an accurate one) of how the need must be satisfied rather than a definition of the need. For example, a client may express an absolute need to have a certain project completed and delivered in 30 days, whereas I know I will need at least 45 days to get the job done without working nights and weekends, and I am unwilling to give up my nights and weekends for the project. We are soon deadlocked on the issue. But now I probe, trying to determine what my client's real need is. *Why* does he "need" the product in 30 days? What does he plan to do with it? I soon learn that he has an important meeting scheduled with the top brass in his company's home office for the following month and believes he needs at least 15 days to become completely familiar with the system I am to develop for him. His real need is to present this new system and discuss it in detail in about six weeks. I offer to spend a full day going over the system and briefing him in all its details if he allows me 45 days to do my work. We both win—i.e., get what we need—without injuring each other.

This kind of negotiating in its essence consists of identifying each party's need, as distinct from want, and then seeking solutions that satisfy the needs. Problem solving is integral to this mode of negotiating. The chief problem in a great many cases is learning what the *true* needs are and not allowing yourself to be misled by expressed wants that are actually presumptions of how to satisfy the true need. However, even in the most cooperative negotiation, your interests are adverse to those of the other party. One party gains at the expense of the other party.

DO AND DON'T GUIDELINES FOR NEGOTIATING

These discussions have, of necessity, not gone far beyond touching on the main themes and issues of negotiating contracts. Perhaps the most useful guidance on the subject is to point to a few do and don't principles to avoid the most common errors and pursue some basic approaches that work best in most negotiating situations.

Ultimatums and Deadlines

If you say to the other party words such as "That's my best offer. Take it or leave it," you foreclose negotiations immediately. You have announced your final position in advance. What is left to negotiate? The only way such a negotiation can be salvaged is for the other party to ignore the ultimatum— i.e., pretend it was never said—and continue as though it had indeed never been said.

Announcing a deadline is equally self-defeating as it eliminates uncertainty, the chief reason for negotiation. Both parties undoubtedly have deadlines; but shrewd negotiators, even in win-win negotiating, don't reveal more than the other party needs to know as discussions continue.

The essence of any negotiation is the continuing possibility that the other party will yield or cooperate a bit more—that there is still *room* for negotiation. When you eliminate that possibility, you end the negotiation. You either have come to final agreement or you have reached deadlock. Deadlocks can be broken, but it is best to avoid them if possible. (And it usually is possible.)

Early Concessions and Giveaways

One mistake some negotiators make is to open discussion with a concession or to make it early in the discussion with the avowed purpose of saving time. It may indeed save time but probably at great cost to the party who made the unnecessary concession or made a necessary concession unnecessarily soon in the process. For example, suppose you propose a price of $40,000 in your proposal and the client calls on you to come in for "best and final" discussions (a common step in many government contracting processes). You know that your proposal was in the ballpark, and the client took it seriously enough to want to discuss contracting with you. You don't know whether the client is also having similar discussions with others. You also don't know whether the client finds your price a bit too high or is going to negotiate with you as a matter of policy and try to get better prices. Asked if that is your "best price," you respond immediately with "Well, let's save time. I can sharpen my pencil a bit." You have conceded that your price was on the high side. From here on, the chief discussion and interest of your opponent is how much you can sharpen your pencil—i.e., how much you can be driven to further sharpening of your pencil.

You should have fought hard before making that concession. You should have made the other party work hard for it. And you should not have made it without getting something in return. If you get even a ten-cent reduction in what you must deliver for every ten-dollar concession you make, you must do that. You must make your opponent trade with you and pay something for everything you yield.

Be Patient and Keep Your Temper

There are negotiators who will deliberately try your patience by provoking you. They will assume an arrogant attitude, speak to you sneeringly and otherwise work at making you lose your cool. That puts you at a disadvantage in more than one way, if it succeeds in making you respond in kind. When you get angry, your judgment is affected. And if you get angry, the other party feels that he or she is justified in taking advantage of you at every turn and without the slightest mercy. If you meet such an opponent, assume that the bad temper displayed is an act, a deliberate ploy, and ignore it.

Anticipate and Prepare for Possible Changes in Scope

You may recall the discussions of what changes in scope mean for you (See Chapter 5). They mean that you have grounds for renegotiating your contract, which normally means more money for you and possibly contract extensions in time. Changes in scope ordinarily work to your benefit as a contractor because they justify and open the door to renegotiation for added work and added money. However, there is one condition. You must be able to demonstrate that what the client asks does represent a change in scope—i.e., it calls for more than you contracted for originally. (In fact, many contractors are quite easy to negotiate with when they foresee an almost certainty that there will be extensive changes in scope before the contract is over. They can then negotiate the changes—in fact, *renegotiate* the contract—from a position of much greater strength as the incumbent contractor.)

The necessary caveat is to consider the specification of work quite closely in negotiating the contract (and/or in writing the original proposal) to ensure that (1) there is the possibility/probability that there will be changes and (2) the specification of work is quite detailed so that you will have no difficulty later identifying changes and proving that they are changes to the original contract. The main point here is quantification. If you have not quantified what you contracted for (e.g., a particular number of hours or days, pages, engineering drawings, etc.), you probably will have a rather difficult time establishing any request as a change or increase in contracted-for quantities. Fight hard to specify numbers, even if they are the roughest of estimates. They become what you contracted for.

Avoid Deadlocks or, at Least, Manage Them

Deadlocks are where a negotiation is most likely to founder. The irresistible force meets the immovable object and all movement stops. The irresistible force will not stop pushing, and the immovable object will not give way. Even with the greatest diplomatic skills, the most artful problem-solving efforts and the maximum effort to identify and define the true needs of the parties, neither will yield a micron. Negotiations are at a standstill.

It is important to recognize the impending deadlock as soon as possible, and manage it. Anticipate the deadlock and take some kind of action before the polarization becomes too rigid—i.e., before both of you have become too emotionally involved in defending your positions. The more entrenched you become in the defense, the more difficult it becomes for you to negotiate your way out of it. Western society does not attach as much importance to "face" and losing as Eastern society perhaps does, but it is not an unknown factor here either. When you see a deadlock as inevitable, managing it means maneuvering out of it as soon as possible.

As mentioned earlier, the smart move is to agree to shelve the issue, for the moment, and move on to other matters, resolving to return later to the sticky wicket. This is especially important if the issue that causes the deadlock has come up at an early stage in the negotiations. With comparatively little time invested and the other party still a stranger, it is relatively easy to abandon the negotiation as a waste of time. When a deadlock comes up late in the negotiation, there is some reluctance to abandon it. Thus, it is wise to postpone the return to the major problem until every other issue has been settled. Perhaps some of the events that transpire in the meantime will create a better basis for solving the problem over which negotiations reached a deadlock earlier. Perhaps a better understanding between the parties will make them almost friends and more disposed to finding a solution. And perhaps with so much time invested, so much accomplished and agreement so close, there is great reluctance to cast it all out and suffer the feeling of failure with success so close.

Special Measures

These measures are general in that they can and should apply to negotiations to defend against the problems that arise as a result of naiveté or excessive trust to luck. There are, however, certain special clauses and considerations that are pertinent in many cases and that are specific defenses against the mistakes of both accepting language that is injurious to your own interests and failing to take advantage of some clauses that you can turn to your advantage. Some are clauses and conditions to watch for and guard against. Others are clauses and conditions to include in your contracts whenever possible. Still others can be helpful or injurious, depending on how they are written, so you must make sure they are written to your advantage, if they are to be used at all. Some of these have been mentioned in passing in this and previous chapters. In the next chapter we will take a much closer look at these special and specific defensive measures.

10

The Fine Print

With reference to contracts, jesters have said that the large print giveth and the fine print taketh away. The print that "taketh away," however, need not be small, even in a metaphorical sense, to present terms and conditions that turn out to be booby traps.

LANGUAGE, CONDITIONS AND CLAUSES

As an independent consultant and contractor, many of your most important agreements will be service contracts involving services only. Depending on how specialized your practice is and the bounds you observe in what you offer clients, you may encounter only a limited number of types of contracts in the course of pursuing your practice. Nevertheless, those contracts will inevitably—and properly—include a diverse array of clauses, language, conditions and provisions. The number and variety of possible permutations and combinations for even a single contract for well-defined services is rather large; it is thus easy enough to overlook or be blissfully unaware of the profound effect a few apparently harmless words can have. Even a single phrase or word may have great advantages or disadvantages for you. Bear in mind that the words recorded as the mutual agreement are the chief and often only evidence upon which disputes can be settled in courts, arbitration or even in friendly and informal negotiations between parties. It is necessary to both include and specify the full agreement in all its detail, as already stressed many times, but that is not enough. It is equally necessary to be cautious when confronted with standard clauses that are airily brushed aside as being "just boilerplate." Boilerplate clauses are not always innocuous; they can become deadly quicksand. Standard or not, they merit close reading and careful consideration.

CLAUSES IN GREAT ARRAY

The number of possible clauses, even those accepted as more or less standard elements, is itself large; and when multiplied by the many possible variations, it can become even larger and more bewildering. Moreover, the tendency to use different headings or captions to identify and define the subject matter of any given clause adds to the confusion. For example, "Indemnification" and "Hold Harmless" may cover the same ground. And finally, the need to create special clauses or classes of clauses for given applications is a further complicating factor. There is almost no limit to the number and variety of contract clauses that may be relevant and appropriate in any given situation. You must therefore be guided by what the words themselves say and not by any other consideration. As semanticists say, the word is not the thing; but it is words with which we must deal in contracting, and we must weigh them carefully in making commitments.

There are many possible contractual situations, and some clauses are appropriate to all or almost all situations (e.g., clauses covering confidentiality), but others are appropriate to only certain kinds of situations or uses. For example, if you hire out as a temporary, you may be asked to sign an employment contract or confidentiality and other agreements appropriate to employment contracts but not appropriate to consulting contracts. Even as an independent consultant, such matters as licensing and rights to products you develop under contract may become the subject of contracts. Of course, certain clauses are relevant to only certain types of contracts, too. For example, a clause specifying a maximum response time to the client's request would be appropriate to a task order contract or basic ordering agreement but would not normally be appropriate to a fixed-price contract for one specific project.

Service contracts are the most appropriate and most commonly used consulting contracts. That is not surprising in a profession that is basically one involving services. Many consultants, however, deal also in products and thus need purchase and sales agreements. And since consulting is after all a business with typical business needs, you may find yourself in need of contracts to finance business operations, rent or buy real estate, make assignments or license or sell under royalty agreements. Even if you do not need these kinds of contracts initially, you cannot predict where your practice will lead you in a business sense, and those needs may surface later.

To some degree, *clause* and *contract* are interchangeable. That is, almost any agreement may be covered by a separate and complete contract, such as one for finder's fees or indemnification, or by a single clause in a larger contract.

Therefore, don't be surprised if you encounter clauses that have the same impact as contracts you encountered elsewhere or vice versa.

The following is a list of just a few clauses you are likely to encounter under these and other names:

Best efforts	Disputes
Pricing methods	Arbitration
Governing law	Training services
Term	Maximum response time
Termination	Task disputes
Indemnification	Finder's fee
Warranty	Commissions
Consequential damages	Expenses
Payments	Subcontracts
Pricing methods	Rights
Schedule/proposal	Relationship
Custom work product	

Models and Samples

In the rest of this chapter, I will present the most important clauses you are likely to encounter or have need of, especially those requiring the most careful consideration (i.e., those with potential hazards). For the most part, however, model contracts and clauses will be presented in the Chapter 11.

A Few Cautions

You must be aware of the many typical and allegedly standard clauses you are most likely to encounter in negotiating contracts for your services. Therefore, observe these cautions and practices in creating and negotiating agreements of all kinds:

- Never allow anyone to brush your question aside and persuade you to skim over clauses casually. You may find it wise to exclude them or modify the language. Even the most timeworn and commonly accepted clause is not chipped in granite: the language can and should be modified when necessary.
- Don't become confused by headings in contracts that are different from the headings you have encountered in other contracts. Be guided by the content of the clause, not its heading.
- Don't leave things to chance or accept verbal assurances. Don't hesitate to insist on the inclusion of any clause you think is necessary to protect your own interests, even if it means writing a new, special clause.

Adapting the Clause to Your Need

In earlier chapters we discussed clauses from the legal viewpoint, covering such concerns as legitimacy of contract and enforceability. In this chapter we will discuss clauses from the viewpoint of strategic significance. There are three major purposes for presenting and discussing these clauses: (1) to suggest some of the ways in which many clauses may be modified to suit your needs (e.g., note the discussion in this chapter of contract *term*); (2) to make you aware of the principal clauses you are likely to encounter and to caution you to consider each carefully; and (3) to show you that each clause may become a bargaining chip you can employ and therefore an opportunity for you to negotiate. Remember that you negotiate a contract clause by clause because each clause is itself an agreement. In short, bargaining over clauses is a strategic tool.

Standard May Be Only a Word

Despite these cautions, it is true enough that many of the clauses and conditions that appear commonly in contracts are more or less standard and applicable to many contracts, and some are even of little consequence. Many are rather routine, substantially the same in each use. Clauses covering trade secrets and confidentiality tend to provide pretty much the same requirements, even though the language may vary somewhat from one contract to another.

On the other hand, there are clauses that are standard in that they are found in most or at least in many contracts, but they vary widely in what they specify as duties, rights and/or conditions for any given application. Sometimes it is absolutely necessary to fight hard over wording. Just a little carelessness in agreeing to wording without reading it carefully and thinking it out thoroughly can be quite expensive for you later. To negotiate and contract defensively—i.e., to protect your own interests—you must be conscious of the exact wording of these clauses and conditions, and you must understand both their meanings and implications. (Where meanings are not crystal clear, implications may make a great deal of difference.) There are some clauses, statements and provisions you should exclude if possible but others you should include if possible. There are still others that can be harmful or beneficial, according to how you utilize and word them.

Finally, there are some commonly used clauses that have little real effect, although they are encountered rather frequently. However, those are exceptions; most contract clauses do have great significance. Don't be lulled into regarding them as anything else. Most of the clauses are deadly serious in what they provide, and they can have serious impact on what you have agreed to and are obliged to do and accept.

Some people have the foible of incorporating into their contracts clauses and language that are inappropriate, either because they call for conditions or obligations that cannot be enforced under common law or statutory law or they have no significant effect on the rights and duties of the contracting parties.

In this chapter you will encounter a potpourri of clauses, phrases, conditions and provisions you are likely to encounter in your practice when negotiating contracts with clients. Some of the items mentioned will be familiar to you because they were discussed at some length earlier. Others will be new. The purpose is to help refresh your memory as well as introduce you to some new information and alert you to some of the hazards you may encounter. It will serve as a reference file for occasions when you must draft a contract. At the same time it will also help you understand the model contracts and clauses presented later. In some cases exemplary illustrations will appear; in other cases reference will be made to illustrations already included elsewhere.

There is no particular significance to the order in which these items are presented, for there really is no logical relationship among them. Even an alphabetical order would serve no real purpose because a given clause may be known by different names. For example, one contract may have a "trade secrets" clause that covers the same ground as a "confidentiality of information" or "proprietary data" clause in another contract, and the label "governing law" is about the same subject as "choice of forum." The important thing is what the clause or condition is about, not what it is called. Judge each clause by its content, not by its label. Conditions and provisions may be stipulated in various ways and places. Breaches of contract, defaults and remedies, for example, may be explained in clauses that are labeled as such or in other clauses directly or indirectly related to the matter. Thus, the word *potpourri* is most appropriate to use in alerting you to what is to come. The organization of items in this chapter is chosen by this author, and I accept full responsibility for it.

Best Efforts

One clause mentioned earlier is the "best efforts" clause. Often cited in agreements, this clause is where the party performing the service pledges his or her best efforts as a warranty for the undertaking. It is a warranty that in reality has little substance as long as the party can be shown to have made some reasonable effort. Best efforts is not a truly definable or measurable item, and it therefore provides substantial warranty or assurance that the contractual objectives will be met.

If you are contracting for someone's services (e.g., a subcontractor you are engaging to assist you in some contractual obligation), a pledge by that individual or organization should, of itself, mean little to you. On the other hand, as the service provider you should feel free to offer that pledge freely, since it imposes no burden on you that you would not be undertaking anyway. If a client wants that kind of clause, you have little reason to oppose it. See Figure 10.1 for an example of a best efforts pledge included in a lengthy clause that covers the subject of warranty.

BEST EFFORTS PLEDGE AND WARRANTY

(b) Limited Performance Warranty. Contractor represents and warrants for a period of ninety (90) days ("Warranty Period") that all services rendered hereunder shall be performed with due diligence and with Contractor's "best efforts" to ensure that any resulting Custom Work Product and Embedded Software (as defined in Section 5) have been prepared in accordance with sound engineering standards.

Courtesy QuickForm Contracts, Invisible Hand Software

Good Faith

Another phrase some people find comforting is one expressing assurance that the other party is bargaining with you in good faith—i.e., with the sincere intention of reaching a mutually acceptable agreement and honoring that agreement faithfully. You may encounter some negotiators who wish to record the pledge of good faith by incorporating it into contract language. There is no true benefit to be derived from this pledge, but there is also no harm in agreeing to its inclusion in a preamble to a contract.

Headings and Captions

Another clause that is commonly found (but is of doubtful value) is one that stipulates that the various headings and captions found throughout the contract are for ease of reference or convenience and as such are only labels and imply no special meaning or interpretation.

Good Commercial Practice

The concept of good commercial practice has been mentioned several times in earlier chapters, especially in Chapter 5. It has its shortcomings as an assurance of proper workmanship, technique and service because it does not offer measurable standards. However, as explained in Chapter 5, it does have some usefulness and force in that it is usually possible to establish that a service performed or product developed meets the implied standard of that phrase. Whether you are the client or contractor, it is far better for you to have every duty and product spelled out in measurable terms. But since it is not always possible to do this, the phrase "good commercial practice" affords some standard for validating work and products.

Term

Every contract has a term, and it is normally defined. There are many variations possible, ranging from a definite date to a given period of days, months or years. The term may be conditional on some event or condition, such as reaching a specified goal or achievement; or it may be indefinite, to be terminated at the option of one or both parties. The term also may be indefinite with annual options that must be exercised by the client and contractor or definite, with periodic options to renew.

Termination

In Chapter 8 we discussed termination as defined legally under various conditions and circumstances. Provisions for termination of a contract may be defined in a separate clause or included in a single clause in which the contract's term is also defined and specified. It is important that if termination is to be arbitrary (e.g., the client may terminate the contract at his or her own pleasure and convenience), you must protect your interest by specifying in the clause that you must be given a suitable notice, a liquidated damages specification (often a separate clause) or other safeguard, as well as a similar right to terminate the contract at your own convenience. (See the discussion of termination and liquidated damages in the section in this chapter entitled "Defaults and Remedies.")

Severability

A severability clause is one that states that if some part of the contract is found to be invalid or unenforceable, it will not invalidate the remainder of the contract provisions and make the contract overall invalid. It is only occasionally necessary or appropriate, experienced lawyers assure us, although it is commonly used.

Specification

Such terms as *specifications, schedule, exhibit* and *statement of work* are used to refer to a detailed statement of what the consultant agrees to do in earning the consideration. When the work can be explained in a brief paragraph or two, it may be included in the body of the contract. However, the explanation of the work frequently is lengthy, and is usually then included as an exhibit or ancillary document, such as a proposal (discussed in Chapters 3 and 5).

Price and Payment

The consideration—what the client agrees to pay you—usually is a basic requirement of any contract and must be stipulated clearly. What is too often not stipulated is precisely *when* the client is to pay you. That is not a matter to be left to chance or blind faith in the client's business practices. It is necessary to state just how and when you are to be paid. For example, if you are to invoice the client periodically, the periods must be stated and the client must agree to pay your invoices within some specified time, such as 15 or 20 days after receipt of the invoice. In these days of cash flow problems and aging payables, that stipulation is a serious concern.

Choice of Law and Choice of Forum

When your client or subcontractor is in another state, there is the question of which state's laws will govern and apply to your contract. Moreover, in the event of a dispute, you must determine which state shall have jurisdiction (i.e., in which state the matter will be litigated or arbitrated). You have the freedom to reach agreement on this in advance by inserting a clause that specifies the choice of forum. It is, of course, very much to your advantage to make your own state your choice of forum (considering travel and other costs, if a dispute or an arbitration arises). If the other party has a conflicting wish, this may be an item to be negotiated. (Normally, both parties would prefer to name their own states as the preferred forum.) The clause labeled "Governing Law" in Figure 7.3 is an example of a simple clause stipulating the choice of forum. Note that the same label is used in the contracts in Figures 8.1 and 8.2.

Confidential Information/Trade Secrets

Most businesses have some information that management considers confidential and proprietary data that it values as trade secrets. A company does not have to be in a highly technical field to possess trade secrets. Almost anything that the management believes has special value for them and provides some competitive advantage qualifies as a trade secret, which makes it proprietary and confidential. It can be a process that provides the company greater efficiency than its competitors, a unique marketing method or even an advantageous source of supply that competitors do not know about. In addition, such things as customer lists, sales figures, overhead rates, profit margins and other such information is held closely by every business, especially with regard to keeping it from competitors. It is therefore quite common for companies to require employees to sign pledges to honor confidentiality and to include such pledges in contracts that consultants are asked to sign. Labels and language used in contracts to identify relevant clauses may vary widely from one case to another, with the labels using such words as "confidential, proprietary" and "trade secret," but the practice and principle is much the same in all cases. It is also a pledge that must cut both ways: both parties normally pledge nondisclosure of the proprietary and confidential information of the other party. The mutual pledges of nondisclosure may be covered in a single clause or in two separate clauses, as in Figure 7.3, where the two clauses are labeled "Nondisclosure by Contractor" and "Nondisclosure by Client," or as in Figure 7.2, where one clause acknowledges and defines confidential information and a second clause imposes the mutual pledge to maintain confidentiality. However it is done, if the pledge is to appear, be sure that it is mutually applicable.

Defaults and Remedies

When one party to a contract fails to live up to its terms—i.e., breaches the contract—the other party may declare that the first party is in default. Some contracts include a specific default clause that provides remedies, such as a given number of days in which the offending party must cure the default. A default clause may list general occurrences that are to be considered breaches, or it may list specific ones. It may specify a number of days in which the offending party can be permitted to cure the breach, with or without penalty, as well as specify penalties or a formula for assessing penalties. These items can all be defined under a separate clause, more than one clause or under a related clause, such as one providing for termination. For example, the following is a portion of a contract clause:

> Termination. Either UST or Consultant may terminate this agreement in the event of a material breach that is not cured within thirty (30) days of written notice of such breach. Material breaches include but are not limited to the filing of bankruptcy papers or other similar arrangements due to insolvency, the assignment of Consultant's obligations to third parties or acceptance of employment or consulting arrangements with third parties which are or may be opposed to UST's interests.

There are many other remedies, which may or may not be stipulated in specific clauses.

Stop Work. When a buyer defaults on a sales contract, the seller often resorts to repossession of the item sold, usually after one or more notices of default if repossession is a suitable remedy, as in the case of real property and major items such as automobiles. In the case of a service contract in which the buyer is delinquent in payments, the obvious analog of repossession is cessation of the service after suitable notice of default. Failure to pay as scheduled, *if scheduled,* is a contract violation. To avoid a challenge of your right to stop work when the client has failed to pay your invoices when due, it is wise to include a clause that stipulates such a remedy.

Injunctive Relief. It is possible to solicit a court of equity to issue an injunction to the offending party to correct the breach by doing or not doing whatever is necessary to effect a cure. Some contracts include a clause acknowledging acceptance of the injunctive cure as a remedy, but it does require that the court agree to issue the injunction and is thus not entirely within the discretion of the contracting parties to turn to this as the best remedy.

Consequential Damages. The concept of paying damages to the injured party for breach of contract or other wrongs was discussed earlier in Chapters 4 and 8, and there are a number of different types of damages that one party may be required to pay to the other. Consequential damages are often the subject of a special clause in a contract. It calls for the payment of damages to compensate for a loss sustained as an indirect result of a breach of contract—as a *consequence* of that breach. It may be a loss of profit due to a contractor's failure to perform, lost goodwill of clientele and almost any other result. In fact, the hazard is quite a serious one, and you can easily note in the warranty language accompanying most products a disclaimer of any potential liability for consequential damages. To agree to be liable for consequential damages is equivalent to signing a blank check in the opinions of many experienced consultants and contractors, and they will normally resist efforts to agree to such commitments. In fact, many contracts include a clause specifically disclaiming responsibility for consequential damages.

Liquidated Damages. There are other kinds of damages—nominal, compensatory, punitive and liquidated. *Liquidated damages* are those to which the contracting parties have agreed in advance as an equitable means of settling up—liquidating the contract—in the event the contract must be terminated before it runs its full term. Thus, there must be at least one clause or portion of a clause devoted to defining this matter if it is to be a means of resolving the termination of an uncompleted contract. That may take the form of a specific figure, or it may be a formula. It is also possible to provide a remedy for breach of a specific clause or provision of a contract, such as is shown in Figure 7.3, where provision is made for liquidated damages in the event of breach of the confidentiality clause. If there is a dispute that must be settled in court, the court will accept the terms of the liquidation agreement only if it appears to be reasonable.

Warranties

Warranties were discussed earlier (principally in Chapter 8), where it was explained that there are several types of warranties and that there is relevant statutory law, including the UCC. Warranties apply to goods rather than to services. However, many consulting projects do produce an end item, such as a report, manual, computer program, design package or other custom work product, and the client usually will want a warranty specified in the agreement. The warranty may take several forms, however, such as warranty of performance, warranty against defects or warranty against patent or copyright infringement. There is also the period of warranty, which may be covered in a separate clause or included in a general clause. In addition, there is the remedy offered in the event of a defect covered by warranty.

It is easy to put your foot in it here; you must be cautious in extending an expressed warranty or limiting an implied warranty (which you can do). You will probably find it wise to limit the kind and period of warranty coverage, but you must know what is accepted practice in your industry to adopt a viable negotiating position in this regard. If you do not know what are the standard practices in your industry, consult with others (e.g., professional associations to which you belong) and gather up recommendations.

Finally, note how warranties verge into other areas. The matter of a warranty against patent or copyright infringement, for example, may also be the subject of or covered by a hold harmless clause (which may be labeled "Indemnification," "Release" or "Liability").

Relationship Between Parties

The question of your position as an independent contractor vis-à-vis the IRS and its practice of challenging many consultants' claims to that status was discussed at some length in Chapter 7. This has become a matter of great interest, and it is quite common today for consulting contracts to bear a clause specifying the relationship between the parties to be that of client and contractor (e.g., the clause may be labeled "Independent Contractor Status"), insisting quite plainly that it is not one of employer and employee. A suggested clause to that effect was included in Chapter 7.

Rights and Work Made for Hire

Under the federal copyright laws, copyrights in copyrightable properties made by employees belong to the employer unless specifically reserved to the employee by contract. The reverse is also true. Copyrights to work created by an independent contractor belong to the contractor unless specifically assigned to the client as a work made for hire. You must be careful to preserve your rights to anything you produce that can be copyrighted or to reach agreement for proper compensation if you are surrendering those rights to a client. It is possible to assign rights to a client, however, under work made for hire while still maintaining your claim to independent contractor status. The two propositions are not linked.

Custom Work Product

Related to the concept of work made for hire and rights (copyrights, patents and ownership generally) are such terms as *custom work product, intellectual property,* etc. A custom work product is one made specifically for the client under contract, as distinct from a commodity, as the term suggests. If a product of some intrinsic value is to be the result of the services you perform, rights to and ownership of the product must be addressed.

Assignments, Licensing and Royalties

The right to make assignments was discussed at some length in Chapters 3 and 7, and mention was made of assigning intellectual property. Of course, there usually is a consideration of money paid. An assignment may represent a complete and permanent transfer of all rights to the trademark, literary work, patent or whatever rights are being transferred, with a single payment. However, the consideration may be in the form of royalties also, with or without an advance payment. That is most often the case with literary and other artistic properties. For intellectual property of another kind, such as trademarks and patented inventions, licensing is a common arrangement for permitting others the use of rights to the item. In both cases the contracts (specimens appear in Chapter 11) must stipulate the various allowable uses and restraints thereto.

As in other contractual concerns discussed here, each industry has its usual practices, many with standard contracts, and it is necessary to either be familiar with those common and typical practices or to take steps to become familiar with them before attempting to negotiate a contract.

Arbitration

Arbitration, as a method for settling disputes without litigation, was discussed rather briefly in Chapters 6 and 8. It is not uncommon to include a special clause that provides for arbitration in the event a dispute arises. Such a clause normally specifies what matters are to be arbitrated, if the clause is not to cover all elements of the contract; whether the findings are to be binding or not binding; and by whom and where the arbitration is to be conducted (quite often it is the American Arbitration Association). The clause required is a rather simple one. The following model is for a general clause specifying arbitration of disputes in all contractual matters, as recommended by the American Arbitration Association.

> Arbitration. Any controversy or claim arising out of or relating to this contract or the breach thereof shall be settled by arbitration in accordance with the Commercial Arbitration Rules of the American Arbitration Association, and judgment upon the award rendered by the arbitrator(s) may be entered in any court having jurisdiction thereof.

Indemnify/Hold Harmless

Indemnification, also referred to or included under such captions as hold harmless, save harmless, release and liability, is a clause commonly included for the protection of the buyer, your client, from claims arising out of your work, presence on the client's site or use of the client's facilities. The blanket release from liability this clause provides normally covers a variety of possible losses, including property damage and personal injury, and is written to indemnify the client against any claims arising out of anything done by you, your employees, your associates or your subcontractors.

Entire Agreement and Modification

This is virtual boilerplate that states simply that the agreement is the entire agreement between the parties and may be modified only in writing consented to and signed by both parties. It is appropriate in many cases, especially where a new agreement replaces an older one.

Survival of Terms

A clause stating that the representations and warranties of the agreement shall survive the expiration or termination of the agreement is used to ensure that certain agreements, such as confidentiality and liability, will continue and survive the contract for some period.

Waiver

A waiver can be tricky and requires careful thought as to whether it is in your interest to include one. It stipulates that although you may waive your rights under the contract in one case, you are not waiving your rights under any subsequent case. For example, you may have the right to stop work when the client is delinquent and may decide to waive the right, but you are still entitled to exercise that right in a subsequent delinquency. You will have to consider whether you want that clause, bearing in mind that it confers the same right on the other party.

Audit of Books and Records

In a partnership, consortium or joint venture or where you are entitled to collect royalties, license fees, commissions or other such payments, you will probably want the right to examine the books to ensure that you are getting what your contract calls for. You need a clause that stipulates that right.

Force Majeure

Force majeure is a general escape clause to protect you from major events that are beyond your control and might interfere with or prevent you from performing the services for which you contracted. It states that you shall not be liable for any losses or damage resulting from acts of God and other disasters listed in the clause. The clause should be worded, however, to make it clear that the client must still pay you any money that was due or would have come due for work completed before the event causing the stoppage.

Notices

The notices clause simply provides the conditions under which notices of any sort shall be delivered to either party. Such clauses typically require notices to be in writing and delivered in person or by mail (certified, registered or otherwise) and specifies the individuals to whom notices shall be addressed and the address to which they are to be sent.

Noncompete Clause

Noncompete agreements have been mentioned several times, and as in the case of other considerations, may be separate agreements or clauses within larger agreements. Their purpose is simple enough: they are intended to restrain an employee or contractor from exploiting the employment or contract conditions by using information gained thereby to compete with the employer or client. The agreement normally provides that the consultant/contractor or employee will not engage in business with customers of the client or employer for some specified time, usually for the term of the employment or contract and for six months or a year following the end of that term. The noncompete clause is commonly applied by labor brokers or other third parties who place consultants on client's projects, either as subcontractors to or temporary employees of the broker. Brokers ask those consultants to agree in writing to refrain from accepting direct employment or independent contracts with the broker's client during and for some period following the contract or temporary employment. It is also not uncommon for the brokers to ask their clients to agree in writing that they will not attempt to hire or contract directly with the consultants placed on their projects by the brokers. (In some cases, I have known brokers to agree to insert a clause in which the client may hire the broker's temporary employee or subcontractor by paying the broker a kind of headhunter's placement or finder's fee.)

Miscellaneous and Special Clauses

Finder's fees may be the subject of many kinds of agreements. Most commonly, they are fees or commissions the consultant is willing to pay anyone who "finds" and helps the consultant win a contract with a client. However, there are other finder services for which individuals are often willing to pay. A person in need of financing who is having difficulty getting it from the usual sources may pay a fee to a finder who can arrange the financing. (Many finders specialize in this field.) In many fields of trade and commerce, finders earn substantial fees bringing buyers and sellers together and may be working on behalf of and being paid by either party.

This is by no means the entire array of clauses you may encounter in different agreements, especially since many contract clauses are drawn up to cope with unique problems and situations. You may have to draft special clauses when you encounter situations for which no standard or commonly used clauses exist. But even then it may be much easier to find a clause that is reasonably close to your need and revise it to fit.

In the next chapter you will find a broad sampling of models that can be used as complete agreements or as clauses within larger agreements.

11

Contract Models

No cookbook could present every dish and recipe cooked every day in the United States (let alone, the entire world), and no book on contracts can offer anything approaching a complete array. However, the following selection models most commonly used should help you satisfy the vast majority of your needs.

CONTRACTS ARE CONSTRUCTED FROM BUILDING BLOCKS

In some respects reaching agreement so that you can write a contract has some of the overtones of a Chinese dinner menu. (But remember, you cannot even begin to write a contract until you have reached agreement at least on the major questions and concerns.) There are options to select appetizers and main dishes from several columns: a clause here and a phrase there until the entire meal of agreements—clauses and phrases—is assembled and accepted.

Contracts must include certain key elements, but beyond those minimum requirements, most contracts are assemblages of many agreements and provisions, called *clauses* (often modified with phrases). As I noted earlier, many concerns and considerations (e.g., maintaining the confidentiality of proprietary data and agreements to refrain from competing with another party) can and do appear both as complete agreements in themselves and as clauses in larger agreements. (Most clauses, in fact, are themselves agreements and are often made the subject of separate contracts.)

However, sometimes there are concerns and considerations that appear as contract clauses and otherwise in connection with contractual relationships that do not constitute agreements or contracts. In this chapter you will find a number of model contracts. Many are especially appropriate to consulting, but others are appropriate to business ventures in general and are thus of interest to consultants, as well.

There will be no attempt to present models of every possible contract form in all its possible variations, but there is a representative sampling of those contracts most commonly needed or likely to be needed by independent consultants. This includes such items as service contracts, finder's fee agreements, partnership agreements and joint venture agreements, among others. Most models presented are easily adaptable to your own needs, and you may feel free to modify the forms to cover your own needs and preferences.

A few models of contracts and clauses have already appeared in earlier chapters, including models of purchase orders and complete service agreements as well as the wide array of clauses. This chapter will deal principally with examples of complete contracts.

FORMS, FORMATS AND LANGUAGE

You may be somewhat surprised at both the great variety of contract forms and formats and the simplicity of style, format and language used. In his book *Small Business Legal Forms,* attorney-author Daniel Sitarz adds his voice to the steadily rising chorus of today's lawyers who decry the difficult-to-understand (even for lawyers), antiquated jargon, and he champions the writing of forms and agreements in the simplest of everyday English. He also notes that legal-sized paper (8½-by-13-inch and 8½-by-14-inch paper) is used less today as the legal profession turns to the popular paper used in most offices today, the standard 8½-by-11-inch-paper.

There really is no such thing as a required form or format, and there is really no de facto standard, except in the most general terms. Therefore, formats and layout of contract forms vary widely, and a wide variety of formats are used deliberately in the models offered in this chapter to reflect that variance and stress the fact that format has nothing to do with the legal impact of the form. It is the clarity of communication—the words—and the signatures that are important, and formats thus inevitably vary a great deal, according to individual preference.

I have deliberately gathered contracts and forms from as wide a variety of sources as possible and have even adapted them to the needs of this book in various ways to heighten that truth. I heartily endorse the idea of using the simplest and most direct language possible, but I want the models to reflect reality. You will inevitably encounter contracts with overblown, ornate and antiquated terms, and so I have resisted the normal writer's temptation to render all the models into the simplest forms possible.

CONTRACT TYPES AND MODELS

The variations in basic form are relatively superficial. Service contracts do not vary greatly, despite differences in language, and they appear to be at about three levels of complexity. The simplest level is the letter of agreement or letter contract of one or two pages that originates with either consultant or client and is countersigned by the other party. The next level is the more formal, yet simple agreement of a few pages. Finally, there is the full-blown formal contract, a formidable document of many pages and clauses, with many signatures and seals.

Letter Contract

For the average small consulting projects, many of which will be of only a few days' duration, it is hardly necessary or practicable to draft lengthy agreements and undertake formal negotiations to arrive at terms. In fact, most clients will issue a purchase order or accept your standard contract form for such tasks, although minor changes may be necessary. Two examples (Figures 11.1 and 11.2) are offered here as models. You can adopt or adapt these models freely for your own use. (If the client is to issue a purchase order, you may have to write a statement of work to appear on the purchase order.)

Figure 11.1 illustrates a simple, informal contract that is suitable for small projects and presented in the form of a letter. (At one time, some rather large government projects were contracted out with relatively simple letter contracts.) The letter contract may be prepared on plain paper or on your letterhead. The client who retains a consultant only occasionally would not normally have a standard form for this contract, whereas you, as a consultant, have frequent need for such a form and may benefit from having a standard letter contract that you can adapt readily to each situation. Quite often, however, the client prefers the letter of agreement to be on his or her own letterhead, although the client may be willing to use your form. In that case you furnish the client a copy penciled in for his or her secretary to type up, usually using the client's own letterhead for the first page. Note that the basic requirements of a contract are met in this simple form: the consideration is stated, the rights and duties are defined and the independent consultant status is affirmed.

Figure 11.2 illustrates another letter-sized contract document but one more formal in its presentation. Either of the contracts in Figure 11.1 and 11.2 may be used, on plain paper or on a letterhead of the client or the consultant, and may be modified and adapted to any special needs you may have. If the contract forms do not provide space for explanation of the work to be performed, a work

LETTER OF AGREEMENT

Dear _____:

The following constitutes our entire agreement for services to be provided by _____, Consultant, to and for _____, Client. Services to be provided/products to be developed under this agreement include the following:

The services will be performed on the following schedule:

Fees and expenses agreed upon and schedule for payments are as follows:

Client shall have full ownership of and all rights in and to the work product(s) after full payment has been made.

Consultant is an independent Consultant, not entitled to any benefits or privileges as an employee. Consultant alone is responsible for maintaining proper insurance and for compliance with federal, state, and local laws and regulations relating to taxes and Social Security payments.

This agreement represents the entire agreement between us and shall not be subject to any waiver, modification, or discharge except in writing signed by both of us. No representations or conditions are made by either of us except as expressly contained in this agreement. This agreement shall be interpreted in accordance with the laws of the State of _____.

If the above terms are in accordance with our understanding and agreement, please sign where indicated below and return one copy to me.

Sincerely,

_____
Consultant/Client

Agreed to/accepted: (Date)

_____
Consultant/Client

AGREEMENT

*Client:*_____

Consultant: _____

Services to be provided or relevant specifications/proposal, if applicable:

_____
_____
_____
_____
_____

*Reports/presentations:*_____

On client's premises [ ] On consultant's premises [ ]

Other or special arrangements: _____

Beginning date: _____ *Target completion date:* _____

*Fees: $*_____ *per*_____ *No.:* _____*Total est. fee/cost: $* _____

*Other costs: $*_____ *(for:*_____*)*

*Advance retainer: $*_____ *Terms for balance:* _____

Notes, remarks, special provisions, if any: _____

_____

_____

For _____ (consultant) *For* _____ (client)

_____ (signed) _____ (signed)

_____ (date) _____ (date)

Figure 11.2 One-Page Agreement   175

statement or even a complete proposal can be attached as an exhibit and invoked in the contract language. This is a common practice and greatly simplifies contract negotiation in many situations.

Small Formal Contracts

Where the project is of fairly large proportions and extended term but is small enough to be handled by a single consultant working alone, somewhat greater formality and more detailed coverage may be required, although without all the flourishes and detail of truly large contracts. Figure 11.3 is an example of a contract of medium formality that is suitable for the vast majority of consulting assignments handled by independent consultants.

Figure 11.3, titled "Consulting Agreement," uses few headings, although the major paragraphs are numbered. Headings and captions have no special significance, despite their common usage. They do facilitate reviewing the contract to ensure that major concerns are covered, however, and it is a good idea to employ them. If headings and captions were used in this model, the numbered paragraphs might be designated as follows:

1. Term and Nature of Services
2. Consideration and Rates
3. Independent Consultant
4. Discovery and Rights
5. Proprietary and Confidential Information
6. Conflicts of Interest
7. Termination
8. Survival of Terms
9. Assignment

Headings and captions are not required, but they are useful as road maps through a contract, especially when it is a rather lengthy document (as is Figure 11.4). When they are used, it helps to couch them in simple, descriptive language rather than special legal jargon.

The More Formal Contract

Figure 11.4 illustrates a much more formal and wider-ranging document, headed "Contract for Services," in which headings are used freely and perhaps even excessively. As author E. Thorpe Barrett remarks in *Write Your Own Business Contracts,* the legal profession tends strongly toward redundancy, and this model reflects that truth. For example, it should not be necessary to write separate paragraphs to identify each party's restriction on assignments. A single paragraph making each party's rights to assignments dependent on the other party's agreements would have had the same weight. If you study

CONSULTING AGREEMENT

PREAMBLE: This is an agreement, effective as of (date), between
_____, an individual residing at
_____, _____, (Consultant),
and _____, of _____ (Client).

PURPOSE: Client wishes to retain the services of Consultant to advise and consult Client in technical matters relative to Client's
business, and Consultant is willing to provide such services.

1. Consultant agrees that for a period of twelve (12) months, commencing with the effective date of this Agreement, he will, consistent with his other obligations, render to Client such consulting
services as Client may request relating to the field set forth in Exhibit A, attached (Specification). Consultant shall not be required
at any time to render service that would conflict with obligations
of Consultant undertaken prior to the request for such services by
Consultant.

2. Client agrees to reimburse Consultant for such consulting services at the hourly rates shown in Exhibit B, attached (Rates). Consultant shall invoice Client monthly for services rendered, and such
invoices shall be payable upon receipt. Invoices shall include the
hours worked at the hourly rate, and a brief description of the services rendered. Upon adequate substantiation, Client will reimburse
Consultant for all travel and related living expenses incurred by
Consultant in connection with any travel requested by Client. Prior
written approval by Client shall be required for all travel outside
the United States and Canada in connection with this Agreement.

3. Consultant shall act as an independent Consultant and not as an
agent or employee of Client, and Consultant shall make no representation as an agent or employee of Client. Consultant shall furnish insurance and be responsible for all taxes as an independent
Consultant. Consultant shall have no authority to bind Client or
incur other obligations on behalf of Client.

4. Consultant will promptly disclose to Client each discovery
which he reasonably believes may be new or patentable, conceived by
him in carrying out the consulting services contracted for herein.
Client shall have the right to file a patent application, at Client's expense, on each discovery, and Consultant agrees to cooperate
with Client and to execute all proper documents, at the expense of

Figure 11.3 Typical Consulting Agreement   177

Client to enable Client to obtain patent protection in the United States and foreign countries. Consultant agrees to assign all rights to each such patent application and patent to Client, but Consultant shall have a free, non-exclusive and irrevocable license to use of the patent, with the right to sublicense use in all areas except those of the Specification. In the event Client fails to file a patent application on any such discovery within six (6) months after written disclosure thereof to Client, Consultant shall have the right to file such, at Consultant's expense, in the United States and foreign countries. On each patent issuing from such application, Client shall have a free, non-exclusive, irrevocable license, with the right to sublicense, in the areas of the Specification.

5. In the event Client discloses information to Consultant that Client considers to be secret or proprietary and so notifies Consultant, Consultant agrees to hold the Proprietary Information in confidence and to treat the Proprietary Information with at least the same degree of care and safeguards that he takes with his own proprietary information. Proprietary Information shall be used by Consultant only in connection with services rendered under this Agreement. Proprietary information shall not be deemed to include information that (a) is in or becomes in the public domain without violation of this Agreement by Consultant, or (b) is already in the possession of Consultant, as evidenced by written documents, prior to the disclosure thereof by Client, or (c) is rightfully received from a third entity having no obligation to Client and without violation of this Agreement by Consultant.

6. Consultant warrants that he is under no obligation to any other entity that in any way conflicts with this Agreement, that he is free to enter into this Agreement, and is under no obligation to consult for others in fields covered by this Specification. Consultant shall not, during the term of this Agreement, perform consulting services for others in the field of the Specification but shall have the right to perform consulting services for others outside the Specification.

7. This Agreement may be terminated by Client at any time on sixty (60) days advance written notice. In the event consulting services requested by Client hereunder for immediate performance shall in any calendar month total less than $2,000.00, then Consultant shall have the right to terminate this Agreement by thirty (30) days advance written notice, provided, in the event Client shall within such thirty day period place sufficient requests with Consultant to bring the total for the previous and current month to the minimum amounts set forth above, such notice shall be of no effect.

178   Figure 11.3 Typical Consulting Agreement

8. The secrecy provisions of Section 5 hereof shall survive any termination of this Agreement for a period of three (3) years after such termination.

9. This Agreement is not assignable by either party without the consent of the other.

Signed: _____   Signed: _____

For:_____   For: _____
          (Consultant)   (Client)

Date: _____   Date:_____

Figure 11.3 Typical Consulting Agreement   179

CONTRACT FOR SERVICES

Paragraph 1. Preamble
   This Agreement is made this date (date) between (Client's business name and address), hereinafter known as "Client," and (Consultant's business name and address), hereinafter known as "Consultant."

Paragraph 1. Term
   This Agreement will continue in effect until (date/event/condition) unless terminated earlier in accordance with the provisions of Paragraph 7 of this Agreement.

Paragraph 2. Independent Consultant
   It is the express intention of the parties that Consultant is an independent Consultant and not an employee, agent, joint venturer or partner of Client. Nothing in this Agreement shall be interpreted or construed as creating or establishing the relationship of Employer and Consultant between Client and Consultant or any employee or agent of Consultant. Consultant shall retain the right to perform services for others during the term of this Agreement.

Paragraph 3. Services to be Provided
   3.01. Service Program
   Consultant agrees to provide services per the service program described in Exhibit A. Consultant has the right to refuse to perform specific requests by Client other than as so defined and identified.
   3.02. Service Methods
   Consultant will determine the method, details, and means of performing the above-described services. Client shall not have the right to, and shall not control the manner or determine the method of accomplishing Consultant's services.
   3.03. Consultant's Staff/Associates
   Consultant may, at the Consultant's own expense, employ such assistants as Consultant deems necessary to perform the services required of Consultant by this Agreement. Client may not control, direct, or supervise Consultant's assistants or employees in the performance of those services. Consultant assumes full and sole responsibility for the payment of all compensation and expenses of these assistants and for all state and federal income tax, unemployment insurance, Social Security, disability insurance and other applicable withholdings.
   3.04. Workplace
   Consultant shall perform the services required by this Agreement at any place or location and at such times as Consultant shall determine.

Paragraph 4. Consideration
   4.01. Rates and Payments

In consideration for the services to be performed by Consultant, Client agrees to pay Consultant fees and payments specified in Exhibit A.

4.02. Invoices

Consultant shall submit invoices for all services rendered in accordance with the following schedule: (List billing periods.)

4.03. Payments

Client shall pay Consultant's invoices within _____ days of receipt.

4.04. Expenses

Consultant shall be responsible for all costs and expenses incidental to the performance of services for Client, including but not limited to, all costs of equipment provided by Consultant, all fees, fines, licenses, bonds or taxes required of or imposed against Consultant and all other of Consultant's costs of doing business. Client shall be responsible for no expenses incurred by Consultant in performing services for Client with the following exceptions: (List expenses to be reimbursed, if any.)

Paragraph 5. Consultant's Duties

5.01. Tools and Equipment

Consultant will supply all tools and equipment required to perform the services under this Agreement. Consultant is not required to purchase or rent any tools, equipment, or services from Client.

5.02. Worker's Compensation

Consultant agrees to provide worker's compensation insurance for Consultant's employees and agents and agrees to hold harmless and indemnify Client for any and all claims arising out of any injury, disability, or death of any of Consultant's employees or agents.

5.03. Indemnify/Hold Harmless

Consultant shall indemnify and hold Client harmless against any and all liability imposed or claimed, including attorney's fees and other legal expenses, arising directly or indirectly from any act or failure of Consultant or Consultant's assistants, employees or agents, including all claims relating to the injury or death of any person or damage to any property. Consultant agrees to maintain a policy of insurance in the minimum amount of dollars to cover any such claims.

5.04. Assignments

Neither this Agreement nor any duties or obligations under this Agreement may be assigned by Consultant without the prior written consent of Client.

5.05. State and Federal taxes

As Consultant is not Client's employee, Consultant is responsible for paying all required state and federal taxes. In particular, Client will not withhold FICA (Social Security) from Consultant's pay-

Figure 11.4 Services Contract 181

ments, withhold state or federal income tax from payment to Consultant, make state or federal unemployment insurance contributions on
behalf of Consultant, make disability insurance contributions on behalf of Consultant, or obtain worker's compensation insurance on behalf of Consultant.

Paragraph 6. Client's Duties

6.01. Cooperation

Client agrees to comply with all reasonable requests of Consultant
(and provide access to all documents reasonably) necessary to the
performance of Consultant's duties under this Agreement.

6.02. Assignments

Neither this Agreement nor any duties or obligations under this
Agreement may be assigned by Client without the prior written consent of Consultant.

Paragraph 7. Termination Due to Special Events

7.01. Termination

This Agreement shall terminate automatically on the occurrence of
any of the following events:

Bankruptcy or insolvency of either party;

Sale of the business of either party;

Death of either party.

7.02. Termination by Client for Default by Consultant

Should Consultant default in the performance of this Agreement or
materially breach any of its provisions, Client, at Client's option,
may terminate this Agreement by giving written notification to Consultant. For the purposes of this section, material breach of this
Agreement shall include, but not be limited to the following: [Spec-
ify]

7.03. Termination by Consultant for Default of Client

Should Client default in the performance of this Agreement or materially breach any of its provision, Consultant, at the Consultant's
option, may terminate this Agreement by giving written notice to Client. For the purposes of this section, material breach of this Agreement shall include but not be limited to the following: [Specify]

7.04. Termination for Delinquencies

Should Client fail to pay Consultant all or any part of the compensation set forth in Paragraph 4 of this Agreement on the date due,
Consultant, at the Consultant's option, may terminate this Agreement
if the failure is not remedied by Client within [thirty (30)] days
from the date payment is due.

Paragraph 8. General Provisions

8.01. Notices

Any notices to be given hereunder by either party to the other may
be effected either by personal delivery in writing or by mail, registered or certified, postage prepared with return receipt requested.

Mailed notices shall be addressed to the parties at the addresses appearing in the introductory paragraph of this Agreement, but each party may change the address by written notice in accordance with this paragraph. Notices delivered personally will be deemed communicated as of actual receipt; mailed notices will be deemed communicated as of two days after mailing.

8.02. Entire Agreement

This Agreement supersedes any and all agreements, either oral or written, between the parties hereto with respect to the rendering of services by Consultant for Client and contains all the covenants and agreements between the parties with respect to the rendering of such services in any manner whatsoever. Each party to the Agreement acknowledges that no representations, inducements, promises, or agreements, orally or otherwise, have been made by any party, or anyone acting on behalf of any party, which are not embodied herein, and that no other agreement, statement, or promise not contained in this Agreement shall be valid or binding. Any modification of this Agreement will be effective only if it is in writing and signed by both parties.

8.03. Severability

If any provision in this Agreement is held by a court of competent jurisdiction to be invalid, void, or unenforceable, the remaining provisions will nevertheless continue in full force without being impaired or invalidated in any way.

8.04. Attorneys' Fees

If any action at law or in equity, including an action for declaratory relief, is brought to enforce or interpret the provisions of this Agreement, the prevailing party will be entitled to reasonable attorneys' fees, which may be set by the court in the same action or in a separate action brought for that purpose, in addition to any other relief to which that party may be entitled.

8.05. Governing Law

This Agreement will be governed by and construed in accordance with the laws of the State of

Executed at (city and state).

Figure 11.4 Services Contract   183

this contract closely, you will see many other areas that could have been simplified by eliminating what are essentially redundancies.

Even more interesting and noteworthy are the provisions of paragraphs 2 through 5, with all the subparagraphs. These provisions are clearly designed to support the consultant's claim to the status of independent consultant and are influenced heavily by the provision of the well-known 20 questions of Section 1706 of the current Tax Reform Act. These paragraphs constitute direct responses to the most important of those questions.

Note that the order in which the various clauses appear has no special significance and varies widely from one contract to another. The model in Figure 11.4 has the termination clauses near the end of the contract, for example, whereas most contract documents place them near or even combine them with the clause defining the term of the contract. The order in which the clauses appear makes little difference legally, but in terms of good organization and the logical flow of ideas, some thought should be given to the organization.

Sales Contract

The model in Figure 11.5 is that of a contract to sell a business, which could easily be a consulting practice or almost any other kind of business. Note that once again, the drafter of this agreement is safeguarding against the possibility that something illegal may have inadvertently found its way into the contract, so the contract includes a severability clause (clause 13). And if you examine the agreement carefully, you will find that once again, author E. Thorpe Barrett is proven right: contracts drafted by lawyers tend to include many redundancies.

A clause I once encountered that illustrates the typical redundancy introduced the subject of indemnification with the following words:

> Licensor hereby agrees to indemnify, hold harmless and defend Licensee from and against any claim, action, loss, liability, expense, damage, or judgment, including costs and attorney's fees, that . . .

The clause goes on to elaborate further on each of these terms, devoting entire paragraphs to them. Asked why the redundancy was required, a practicing lawyer assured me that each term was "technically different," and it was thus important to name each one. I would bow to his judgment if many other lawyers had not assured us in writing that such redundancy is not necessary.

The agreement to sell a business is followed by a simpler model in Figure 11.6 of a contract to sell goods, on the reasonable assumption that most consultants do not get involved deeply in selling goods, if they do so at all. (Other agreements to sell goods will appear later in this chapter.) Many consultants, especially those who lecture and present seminars or training courses, support their clients by selling items closely related to their consulting practices, such as books, tapes, newsletters and other information and instruc-

AGREEMENT TO SELL BUSINESS

This Agreement is entered into this _____ day of
_____, 19____ by _____, Seller, of
_____, doing business as
_____, and _____, Buyer, of
_____, doing business as
_____.)

   Seller agrees to sell and Buyer agrees to buy the business
of a certain _____ now being operated at
_____ and known as _____
and all assets thereof as contained in Schedule A attached here.
The parties agree and hereby covenant as follows:
   1. The total purchase price for all fixtures, furnishings and
      equipment is _____ dollars, payable as fol-
      lows:
      (a) $ _____ in cash, certified or cashier's check, as
          a deposit upon execution of this Agreement, to be held by
          _____.
      (b) $ _____ additional to be paid in cash, certified
          or cashier's check, at the time of passing papers.
      (c) $ _____ to be paid by a note of Buyer to Seller,
          bearing interest at the rate of ____ percent per annum
          with an option of Buyer to prepay the entire outstanding
          obligation without penalty. Said note shall be secured by
          a chattel mortgage and financing statement covering the
          property to be sold hereunder, together with any and all
          other property acquired during the term of said note and
          placed in or within the premises known as
          _____.
   2. The property to be sold hereunder shall be conveyed by a stan-
      dard form Bill of Sale, duly executed by Seller.
   3. Seller promises and agrees to convey good, clear, and market-
      able title to all the property to be sold hereunder, the same
      to be free and clear of all liens and encumbrances. Full pos-
      session of said property will be delivered in the same condi-
      tion that it is now, reasonable wear and tear expected.
   4. Consummation of the sale, with payment by Buyer of the balance
      of the down payment and the delivery by the Seller of a Bill
      of Sale, will take place on or before
      _____, 19____.

Figure 11.5 Agreement To Sell a Business 185

5. Seller may use the purchase money, or any portion thereof, to clear any encumbrances on the property transferred and in the event that documents reflecting discharge of said encumbrances are not available at the time of sale, the money needed to effectuate such discharges shall be held by the attorneys of Buyer and Seller in escrow pending the discharges.

6. Until the delivery of the Bill of Sale, Seller shall maintain insurance on said property in the amount that it is presently insured.

7. Operating expenses of $ _____ including but not limited to rent, taxes, payroll and water shall be apportioned as of the date of the passing of papers and the net amount thereof shall be added to or deducted from, as the case may be, the proceeds due from Buyer at the time of delivery of the Bill of Sale.

8. If Buyer fails to fulfill his obligations herein, all deposits made hereunder by the Buyer shall be retained by Seller as liquidated damages.

9. Seller promises and agrees not to engage in the same type of business as the one being sold for _____ years from the time of passing, within a _____ radius of
_____.

10. A Broker's fee for professional services in the amount of ($_____) is due from Seller to _____, provided and on condition that papers pass.

11. Seller agrees that this Agreement is contingent upon the following conditions:
    (a) Buyer obtaining a Lease on the said premises or that the existing Lease be assigned in writing to the Buyer.
    (b) Buyer obtaining the approval from the proper authorities Town and State) of the transfer of all necessary licenses to Buyer.
    (c) The premises shall be in the same condition, reasonable wear and tear expected, on the date of passing as they are currently.

12. All of the terms, representations and warranties shall survive the closing. This Agreement shall bind and inure to the benefit of Seller and Buyer and their respective heirs, executors, administrators, successors and assigns.

13. If this Agreement shall contain any term or provision which shall be invalid or against public policy or if the application of same is invalid or against public policy, then, the remainder of this Agreement shall not be affected thereby and shall remain in full force and effect.

In witness whereof, the parties hereto have caused this instrument to be executed in triplicate on the day and year first above written.

_____   _____
SELLER: BUYER:

_____   _____
SELLER: BROKER:

Figure 11.5 Agreement To Sell a Business   187

CONTRACT FOR SALE OF GOODS

Agreement is entered into this _____ day of _____,
19_____ by _____, Seller, with offices at
_____ and _____, Buyer,
with offices at _____.

1. SALE
Seller has agreed to sell and Buyer has agreed to purchase goods
described in Schedule A attached.

2. PRICE
The total price for the goods is $ _____, (including) (not
including) freight, shipping, and insurance costs.

3. PAYMENT
Payment shall be made as follows: The entire amount due shall be
paid in full (not later than _____ days after receipt by Buyer)
(upon signing of this agreement).

4. DELIVERY/SHIPPING/ACCEPTANCE
(A) Delivery of the goods purchased shall be set forth in the at-
tached Schedule B.
(B) Shipment of the goods purchased shall be _____.
(C) Buyer shall examine each shipment promptly upon receipt and will
advise Seller in writing of discrepancies, if any.

5. SELLER'S WARRANTIES
It is understood and agreed by the parties that Seller does not
warrant the Buyer's use of the items purchased and does not warrant
to Buyer or any other that the items are merchantable or fit for any
particular purpose.

In witness whereof, the parties have signed this agreement on the
date first written above.

By _____
   (Seller)
By _____
   (Buyer)

tional items. Some, such as computer consultants, sell more highly priced goods—hardware and software—and therefore may need to use more or less formal written sales contracts. Of course, you are also a buyer, and from that viewpoint you need to be familiar with relevant contract forms, along with standard warranty clauses and disclaimers.

Finders and Their Fees

There are many individuals who are self-employed as finders. They usually operate in somewhat specialized fields, such as financing, buying and selling businesses and real estate. Sometimes they specialize in whatever current conditions dictate. Thus, at the height of the energy crisis, many finders were commissioned to find buyers and sellers of fossil fuels and related technology.

The most immediate reason for using finders to aid you in your consulting practice is for marketing support. Working in this kind of effort, finders act as salespeople, usually on a commission basis. Their most frequent role is to introduce you directly to prospective buyers of your services, either in person or by arranging a meeting. They may also arrange a meeting indirectly by furnishing you with a lead, identifying the parties you want to address and paving the way so that the prospective buyer is waiting to hear from you. At that point the finder has done his or her job, and the rest is up to you.

Finders work under written contracts for their protection. The model in Figure 11.7 is for the retention of a finder to help win new clients. Finders may be employed for a single objective or on an ongoing and indefinite basis, to help you get financing, find special equipment or find sellers (e.g., to buy or sell a business). Figure 11.7 may, of course, be adapted to these or other purposes.

Licensing Agreements

Depending on what you do as a consultant, you may find yourself in a position where you must consider a licensing or royalty agreement. Among the items you might license are computer software; mechanical, electrical, electronic or other engineering designs; patents; and trademarks. An analogous arrangement often occurs with regard to expressions of art (e.g., writing) that are copyrighted. Figure 11.8 is a general model of a licensing agreement.

Partnerships and Joint Ventures

As in other businesses and professions, consultants may enter into partnerships. Many consultants use the word *associates,* as in John Doe Associates, without having partners, except in the loose and informal sense of sharing office expenses and supporting one another as necessary. However, many do enter into formal partnerships and share investments, expenses, risks and benefits. The model in Figure 11.9 is a partnership agreement for multiple partners. It is followed by Figure 11.10, which is a partnership agreement for

FINDER'S FEE AGREEMENT

This Agreement is hereby entered into between HRH Communications, Inc. (Client) and Harvey Katzenjammer (Finder) on the following terms and conditions:

1. Services and Term

General. During the Term, which shall be indefinite, subject to termination by either party on 30 days' notice, Finder shall act as a nonexclusive finder of buyers for professional services of Client and shall be paid the sales commissions described in paragraph 6.1. Services of Finder to include introduction of Client to buyers or furnishing of sales leads that result directly in sales of Client's services to a buyer. It is specifically understood and agreed that the dominant purpose of this Agreement is the entry by Client into a contract for sale of Client's services to a buyer.

2. Buyer Agreements. All deliverable items shall be provided under separate agreement between Client and buyer. Finder shall not be a party to any buyer agreement.

3. Best Efforts. Finder shall use his best efforts to promote Client's services in the market areas defined by Client. Finder will not, and is not required to, take part in negotiations with customers.

4. Conditions of Payment. HRH Communications, Inc. shall be under no obligation to pay any fee or other monies whatsoever to Finder on account of this Agreement until any sale or contract contemplated by this Agreement has closed with any buyer of Client's services, resulting from either the introduction by Finder to the buyer or the furnishing of a sales lead that results in a sale to the buyer. Finder shall not be entitled to any fee or other monies until Client has entered into a binding arrangement with the purchaser and/or investor. For purposes of this Agreement, the total amount of the fee due Finder shall be due and payable on the date of the closing or, in the event that any such purchase and/or investment shall be of payments over time, on the date of the first payment made by such buyer.

5. Finder's Rights Non-Exclusive. Nothing contained in this Agreement shall be construed to give Finder any exclusive rights, it being understood and agreed that Finder shall be entitled to a fee only in connection with the entry by Client into a binding agreement with a buyer introduced by Finder or resulting directly from a lead supplied by Finder.

6. Fees

6.1 The fee for introduction by Finder to a buyer or furnishing of a direct lead resulting in a sale to a buyer pursuant to this Agreement, shall be a sum computed on the total contract price as follows:

less than $50,000	5%
$100,000 but less than $200,000	4%
$200,000 but less than $300,000	3%
$300,000 but less than $400,000	2%
$400,000 or more	1%

6.2 Finder shall not be entitled to any fee or other monies until Client has entered into a binding arrangement with a buyer resulting directly from Finder's efforts.
OTHER

6.3 Any arrangements made by Finder with any broker or other persons with whom Finder is or may be involved are the total responsibility of Finder. Upon payment made by Client to Finder of the Finder's fee, Finder will hold Client free and harmless from any and all claims, liabilities, commissions, fees or expenses in connection with the transaction from any party who alleges a relationship with or through Finder and the buyer.

7. Arbitration. In the event of any dispute between Client and Finder arising under or pursuant to the terms of this Agreement, or any matters arising under the terms of this Agreement, the same shall be settled only by arbitration in the City of New York, State of New York, in accordance with the rules and regulations of the American Arbitration Association. The determination of the arbitrators shall be final and binding upon Client and Finder and may be enforced in any court of appropriate jurisdiction.

8. Governing Laws. This Agreement shall be construed by and governed under the laws of the State of New York.

9. Complete Agreement. This Agreement contains the entire agreement between Finder and Client concerning the introduction of a buyer or furnishing of a lead resulting directly in a sale of Client's services to a buyer and correctly sets forth the rights and duties of each party to this Agreement. This is the complete Agreement between the parties named herein.

IN WITNESS WHEREOF, the parties have signed this Agreement on the date first written above.

_____   _____
For HRH Communications, Inc., Client   Date

_____   _____
For Harvey Katzenjammer, Finder   Date

Figure 11.7 Finder's Fee Agreement   191

GENERAL LICENSING AGREEMENT

Agreement made this _____ day of _____, 19_____
by and between _____ (Licensor) and
_____ (Licensee).

Licensor has the exclusive rights to
_____ (Product) and Licensee is desir-
ous of obtaining a license to (sell/manufacture/use) the Product.
Therefore, in consideration of the mutual terms, conditions and covenants hereinafter set forth, Licensor and Licensee agree as follows:

1. (a) Licensor grants to Licensee the (exclusive/non-exclusive)
and nontransferable right to (sell/manufacture/use) the Product for
a period commencing on _____ (the Effective Date)
and ending _____ years from the Effective Date (the Initial
Term) unless sooner terminated pursuant to the provisions of this
Agreement.

(b) It is mutually agreed that either party may terminate this
Agreement at the end of the Initial Term by giving the other party
written notice thereof at least six (6) months prior to the end of
the Initial Term. Should either party fail to give such notice, this
Agreement shall continue upon the same terms and conditions in force
immediately prior to the expiration of the Initial Term, for an additional period of _____ years. After the Initial Term, either
party may terminate the renewal of the Agreement by giving six
months' written notice of its intention to terminate at any time
prior to the expiration of the then current term.

2. (a) Licensee hereby accepts the right to (sell/manufacture/use)
the Product and agrees to do so in accordance with this Agreement.

(b) Licensee shall (purchase all of the Licensee's requirements
for the Product from Licensor and not directly or indirectly from
any other person, firm or corporation) (manufacture the Product in
strict conformity with the specifications and standards provided to
Licensee by Licensor). Licensor reserves the right to amend the
specifications and standards from time to time.

3. Licensee is an independent Consultant and nothing contained in
this Agreement shall be deemed or interpreted to constitute Licensee
to be the agent or legal representative of Licensor for any purpose
whatsoever. Licensee is not granted any right or authority to assume
or create any obligation or responsibility, express or implied, on
behalf of or in the name of Licensor, or to bind Licensor in any manner or fashion whatsoever.

4. Commencing with the Effective Date, Licensee shall (sell/
manufacture/use) _____ units of Product per twelve-month period.
Licensee may consider the total units of Product in any twelve-month

period over and above the specified volume as cumulative, to be carried forward to the succeeding twelve-month period.

Licensor shall fill all orders from Licensee with reasonable promptness, except that in case of fire, riots, strikes, accidents, or other conditions, whether or not similar in character to those specifically named, which unavoidably stop the making of deliveries contracted for, orders may be canceled or partially canceled, as the case may require, upon written notice or telegraph notice to Licensee. Such interruption of deliveries, however, shall not invalidate the remainder of this Agreement, but upon removal of the cause of the interruption, delivery shall continue, as before. During the period of interruption, the Licensee's obligations to purchase the minimum units shall abate and, if required to meet Licensee's obligations, Licensee may obtain inventory and goods from such other source as required to mitigate any damages Licensee might sustain by virtue of the interruption.

5. Licensee shall pay to Licensor a royalty for each unit of Product manufactured as follows: (license fees, royalty rates, or other). Licensor shall not charge Licensee a higher price than any other Licensee purchasing equal quantities and making payment on the same terms.

6. The provisions of Paragraph 1(a) and 1(b) notwithstanding, in the event that Licensee shall default in the terms and conditions of this Agreement with which the Licensee is to conform, without limiting the generality of the foregoing prompt payment of all fees and other obligations incurred under the terms of this Agreement, this Agreement shall be subject to cancellation by Licensor upon fourteen (14) days' written notice by Certified Mail, Return Receipt Requested, to Licensee, during which period of fourteen (14) days Licensee shall have the right to remedy such default. Upon the remedying of such default, the cancellation notice shall have no further force or effect.

7. Licensee agrees that it will obtain and maintain during the term of this Agreement and any renewal thereof product liability insurance in the amount of $ _____.

8. In the event of the termination of this Agreement, whether voluntary or involuntary, Licensee agrees that Licensee will not, for a period of _____ years from the effective date of termination, engage in the manufacture, sale, or distribution of a product similar to Product that is the subject of this Agreement.

9. It is agreed between the parties hereto that there are no oral or other agreements or understandings between them relating to the selling or servicing of Product. This Agreement supersedes all prior agreements between the parties, and is intended as a complete and exclusive statement of the full agreement between the parties.

Figure 11.8 General Licensing Agreement 193

10. In the event of any dispute between Licensor and Licensee arising under or pursuant to the terms of this Agreement, the same shall be settled only by Arbitration in the State of _____, under the then pertaining rules and regulations of the American Arbitration Association. The determination of the arbitrators shall be final and binding upon the parties and may be enforced in any court of appropriate jurisdiction.

11. This Agreement shall be construed in accordance with and governed by the Laws of _____.

INTENDING TO BE LEGALLY BOUND, the parties hereto have caused the License Agreement to be executed as of the date first above written.

By _____

(Licensor)

By _____

(Licensee)

PARTNERSHIP AGREEMENT

This Partnership Agreement is made this _____ day of
_____, 19____ by and between _____,
_____, and _____ (individually the Partner
and collectively the Partners).

In consideration of the mutual terms, conditions and covenants
hereinafter set forth, the Partners agree as follows:

1. GENERAL

1.1 The purpose of the Partnership shall be
_____.

1.2 The name of the Partnership shall be
_____, (the Partnership).

1.3 The business address of the Partnership shall be
_____, which address may be changed in
the future by the Partners.

1.4 The Partners shall execute the necessary documents to register
the Partnership's name and existence with the proper governmental offices in the County of _____, State of
_____.

1.5 The Partnership shall continue until, and dissolve upon the
first happening of the death of one Partner; the withdrawal, by written notice, of one Partner; or the affirmative vote of a majority in
interest of the Partners.

2. CAPITAL

2.1 The Partners shall contribute to the Partnership in the following amounts, which shall reflect the Partnership interest of each
Partner:

_____ : $_____ ____%
_____ : $_____ ____%
_____ : $_____ ____%

2.2 No Partner shall receive interest on his capital contribution.

2.3 A separate Capital Account shall be maintained for each
Partner.

2.3 (a) A Capital Account shall be increased by (i) the contribution to the capital of the Partnership, including the initial
contribution, and (ii) the distributive share of the Net Profits of
the Partnership; and decreased by (i) distributions, (ii) the distributive share of Net Losses of the Partnership and (iii) the
distributive share of expenditures of the Partnership not deductible
in computing Net Profits/Losses and not properly treated as capital
expenditures.

Figure 11.9 Agreement for Multiple Partners   195

2.3 (b) Distributions in kind shall be valued at fair market value less any liability which the Partner assumes on the distribution or to which the asset distributed is subject.

2.4 If, in the opinion of the majority in interest of the Partnership, additional capital is needed for the conduct of the business of the Partnership, each Partner shall contribute pro rata according to his or her interest.

2.5 Each Partner shall be indemnified by the other Partners as to excess over the Partner's interest in the Partnership in the event a Partner is compelled to pay and does pay any Creditor of the Partnership in satisfaction of an obligation of the Partnership. It is the intent and purpose of this provision that all of the Partners shall pay their pro rata share of the Partnership debts, regardless of whether a creditor of the Partnership recovers payment from some but not all the Partners.

3. MANAGEMENT

3.1 All matters to be determined by the Partners shall be determined by affirmative vote of a majority in interest of the Partners at a meeting. All matters determined by the Partners shall be recorded in a document reflecting the date, matter discussed, and action taken.

3.2 The Partners shall meet at least once each year. Additional meetings may be held at the request of any member of the Partnership. All meetings shall be announced by written notice sufficiently in advance to permit each Partner to be present in person or by written proxy.

3.3 At the first meeting of the Partnership to be held at _____ AM/PM on _____, 19_____ at _____ AM/PM, the Partnership shall determine and decide on such initial matters as the manner in which the business of the Partnership shall be managed; the hiring of employees; salaries to be paid to employees and the Partners who participate in the day-to-day management of the business of the Partnership; banking procedures; and any other matters which may properly come before the Partnership.

3.4 The fiscal year of the Partnership shall be from _____ first to _____ thirty-first.

3.5 Each Partner shall have the right to inspect the books, records, reports and accounts of the Partnership during normal business hours, which books, records, reports and accounts shall be kept at the Partnership's place of business or at such other place as determined by the partnership.

4. PROHIBITIONS

4.1 No Partner shall sell, assign, mortgage, hypothecate or encumber his interest in the Partnership without the express written permission of all the remaining Partners, without regard to interest.

4.2 All Partners shall meet their personal obligations and debts as they become due and each agrees to save and hold the remaining Partners and the Partnership harmless from all costs, claims and demands with respect to such obligations and debts.

4.3. No Partner shall, except upon the approval of the Partnership by affirmative vote, lend any Partnership funds; incur any obligation in the name of or on the credit of the Partnership; lend any of the Partner's funds to the Partnership, with or without interest; sell, assign, mortgage, hypothecate or encumber any asset of the Partnership; make an assignment of the assets of the Partnership for the benefit of creditors of the Partnership; execute any guarantee on behalf of the Partnership; release, assign or transfer a Partnership claim or any asset of the Partnership; borrow in the name of the Partnership; submit any Partnership claim or liability to arbitration; initiate, conduct or settle litigation in the name of or pertaining to the Partnership; or invest Partnership funds.

4.4 Any Partner who commits a prohibited act shall be individually liable to the remaining Partners, pro rata to their Partnership interest, for any loss caused by the prohibited act.

5. PROFITS/LOSSES AND DISTRIBUTIONS

5.1 Net Profits/Losses shall be determined in accordance with good accounting principles and shall be as finally determined for federal income tax purposes.

5.2 Net Profits/Losses shall be apportioned pro rata among the Partners' capital account, according to each Partner's interest.

5.3. Distribution shall be made upon the affirmative vote of the Partners as provided for in paragraph 3.1 herein.

6. ADDITIONAL PARTNERS/DISSOLUTION

6.1 The Partnership may admit additional Partners upon the affirmative vote of the Partners, as provided for herein. Additional Partners shall then be admitted upon payment of a contribution to capital as determined by the Partnership and each Partner's interest in the Partnership as provided for in paragraph 2.1 shall be redetermined.

6.2 In the event of the dissolution of the Partnership for any reason, the affairs of the Partnership shall be wound up and the proceeds of the Partnership distributed in accordance with the terms of this Agreement and the laws of the State of _____.

7. MISCELLANEOUS

7.1 Arbitration. If any controversy or claim arising out of this Agreement cannot be settled by the Partners, the controversy or claims shall be settled by arbitration in the City of _____, State of _____, in accordance with the rules of the American Arbitration Association then in

Figure 11.9 Agreement for Multiple Partners   197

effect, and judgment on the award may be entered in any court having jurisdiction.

7.2 Governing Law and Severability. This Agreement shall be interpreted under and subject to the laws of the State of
_____. If any provision of this Agreement shall be unlawful, void or unenforceable, that provision shall be deemed separate from and in no way shall affect the validity or enforceability of the remaining provisions of this Agreement.

7.3 Notices. All notices required to be given under this Agreement shall be either delivered in person to the party to whom addressed or sent by mail, postage prepaid, Certified Mail, Return Receipt Requested, addressed to the Partner at the last address for that Partner as maintained by the Partnership.

7.4 Complete Agreement. This Agreement presents the full and complete understanding of all of the Partners with reference to the Partnership and supersedes any prior agreements and understandings, whether written or oral. This agreement may not be amended except in writing and upon the consent of all of the Partners then existing of the Partnership.

7.5 Successors. This Agreement shall be binding on and inure to the benefit of the respective successors, permitted assigns, executors, administrators, personal representatives and beneficiaries of the Partners.

7.6 Subject Headings. The subject headings used in this Agreement are for convenience only and shall not be deemed to affect the meaning or construction of any of the provisions of this Agreement.

Executed by the Partners as of the date first above written.

_____ (signed)

_____ (signed)

_____ (signed)

PARTNERSHIP AGREEMENT

This Agreement made this _____ day of _____, 19____
between _____ of _____,
_____, _____,
_____, and _____ of
_____, _____,
_____, _____, witness and agree as
follows:

1. Name of Business. The parties hereby agree to form a partnership
under the name of _____ for the purpose of con-
ducting a _____ business.

2. Place of Business. The partnership shall conduct its business at
_____,
_____,
_____,
_____, and such other places as the par-
ties shall select.

3. Term. The partnership shall continue until dissolved by mutual
agreement.

4. Capitalization. The capital of the partnership shall be contrib-
uted equally in cash by the partners.

5. Division of Receipts. The net profits of the partnership shall
be divided equally between the partners, and the net losses shall be
borne equally by them.

6. Salaries. Neither partner shall receive any salary for services
rendered to the partnership.

7. Drawing Accounts. Each of the partners shall be permitted drawing accounts as may be agreed upon by them.

8. Full-Time Efforts. Both partners are to devote their full time
and attention to the business. The partners shall have equal rights
in the management of the partnership business.

9. Books and Records. The partnership books and records shall be
kept at the place of business and shall be at all times open to in-
spection by either partner.

Figure 11.10 Agreement for Two Partners 199

10. Partnership Funds. All funds of the partnership shall be deposited in its name in the _____ of _____, and all withdrawals therefrom are to be made upon checks signed by either partner.

11. Voluntary Termination. Either partner may retire from the partnership at any time by giving to the other party _____ days' notice of his desire to do so. The remaining partner shall have the right either to purchase the retiring partners' interest or to terminate the partnership and liquidate the business. If the remaining partner elects to purchase the remaining interest of the retiring partner, the purchase price shall be equal to the book value of the retiring partner's interest in the partnership business as reflected in the partnership books. The purchase shall be financed by payment in full or by an initial payment of $_____, and the balance paid in installments over a period of _____ years, bearing interest on the unpaid balance at the rate of _____ percent per year.

12. Involuntary Termination. Upon the death of either partner, the surviving partner shall have the right either to purchase the interest of the decedent in the partnership business or to terminate and liquidate the partnership business. If the surviving partner elects to purchase the decedent's interest, the terms and conditions shall be those set forth in the preceding clause. If the surviving partner does not elect to purchase the interest of the decedent in the partnership, he shall proceed with reasonable promptness to liquidate the partnership.

In Witness Whereof, the parties have signed this Agreement.

(Witness)   /s/_____
                                   John Doe
/s/_____   /s/_____
                                   Rob Roe

JOINT VENTURE AGREEMENT

This Agreement made this _____ day of _____, 19____
by and between _____, of _____, and
_____, of _____, (individually the
Venturer and collectively the Joint Venturers).

1. PURPOSE

In consideration of the mutual terms, conditions, and covenants hereinafter set forth, the Joint Venturers agree as follows:

The Joint Venturers hereby form a Joint Venture for the purposes of
_____ and shall conduct business under the name
_____.

2. TERM

The term of the Joint Venture shall be _____.

3. REGISTRATION

The Joint Venturers shall execute all necessary documents to register the Joint Venture with the proper governmental offices in the
County of _____, State of _____.

4. CAPITALIZATION

The capital of the Joint Venture shall consist of $_____.
_____ shall contribute $_____ and
_____ shall contribute $_____, which shall
be deposited in the _____ Bank and shall be dis-
bursed only upon the signatures of the Joint Venturers.

5. COMPENSATION

The profits and losses of the Joint Venture shall be determined in
accordance with good accounting practices and shall be shared among
the Joint Venturers in proportion to their respective capital contributions.

Figure 11.11 Joint Venture Agreement   201

6. MANAGEMENT

_____ is named Venture Manager, and shall have at his sole discretion the management and entire control of the conduct of the business of the Joint Venture.

As compensation for his services the Venture Manager shall be paid $_____ per _____ during the duration of the Joint Venture and shall be reimbursed for all reasonable expenses incurred in the performance of his duties as Venture Manager.

Each Joint Venturer shall be bound by any action taken by the Venture Manager in good faith under this Agreement. In no event shall any Joint Venturer be called upon to pay any amount beyond the liability arising against him on account of his capital contribution.

The Venture Manager shall not be liable for any error in judgment or any mistake of law or fact or any act done in good faith in the exercise of the power and authority as Venture Manager, but shall be liable for gross negligence or willful default.

7. LIMIT OF RELATIONSHIPS

The relationship between the Joint Venturers shall be limited to the performance of the terms and conditions of this Agreement. Nothing herein shall be construed to create a general partnership between the Joint Venturers or to authorize any Venturer to act as a general agent for another, or to permit any Venturer to bind another other than as set forth in this Agreement, or to borrow money on behalf of another Venturer, or to use the credit of any Venturer for any purpose.

8. ASSIGNMENTS

Neither this Agreement nor any interest in the Joint Venture may be assigned, pledged, transferred, or otherwise committed without the prior written consent of the Joint Venturers hereto.

9. GOVERNING LAW

This Agreement shall be governed by and interpreted under the laws of the State of _____. Any controversy or claim arising out of or relating to this Agreement or the breach thereof, shall be settled by arbitration in accordance with the Commercial Arbitration Rules of the American Arbitration Association in the City of _____, State of _____, and judgment upon the award rendered by the arbitrator(s) may be entered in any court having jurisdiction thereof.

10. NOTICES

Any and all notices to be given pursuant to or under this Agreement shall be sent to the party to whom the notice is addressed at the address of the Venturer maintained by the Joint Venture and shall be sent Certified Mail, Return Receipt Requested.

11. ENTIRE AGREEMENT

This Agreement constitutes the entire agreement between the Joint Venturers pertaining to the subject matter contained in it, and supersedes all prior and contemporaneous agreements, representations, warranties, and understandings of the parties. No supplement, modification or amendment of this Agreement shall be binding unless executed in writing by all the parties hereto. No waiver of any of the provisions of this Agreement shall be deemed, or shall constitute, a waiver of any other provision, whether similar or not similar, nor shall any waiver constitute a continuing waiver. No waiver shall be binding unless in writing signed by the party making the waiver.

The parties hereto, intending to be bound, have signed this Agreement as of the date and year first above written.

/s/_____

/s/_____

Figure 11.11 Joint Venture Agreement   203

two partners. These figures are followed by Figure 11.11, a model contract for a joint venture.

Figure 11.1 merits a special note. A joint venture is a temporary partnership. If you encounter a project that you know you need help to handle, you have three options: (1) you can hire someone as a W-2 employee, (2) you can subcontract to another consultant as a 1099 subcontractor or (3) you can establish a joint venture with an associate.

It's easy enough to modify joint venture agreements to suit your needs. For example, you might want to form a consortium with several others to undertake a major project. (In one case two small companies established a joint venture together by forming a third company, in partnership, to pursue a major contract. They won the contract, and the third company formed to undertake the joint venture survived for more than ten years.)

There are many items in the contracts in Figures 11.9 through 11.11 that you may wish to modify. The models are fairly stiff and formal, and you simply eliminate some of the clauses if they are inappropriate to your need. Many successful partnerships have been based on simpler agreements. However, it is wise to have a clear written agreement drawn up, and the closest model is a good starting place. It is better to start with too much and edit it down to a suitable size than to discover later that you failed to include some important clause. As in other cases, it is always a good idea to have a lawyer look over your contract, especially in cases where your entire venture is at stake, as compared with a single project. Studying the model, however, is a very good idea because it will alert you to the need to consider many factors you might not otherwise have even thought about.

Brokers and Subcontracting

Many consultants work on subcontracts that support larger organizations holding prime contracts with clients. These may include technical service companies that are overloaded and need help or that need special talents not available in their own companies. In some cases prime contractors are actually brokers—labor brokers, in fact—who do none of the consulting work directly or with employees of their own, but subcontract all work out to independent consultants. The model in Figure 11.12 is an agreement you might encounter with such a broker, but it is easily adaptable to any other situation in which you wish to subcontract your services. Note again the careful effort to support the consultant's claim to independent contractor status. Brokers are especially aware of the perils posed by the IRS's use of the Section 1706 provision for challenging the independent contractor status most consultants prefer to claim.

SUBCONTRACT AGREEMENT

This Agreement is entered into by and between
_____, a corporation doing business at
_____, (Broker) and
_____, of _____, (Consultant).

1. PREAMBLE

1.1 Broker contracts to provide consultants for computer services, engineering, technical writing, training, and other related services to client organizations on a project basis and assignments as needs arise.

1.2 Consultant is an independent Consultant with adequate skills to perform the duties of consultant, with respect to the particular assignment and/or project identified in Attachment A.

1.3 The parties desire to provide in this Consulting Agreement for the provision by Consultant of the services necessary to perform the services as identified in Attachment A, on the terms and conditions set forth here.

1.4 Broker and Consultant hereby agree as follows: Broker and Consultant desire to enter into a working relationship whereby Consultant will provide services as an independent contractor to Broker directly, in support of Broker's contract with Broker's clients. The parties do hereby agree to the following terms and conditions:

2. WORK ASSIGNMENTS: Consultant shall provide services directly to Broker and to Broker's clients, as required, to perform work assignments which require the training, skills, and abilities of the Consultant as represented to Broker. Descriptions of the work assignments are appended to this agreement as Attachment A.

3. COMPENSATION: Compensation shall be determined at the beginning of each work assignment and included in the work assignment appended to this agreement as Attachment B. Consultant shall not be entitled to any other benefit, monetary or otherwise, from Broker or anyone else, on account of or in consideration of the work performed by Consultant. Consultant shall send invoices to Broker for work completed. Broker shall remit payment of invoice within 30 (thirty) days of receipt to Consultant at _____.

4. INDEPENDENT CONTRACTOR: Consultant further represents that he/she is conducting an independent business, located at address given above, that Consultant has performed services similar to those required under this Agreement for the following persons or firms within the past 12 months.

Figure 11.12 Subcontracting with a Broker   205

5. INDEMNITY: Consultant hereby represents that he/she is covered by disability insurance, worker's compensation insurance and other insurance as he/she may deem desirable and prudent. Consultant understands that, as an independent contractor, he/she will make payments against estimated income taxes due federal, state, and other governments. In the event that Consultant's status as an independent contractor should be disallowed, Consultant agrees to bear any and all expenses, including legal and other professional fees, increased taxes, penalties, and interest that he/she may incur and releases Broker, and any third-party business or client for and from all liability in connection therewith, and any client of Broker from all liability incurred or threatened, including interest and penalties, and the costs of defending administratively or judicially, and, if necessary, settling any proceedings attempting to challenge or invalidate Consultant's status as an independent contractor, or to collect any amounts, including interest and penalties, alleged to be due from Broker or any client of Broker. Consultant may deem it desirable to seek legal or other professional advice in order that Consultant may continue to be properly protected in his/her status as an Independent Contractor.

6. CERTIFICATE OF INSURANCE: Consultant shall obtain and submit a Certificate of Insurance naming Broker as an additional insured on Consultant's automobile insurance policy and general business policy, if Consultant carries such insurance.

7. PERFORMANCE AT WORK: Consultant shall have sole discretion and control of his/her work and the manner in which it is performed. Consultant will arrange the schedule of performance as specified by Broker and will handle all details and logistics of performance.

8. TERM OF SERVICES: The term of the services to be rendered by Consultant shall commence on _____ and terminate upon satisfactory completion of the work assignment; written request from the Broker to remove Consultant from assignment; death of Consultant; physical disability of Consultant; or mutual agreement.

9. CONFIDENTIALITY: Consultant understands that he/she will be working with and developing for Broker and/or Broker's clients procedures, processes, information or other items that Broker and/or Broker's clients may consider to be trade secrets. In the event Consultant uses any formats, procedures or other materials furnished to Consultant by Broker and/or Broker's clients, Consultant understands that such materials and information are proprietary and considered to be trade secrets. All work created by Consultant shall be the

exclusive property of Broker and/or Broker's clients, unless otherwise stated in writing. Consultant agrees to treat all such matters as confidential and of value to Broker and/or Broker's clients. Consultant agrees not to disclose any of such confidential information or items to anyone not directly related to Broker and/or Broker's clients' business nor use such items or property for Consultant's own purposes except in connection with Consultant's work for and on behalf of Broker and/or Broker's clients. Consultant agrees to take all steps reasonably requested by Broker and/or Broker's clients to protect Broker and/or Broker's clients' rights to such material and information. Further, Broker shall not request any information about such property from Consultant nor shall Consultant disclose any information to Broker or others.

10. WORK FOR HIRE; LICENSE: Any materials, processes, formats, charts, graphs, illustrations, documentation, and software created or developed by Consultant in connection with services supplied to Broker and/or Broker's clients (collectively referred to as "Works") shall be the property of Broker and/or Broker's clients (as the client and Broker shall agree) and shall constitute "works for hire" under the Federal Copyright Act of 1976. Broker and/or Broker's clients shall apply for and own the copyright in all such items, and have the exclusive right to commercial or other use of said items. To the extent that the Works are not deemed to constitute "works for hire," Consultant hereby assigns in perpetuity and for no additional consideration all copyrights in the Works to Broker and/or Broker's clients, as may be specified by Broker, and agrees to execute any documents as may be requested by Broker to evidence and effectuate such assignment.

11. SEVERABILITY and CHOICE OF FORUM: If any part of this Agreement shall be held invalid or unlawful for any reason, the same shall be deemed severed from the remainder hereof, and it shall in no way affect or impair the validity of the Agreement. This Agreement shall be deemed a contract made under the laws of the State of _____, and the rights and obligations of the parties hereto shall be governed by and construed in accordance therewith. This is the complete agreement between the parties. Unless set forth herein, neither party shall be liable for any representations made and all modifications hereto must be in writing specifically referencing this provision, signed by both parties hereto. Accordingly, no letter, policy or representation made by or on behalf of Broker shall be deemed a modification hereof, and any act or omission by Broker to strictly enforce the terms and conditions herein shall not act as a waiver of a provision.

Figure 11.12 Subcontracting with a Broker 207

Executed this [day] day of [month, year] in the County of
_____, State of _____.

_____
Consultant

_____
Broker

Job Shops and Temporary Employment

The IRS appears to have a great distaste for subcontracting, especially when it involves third-party arrangements (e.g., brokers and subcontractors). Quite evidently, the IRS has ample authority under the current laws to challenge independent consultants' claims to status as independent contractors, so a great many brokers—and clients also—insist on requiring independent consultants to work as temporary employees, especially when working on the client's premises. The contract model in Figure 11.13 covers such employment, probably in much greater detail than necessary, but the model is easily modified. You will note a number of special provisions, such as that explaining the complete lack of fringe benefits. Many suppliers of technical/professional temporaries (e.g., brokers and job shops) do offer limited fringe benefits to temporaries, and the contract model would have to be modified accordingly.

Sales Representative Agreements

Some consultants choose to sell goods related to their consulting specialties. They may do so as dealers, buying at wholesale and selling at retail, or they may avoid most of the investment and other risks of dealership by simply representing manufacturers and wholesalers. For example, a security consultant can also represent a manufacturer of locks, alarms and similar protective devices. The model in Figure 11.14 is an example of a relatively simple sales representative agreement that is in the form of a letter agreement. It is followed by a somewhat more detailed agreement in Figure 11.15, one that looks more like a formal contract and makes the consultant an agent instead of a representative.

EMPLOYMENT AGREEMENT

This Agreement is entered into on _____, 19____, between _____, of _____ (Employer), and _____, of _____ (Consultant), whose Social Security Number is _____, on the following terms and conditions:

1.0 SERVICES REQUIRED

1.1 Consultant agrees to perform services set forth in Paragraph 1 of the attached Exhibit. The services shall be performed by Consultant during the period and at the times and locations set forth in Paragraph 2 of the attached Exhibit.

1.2 Consultant warrants that he/she is entitled under the law to accept employment in the United States.

2.0 COMPENSATION

2.1 Employer shall pay to Consultant for satisfactory performance of the services hereunder, compensation as set forth in Paragraph 3 of the attached Exhibit. Employer shall withhold from Consultant's compensation all applicable federal and state taxes as required by federal, state, and other legal requirement.

2.2 Consultant's compensation shall be paid to Consultant within _____ working days after Employer's receipt and approval of Consultant's weekly statement of services hereunder. Said weekly statement must be signed by Consultant's supervisor.

2.3 Consultant agrees to employment with Employer as a Project Consultant and therefore elects to receive a higher rate of compensation in lieu of receiving any of the other employee benefits typically provided to other Employer's employees. Such benefits include but are not limited to and are identified as holiday, vacation, sick, funeral and personal absence pay; medical, dental, and Life Insurance, education reimbursements and any other benefits provided to permanent employees.

2.4 Employer shall reimburse Consultant for all authorized business expenses incurred by Consultant. Reimbursement shall occur within the next pay period following Consultant's submission of receipts for authorized expenditures. Expense reports shall be submitted weekly.

2.5 Employer shall pay Consultant $ _____ per mile as reimbursement for authorized use of his/her personal automobile for business purposes.

3.0 TERM

3.1 The term of this Agreement shall be for an estimated period of _____ months, commencing _____, unless terminated earlier by either party as provided below in subparagraph 3.2. The Agreement may be extended by mutual consent of the parties.

3.2 Employer or Consultant may terminate this Agreement at any time and for any reason. This Agreement shall automatically terminate on the occurrence of any of the following events:

a) The occurrence of circumstances that make it impossible or impractical for the business of the Employer with the client to be continued;

b) Consultant's (i) commission of any act of dishonesty; (ii) inability or unwillingness to provide adequate documentation of Consultant's right to work in the United States; (iii) unauthorized disclosure of confidential information relating to Employer or its Consultants; (iv) unauthorized disclosure of the contents of this Agreement; (v) death or continued incapacity to fully perform Consultant's duties; (vi) willful breach of duty, gross carelessness or misconduct in the performance of Consultant's duties; (vii) unjustifiable neglect of the duties hereunder; or (viii) other breach of conditions of this Agreement.

4.0 PROGRESS REPORTS

4.1 Upon Employer's request, Consultant shall provide written progress reports of all oral and written observations, opinions, recommendations, analyses, progress and conclusions related to Consultant's services hereunder. Each report shall be in a form acceptable to Employer.

5.0 AUTHORITY

5.1 Consultant agrees that he/she is not authorized to contract, or otherwise bind, Employer with respect to any matter without Employer's own written approval.

6.0 OTHER EMPLOYMENT

6.1 Consultant shall devote his/her full time and energies to the responsibilities of the position and refrain from undertaking any other employment whatsoever which may impede Consultant's ability to perform such duties in behalf of Employer. Consultant shall not, during the term of this Agreement be interested directly or indirectly, in any manner, as partner, officer, director, stockholder, advisor, employee or in any other capacity in any other business similar to Employer's business; provided, however, that nothing herein contained shall be deemed to prevent or limit Consultant's right to invest in the capital stock or other securities of any corporation whose securities are publicly owned or are regularly traded on any securities exchange or in the over-the-counter market.

7.0 NON-COMPETE CLAUSE

7.1 Consultant agrees that for a period of one (1) year after the completion of his/her services hereunder, Consultant shall not work for Employer's client, for whom the services rendered hereunder were

Figure 11.13 Temporary Employment Agreement 211

performed to complete Employer's contract, either as an employee or otherwise, without prior written approval from Employer.

8.0 COPYRIGHT/PATENTS

8.1 Consultant agrees that all rights, title and interest to any and all inventions, ideas or programs developed as a result of the services provided hereunder, whether copyrightable or not, shall be the sole property of Employer and/or Employer's client.

8.2 Consultant agrees that all written records or other data prepared during or evolving from Consultant's performance of services shall be the property of Employer and/or Employer's client. At the completion, or earlier termination of this Agreement, Consultant shall deliver all originals and copies of records to Employer and/or Employer's client.

9.0 TRADE SECRETS AND CONFIDENTIALITY

9.1 In the course of Consultant's employment, Consultant will have access to Employer and/or Employer's client's trade secrets and confidential information, including but not limited to, records and data pertaining to Employer and/or Employer's client's business. Such information is considered secret and is disclosed to Consultant in strict confidence. Such records and data are the property of Employer and/or Employer's client and shall promptly be returned to Employer and/or Employer's client upon the completion or earlier termination of this Agreement. Consultant shall not directly or indirectly disclose or use any such information, except as required in the course of Consultant's employment by Employer and/or Employer's client.

10.0 AGREEMENT BY INCORPORATION

10.1 The parties agree that the Exhibit attached hereto and all provisions of same, shall be incorporated herein by reference.

11.0 CONFLICTS OF INTEREST

11.1 Consultant represents that there is no conflict of interest between services to be rendered under this Agreement and Consultant's services and employment with other parties. If Consultant believes that there is a conflict, or such conflict arises during this Agreement or any extension, Consultant will immediately advise Employer and Employer may, at its sole discretion, immediately terminate this Agreement, without any obligation owed to Consultant.

12.0 SURVIVAL OF TERMS

12.1 Consultant agrees that the terms of Paragraph 7 shall remain in full force and effect for one (1) year from the date of completion, or earlier termination of this Agreement.

12.2 Consultant agrees that the terms of Paragraph 8 shall continue in full force and effect for perpetuity.

12.3 Consultant further agrees that the terms of Paragraph 9 shall continue in full force and effect from the date of completion, or earlier termination of this Agreement until such time that this information becomes available in the public domain.

13.0 ARBITRATION

13.1 Any controversy or claim arising out of or relating to this Agreement, or the breach thereof, shall be resolved by arbitration in _____. Such arbitration shall be conducted in accordance with the laws, rules, procedures, and regulations of the American Arbitration Association. The Arbitrator shall not be authorized to award either party extra contractual damages (i.e., compensatory or punitive damages). In the event of a breach of this Agreement by Employer, Consultant's damages shall be limited to an award of lost wages and benefits, as may be determined by the Arbitrator.

14.0 ENTIRE AGREEMENT

14.1 This constitutes the entire Agreement of the parties hereto with respect to the subject matter hereof. Other than as expressly set forth herein, the parties acknowledge that there are no other promises, terms, conditions, or representations (verbal or written) regarding any matter relevant hereto including, by way of example, the scope of Consultant's duties or the duration of this Agreement. This Agreement shall not be modified, extended or supplemented in any manner, except by a subsequent written contract or amendment signed by both Consultant and Employer.

15.0 GOVERNING LAW

15.1 This Agreement has been executed in the State of _____, and it is expressly contemplated by the parties and agreed upon by them that the interpretation and enforcement hereof shall be governed by the substantive and procedural laws of the State of _____. Any and all disputes hereunder, including applicability of this paragraph, shall be adjudicated in an arbitration proceeding in accordance with the terms of Section 13.0 of this Agreement.

16.0 ATTORNEYS' FEES

16.1 If any proceeding is commenced involving the interpretation or enforcement of the provisions in this Agreement, the party prevailing in such proceeding shall be entitled to reasonable costs and attorneys's fees.

17.0 WAIVERS

17.1 Failure of Employer or Consultant to exercise any right or remedy upon any breach or default with respect to any of the terms of this Agreement, or delay in exercising any such right or remedy, shall not be construed as a waiver of rights in any later breach.

Figure 11.13 Temporary Employment Agreement 213

18.0 NOTICES

18.1 Any notice provided for in this Agreement shall be in writing and shall be deemed to have been properly given, if sent by certified mail, postage prepaid, to the following addresses:

Employer:

Consultant:

18.2 The date of mailing shall be deemed to be the date on which notice is given. Either party may change addresses for purposes of notice by giving the other party written notice of the new address within [number of ( )] days of the change of address.

19.0 INVALID PROVISIONS

19.1 If any provision of this Agreement is held to be invalid, void or unenforceable for any reason, the remaining provisions shall nevertheless continue in full force and effect, without being impaired or invalidated in any manner.

20.0 TITLES

20.1 The titles of the various sections herein are intended solely for convenience of reference, and are not intended and shall not be deemed for any purpose whatsoever to modify, explain or place any construction upon any of the provisions of this Agreement, and shall not affect the meaning or interpretation of this Agreement.

Employer: _____ (signed)

Consultant: _____ (signed)

SALES REPRESENTATIVE AGREEMENT

[Date]

[Address and salutation]

This letter sets forth our agreement of the terms and conditions upon which you agree to act as a direct seller of products distributed by the [company name].

1. Effective as of the date of execution of this Agreement, you are engaged by the undersigned as a non-exclusive direct seller for [product(s) and territory].

2. In this capacity, you will pursue such leads as you may obtain or that we may supply to you for the sale to such individuals who are interested in purchasing the undersigned's products. All sales will be at such purchase price as we shall agree upon.

3. You will use your best efforts to promote sales and get orders for the undersigned and shall at all times maintain the good will between the undersigned and its customers.

4. You will determine the methods of carrying out your obligations hereunder and the number of hours that you will work. At all times you will maintain professional standards of performance and behavior and conduct your activities accordingly. You may employ such individuals as you may desire on such terms and conditions that you may establish, and you alone will be solely responsible for the direction of their activities, for the payment of salaries and/or other compensation to your employees, and for the payment of federal, state and local tax obligations.

In consideration for the services to be rendered by you, you will receive commissions in accordance with the Schedule which is attached hereto and is set forth as Schedule A. This Schedule of Payment is subject to change by the undersigned upon prior written notice. Such commissions will be payable upon delivery of the products sold.

It is agreed that you will not be an employee of the undersigned and will not be so treated for federal and state tax purposes. You will be an independent contractor and will be solely responsible for payment of all federal, state and local tax obligations with respect to all amounts paid to you by the undersigned.

Figure 11.14 Sales Representative Agreement 215

This agreement will continue until terminated by either of us at will.

Any controversy or claim arising out of or relating to this Agreement, or the breach thereof, shall be settled by arbitration in accordance with the then obtaining rules of the American Arbitration Association in the State of _____ and a judgment upon any award rendered by the arbitrator(s) may be entered in any court having jurisdiction thereof.

If the foregoing accurately contains the terms and conditions of our Agreement, kindly execute the enclosed copy of this letter Agreement where indicated and return it to the undersigned.

Very truly yours,

_____

ACCEPTED

_____

Date:

SALES AGENCY AGREEMENT

Agreement made this _____ day of _____,
19____, by and between _____ (Principal) and
_____ (Agent).

In consideration of the mutual terms, conditions, and covenants
hereinafter set forth, Principal and Agent agree as follows:

PURPOSE: Principal appoints Agent as its sales representative to
sell the products of the Principal as listed in the attached Exhibit A.

Agent accepts the appointment and agrees to promote, market, and
sell the products of the Principal at the prices set forth in Exhibit A.

PRICES: The parties agree that the list of products and/or prices
may be amended from time to time as market conditions and fluctuat-
ing costs justify. Principal may unilaterally remove products from
the list or change prices. Additions to the product list shall be by
mutual agreement.

TERRITORY: Agent's territory in which he is authorized to sell
products shall be _____ (Territory), which may be
amended by mutual written agreement.

With Principal's prior written consent, Agent may sell products
outside Agent's Territory or at prices different from those on
Exhibit A. Principal's consent shall be for individual sales only
and shall not be construed to expand Agent's territory or to amend
Exhibit A.

SALES MATERIALS: Principal shall furnish to Agent at Principal's
expense all sales material for the products listed on Exhibit A and
shall keep the material up-to-date.

BEST EFFORTS: Agent agrees to use best efforts to promote, market
and sell the products of Exhibit A within the allocated territory,
devote such time and attention as may be reasonably necessary, and
abide by the Principal's policies.

SURVIVAL OF TERMS: Agent agrees that during the term of this Agreement and for a period of _____ years thereafter, Agent, either
directly or indirectly, shall handle no products within the Territory that are directly competitive with those products listed in
Exhibit A.

LICENSES AND TAXES: Agent shall obtain, at its own expense, all
necessary licenses and permits to permit Agent to conduct business
as described here. Agent represents and warrants that Agent shall
conduct business in strict conformity with all local, state, and
federal laws, rules and regulations.

INDEPENDENT CONTRACTOR: Principal agrees that Agent may employ
representatives in furtherance of this Agreement and Agent agrees

Figure 11.15 Sales Agency Agreement   217

that Agent shall be solely responsible for the payment of wages or commissions to those representatives and that under no circumstances shall Agent's representatives be deemed employees of Principal for any purpose whatsoever.

Agent is an independent contractor and nothing contained in this Agreement shall be deemed or interpreted to constitute the Agent as a partner or employee of the Principal, nor shall either party have any authority to bind the other in any respect, it being understood that any and all orders submitted by Agent are subject to acceptance by the Principal in its sole discretion.

COMMISSIONS: Principal shall pay to Agent a commission on the sale of products as set forth on Exhibit B, which commission rate may be amended from time to time by mutual agreement. Principal shall be responsible for the granting of credit to customers and shall pay commissions to Agent on the 15th day of the month for all merchandise shipped by Principal to Agent's customers in the preceding month.

TERM: This Agreement shall be for a period of _____ years, unless sooner terminated by either party upon _____ days' written notice.

TERMINATION: Upon termination, Agent shall be entitled to receive commissions for all orders accepted by Principal prior to the date of termination. Payment to be made upon shipment.

ENTIRE AGREEMENT: It is agreed between the parties that there are no other agreements or understandings between them relating to the subject matter of this Agreement. This Agreement supersedes all prior agreements, oral or written, between the parties and is intended as a complete and exclusive statement of the agreement between the parties. No change or modification of this Agreement shall be valid unless the same be in writing and signed by the parties.

ASSIGNMENT: This Agreement shall not be assigned by Agent without the prior written consent of Principal.

NOTICES: All notices required or permitted to be given hereunder shall be in writing and may be delivered personally or by Certified Mail, Return Receipt Requested, postage prepaid, addressed to the party's last known address.

GOVERNING LAW: This Agreement shall be construed in accordance with and governed by the laws of the State of _____.

The parties hereto have caused this Agreement to be executed as of the date first above written.

/s/_____
  Principal

/s/_____

12

A Guide to Some Miscellaneous Forms

As author/attorney-at-law Daniel Sitarz notes in *Small Business Legal Forms,* more legal forms are used in and by American businesses than are used in the operation of many foreign governments. "Paper" is largely what business is about, but especially what American business is about.

THE MATTER OF A FEW OTHER FORMS

Useful and necessary as learning about contracts and their clauses is, it is not enough. Aside from the fact that clauses are the components of contracts and themselves the main subject of many contracts, there are a great number of other business forms that are useful and often necessary to the conduct of your consulting practice. Knowledge and use of them can help you anticipate some of the perils of business and avoid the problems or provide ready-made solutions if problems arise. Thus, although our primary focus has been on contracts and the clauses that make up contracts, you would not be well served were I to ignore and neglect the parallel subject of other business forms, some of which are closely related to contracts. The rest of this chapter is devoted to discussing these business forms and presenting a few models of the more common forms.

Note the simplicity of most of the forms. Many are little more than brief letters or memoranda, although they can become much more complex and elaborate. Some lawyers insist that it is essential to dot all the i's and cross all the t's if you are to be secure. Others think it is gilding the lily and not at all necessary. I lean toward the simplistic side and the middle ground after consulting many sources and finding no great preponderance of sentiment or rationale for lengthy discourses on paper in writing these forms.

Power of Attorney

When you entrust a legal problem to a lawyer, he or she is likely to ask you to sign a power of attorney. Most of us who are not lawyers think that the word *attorney* is synonymous with the word *lawyer.* Not so. Lawyers probably act as attorneys far more often than anyone else does, but anyone can be an attorney. An *attorney* is anyone granted the right to act for another person as if he or she were that other person.

You may grant anyone your power of attorney, making that other party your *attorney-in-fact,* with the right to represent you in all or in a limited number of areas, depending on how you write the document granting power of attorney. (Or you may be asked to serve as someone's attorney-in-fact.) You may have anyone represent you and be empowered to act for you. The two models shown in Figures 12.1 and 12.2 represent both the general or unlimited power of attorney (i.e., the right to act for another in all matters) and the limited power of attorney, or the right to act in only those matters or areas clearly specified in the power-granting instrument.

In addition to the models shown in Figures 12.1 and 12.2, there are other ways to qualify the power of attorney. For example, an attorney-in-fact may be appointed to represent another individual or to represent a corporation. Then there is the *durable* power of attorney, which becomes effective only if and when the grantor becomes physically or mentally disabled and incapable of making decisions (and even this may be further modulated as durable unlimited or durable limited power of attorney). And then there are forms for acknowledging the existence of the power of attorney and for revoking it as well. For most business purposes, however, the two models suffice quite well.

Affidavit

The affidavit generally is a simple form. It certifies or affirms a statement made under oath by a party who presents it as fact. Affidavits may be certified by judges, clerks of the court, justices of the peace or notaries, among other officials. Figure 12.3 offers the simplest format, although you may encounter affidavits with far more complex and detailed statements.

Breaches and Disputes

A breach of contract, no matter how minor, can lead to dissolution or invalidation of the contract. However, many breaches of contract are only technical breaches that are minor in nature, and neither party wishes to invalidate the

GENERAL POWER OF ATTORNEY

State of

County of

Know all men by these presents that I, [name], the undersigned, of [full address], hereby make, constitute, and appoint [name] of [full address] my true and lawful attorney-in-fact for me and in my name, place, and stead, giving to the said attorney-in-fact full power to do and perform all and every act that I may legally do through an attorney-in-fact, and every proper power necessary to carry out the purposes for which this power is granted, with full power of substitution and revocation, hereby ratifying and affirming that which he or his substitute shall lawfully do or cause to be done by himself or his substitute lawfully designated by virtue of the power herein conferred upon him.

Witnesses: /s/_____

_____   Date:

_____

Figure 12.1 General Power of Attorney   221

LIMITED POWER OF ATTORNEY

To all persons, be it known that [name], undersigned, hereby empowers [name] to act for me as my attorney-in-fact.

My attorney-in-fact shall have authority to perform the following acts on my behalf as I would do personally:

My attorney-in-fact hereby accepts this appointment subject to its terms and agrees to act and perform in said capacity consistent with my best interests as he in his best discretion deems advisable.

This power of attorney may be revoked by me at any time, and shall automatically be revoked upon my death, provided any person relying on this power of attorney before or after my death shall have full rights to accept the authority of my attorney-in-fact until in receipt of actual notice of revocation.

Signed under seal this _____ day _____, 19____.

Grantor: _____

Attorney-in-Fact: _____

State of

County of

Then personally appeared before me [name], Grantor, and [name], Attorney-in-Fact, who acknowledged the foregoing before me.

_____
Notary Public

My Commission Expires: [date]

AFFIDAVIT

State of
) ss.
County of

   John Doe, being duly sworn, deposes:

   [Statement(s)]

   Sworn to before me on this _____ day of _____,
19____.

(SEAL)   /s/_____
                              Notary Pubic

My commission expires:

Figure 12.3 Short-Form Affidavit   223

contract over such a minor infraction. Thus, when a breach occurs, the offending party is generally notified of the breach and asked to cure the breach promptly. There are several forms employed to accommodate these purposes. They generally are simple forms but are necessary, nevertheless, for such purposes as advising the offending party of the breach, waiving one's right to such action as invalidating the contract and/or demanding damages and other relevant actions. These forms are often presented as letters between the parties, as shown in Figures 12.4, 12.5 and 12.6. (Figure 12.5 illustrates a notice alleging breach of warranty, although the warranty technically is itself a contract.) These are not all the forms you may encounter, but they are the ones most likely to surface during the life of a contract should there be a breach, even a technical one.

Releases

In the course of a dispute of any kind, the offended party may allege damages and seek compensation or use the allegation of damage and threat of further action as a weapon, or may even enter a lawsuit. Disputes do not always end up in court. Quite often they are settled out of court by one means or another. In any case, when a dispute is settled in some manner other than a formal lawsuit, it is customary for the party making an out-of-court settlement to seek a release from current claims, now and forever. Whenever a dispute is settled in any manner other than a formal suit, one should get a formal release to prevent later action seeking compensation for some alleged damage. Figure 12.7 is a simple general release form. Again, according to the circumstances, there are a number of forms releases can take. There is, for example, the general release, but there are also such variants as specific releases of various kinds relinquishing claims or grounds for future claims in re specific causes deemed actionable.

Temporary Employment

Many independent consultants accept temporary employment from time to time and work most of the time as W-2 temporaries rather than Form 1099 contractors and subcontractors. Should you accept such employment, you may be asked by a client-employer to sign an agreement acknowledging the conditions of your employment. (See Figure 12.8.)

Employee Noncompete Clause

When and if you sell a business, particularly one built around and dependent on your personal services, the buyer generally wants assurance that you will not go out and compete directly with him or her, especially not by soliciting the business of your former clients. In some cases employers ask for a similar assurance from their own employees. This is an especially sensitive issue when

NOTICE OF BREACH OF CONTRACT

On _____, 19____ we entered into agreement to

You are now in breach of our contract as follows:

You have ____ days to cure the breach and avoid termination and other possible action by taking the following measures:

Sincerely,

_____

/s/_____

Figure 12.4 Notice of Breach of Contract   225

NOTICE OF BREACH OF WARRANTY

Date:

To:

Please take notice that the work product described below, furnished by you to me under our contract entered into by and between us at _____ on _____, 19____ is defective in the following respects:

This is unacceptable, per our agreement.

Please cure this breach of warranty within _____ days to prevent further action seeking compensation for damages.

Sincerely,

/s/_____

WAIVER OF BREACH

Date:

To:

1. I, _____, hereby waive my right to action which I may have because of the breach committed on or about _____, 19____ by _____ of the contract between us dated _____.

2. I do not waive my right to action for any other breach that may be hereafter committed under our agreement.

/s/_____

Date:

Figure 12.6 Waiver of Breach   227

RELEASE

BE IT KNOWN, for good consideration, that the undersigned hereby jointly and severally forever releases, discharges, acquits and forgives [name] from any and all claims, actions, suits, demands, agreements, liabilities and proceedings of every nature and description both at law and in equity arising from the beginning of time to the date of these presents and more particularly related to an incident or claim that arose out of the following circumstances:

This release shall be binding upon and inure to the benefit of the parties, their successors, assigns, and personal representatives.

Signed under seal this _____ day of _____, 19____.

By:_____   Witnesses:_____

_____   _____

TEMPORARY/PART-TIME EMPLOYMENT
ACKNOWLEDGMENT

ACKNOWLEDGED by [Employee].

I understand that I am being employed by [Company] in a temporary or part-time position only and for such time as my services are required. I understand that this may be temporary and remain part-time and said employment does not entitle me to any special consideration for permanent or full-time employment. I further understand that my temporary or part-time employment may be terminated at any time without cause or pursuant to disciplinary procedures set forth for permanent or full-time employees. I also understand that I am not eligible to participate in any fringe benefit programs or retirement programs or any other programs available to permanent or full-time employees (unless required by law) and in the event I am allowed participation in any benefit or program, then my continued participation may be voluntarily withdrawn or terminated by the Company at any time.

_____
Employee

_____
Company

Figure 12.8 Acknowledgment of Conditions of Temporary Employment   229

the employee is a temporary one who is also an independent consultant; the employer fears that the employee may utilize what he or she has learned while in the employment to compete with the employer. Thus, employers are motivated to ask employees to sign a noncompete clause or to include one in an acknowledgment of temporary employment. (See Figure 12.9 for an example of a noncompete clause.)

Credit References

One problem you may encounter as a consultant or contractor is that of getting paid promptly and in full. It is one thing to do business with major corporations, but it is quite another to deal with small companies. In the case of small companies, you should check their credit to assure yourself that you are likely to get paid or, at least, to guide you in setting the terms of payment. Figure 12.10 is a suggested form for requesting credit information from the credit references a client offers.

Exhibits, Specifications and Proposals

An essential item that may be an element of a contract by actual incorporation into the text of the contract or included virtually by reference is the detailed statement of what is to be done by you under the terms of the contract. This is referred to variously as the *schedule, specification, statement of work, exhibit* and/or *attachment.* The terms *exhibit* or *attachment* merely indicate where and how it becomes a part of the contract, however, and not what it is. For large and complex projects, a full-scale proposal is requested by and prepared for the client's study to help the client decide on an awardee and determine what the terms of the contract should be.

An example of such an exhibit appears in Figure 7.3 as two pages following the main text of the contract. In the case of a large project the formal proposal used as an exhibit may be considerably more than two pages. Many proposals run to dozens of pages and even to more than one volume for truly major contracts, which are normally never assigned to an independent contractor. However, relatively large proposals are written often for projects running to six figures.

There is the problem of how to define the word *proposal.* Many independents are understandably reluctant to expend the energy and time required to create substantial proposals such as those of larger organizations. These proposals go into extensive sales arguments, descriptions of their facilities and experience, accounts of past projects and other such peripheral subjects before getting down to the meat of exactly what they propose to do for the client. That is a standard practice for certain kinds of work, and many clients require and specifically request the information. Many consultants, however, write a completely objective specification of what they propose to do, with no special effort to sell it to clients. In any case, it is that portion of even the most elaborate proposal that will be included in the contract by reference or actual attachment. As mentioned in earlier chapters, it should include quantified data that specifies the deliverable items and schedules. Thus, remember to specify the hours/days/weeks of labor; deliverable items, if any; schedules; rates; schedule of payments; and anything else that can be cited as part of the statement or description of work.

EMPLOYEE NONCOMPETE CLAUSE

In consideration of my being employed by _____
(Company), I, _____ (Name), agree that following termination of my employment and regardless of the cause of my termination, I shall not compete with the business of the Company or its
successors or assigns within an area of _____ miles from
_____ , _____ , to wit:
_____ and shall not directly or indirectly own, be
employed by or work on behalf of any firm engaged in the business of
_____ or any business substantially similar and competitive with the Company.

This agreement shall remain in full force and effect for _____
years commencing with the date of employment termination.

Signed and sealed this _____ day of _____ , 19____ .

_____
Employee

REQUEST FOR CREDIT REFERENCE

                              Date:

To:

Re:

    The party named here has given your name as a reference for
credit. Your assistance in furnishing the following information
about the party will be greatly appreciated:

    High credit limit:
    Terms of sale:
    Present balance owed:
    Payment history:

    Please note other credit information you may believe useful on the
reverse side.
    This information shall, of course, be held strictly confidential.
    A stamped return envelope is enclosed for your convenience.

Very truly,

_____

Figure 12.10 Request for Credit Information   233

A Special Index to
the Models

WHY A REFERENCE GUIDE TO THE MODELS

Because "facts on the ground" vary a lot from case to case, there are no perfect models and solutions for every contract. Each contract is unique (or should be) and fashioned carefully to suit individual needs and circumstances. Models are thus useful as general guides only; you must select the contract and clause that is closest to your needs and then adapt them as your needs indicate. This chapter is designed to facilitate that process.

WHY A SPECIAL INDEX FOR THE CLAUSES

By now you know that the factor that makes an almost limitless number of contracts and contract forms possible is the large number of standard and quasi-standard contract clauses, most of which are flexible and easily modified to adapt to individual situations and needs. Clauses are the building blocks from which contracts are assembled. In this book you have encountered samples and models of probably all, or certainly most, of the kinds of clauses you are likely to encounter in the contracts you will negotiate, sign and follow as a consultant and independent contractor. As you have learned, clauses are versatile tools for fashioning contracts. They can be labeled as you please, modified in almost limitless ways to suit your needs and reach agreement with your clients, combined or used separately and made into separate and independent contracts. Therefore, once beyond the general information about contracts and contract law, familiarity with and knowledge of clauses is what contract "lore" is all about.

CONTRACT CLAUSES ARE ALSO A TROUBLESHOOTING GUIDE

Clauses are or can be the booby traps of contracts. It is thus necessary to be knowledgeable about them for defensive purposes. But there is another side to this issue. A good knowledge of clauses represents at least two major assets for you as a consultant: (1) it enables you to draft, review, evaluate and negotiate effective contracts and (2) it provides you with insight into the majority of consulting problems and the solutions to those problems. Thus, remember to know what the clauses are, what they say and what they mean, and you will block some of the most difficult problems of independent consulting and contracting.

The clauses that have appeared in this book are used over and over in writing contracts. They have been developed over the years because certain problems have cropped up repeatedly and it has become necessary to devise contract language to solve, overcome or avoid them. Each clause represents a problem, was born out of a past problem and is thus the key to some potential problem and its solution. Often the lack of the right clause is the root of a problem. Thus, it is wise to study these clauses to become alerted to problem areas and to learn how to cope successfully with them.

Note that few contracts shown incorporate every clause that is important to consulting contracts. Clauses covering disputes and arbitration, for example, appear less often than seems advisable; but many models do have clauses covering the governing law and jurisdiction of choice, so perhaps that is deemed adequate for accommodating the settlement of disputes. On the other hand, take note of which clauses appear in virtually all contracts. That is a direct indication of how important these clauses and the matters they cover are to contractors and lawyers.

You don't have to memorize all the data and formats represented by these contracts, clauses and other business forms; even practicing lawyers do not attempt to memorize all the data but turn to their reference books whenever the need arises, a practice you should emulate. In the pages that follow you will find listings of these items, with some of their variant names to help you identify them readily. Special indexes will help you locate the contract models in this book. If, for example, you wish to see how others have written noncompete clauses or agreements, you can easily find such clauses and review them to get ideas for the several ways in which they can be written and the typical terms of noncompete agreements. Or if you want to determine how to protect your interest in computer software programs you write, you can review all clauses relevant to that need.

The three lists that follow are special indexes to the contracts, clauses and other forms you will encounter and have at least occasional need for as a consultant, independent contractor, business owner or temporary employee. They are listed by the titles used as headings, with an attempt to put them into alphabetical order. But remember that there are several different headings that can be used to describe contracts or clauses, so you cannot rely too heavily on the alphabetical listings for complete guidance. And in some cases there are no headings or captions used in the contract to identify the subject of the clause, but the figure and page reference will be supplied, nevertheless. A few clauses are inevitably included in every contract. For example, you can always find samples of *term, termination, preamble* and other such headings, whether they are so labeled or not. There is no reason to include them in these indexes, nor is there any point in including the special clauses that cover minor points. However, an effort is made here to include all major clauses you are likely to need.

Remember that clauses may be combined. A "Governing Law" clause, for example, often includes a "Choice of Forum" clause, which may be known as a clause covering "Jurisdiction for Court Action." You can survey this list whenever you are about to conclude a contractual arrangement to jog your memory and alert you to probable contract needs. You can then go to the special index of clauses to find all the samples of the clause under its various names and headings.

OTHER SPECIAL INDEXES

Although of lesser importance in adapting the models to your needs, special indexes to contract models and miscellaneous forms also follow. But remember: your chief objective is to find the proper clauses for your needs and purposes.

INDEX TO THE CONTRACT MODELS

INDEX TO THE CLAUSES

INDEX TO THE MISCELLANEOUS FORMS

Resources

Some Useful Books

Chernofsky, Charles B., and Griffith G. deNoyelles, Jr. *Legal Forms and Agreements*. Ridgefield, N.J.: Round Lake Publishing, 1991.

Cohen, Herb. *You Can Negotiate Anything*. New York: Bantam Books, 1988.

Consumer Law Foundation. *The Complete Legal Kit*. Philadelphia: Running Press, 1988.

Davidson, Daniel V., Brenda E. Knowles, Lynn M. Forsythe, and Robert J. Jesperson, *Comprehensive Business Law, Principles and Cases*. Boston: Kent Publishing Co., 1987.

Fuller, George. *The Negotiator's Handbook*. Englewood Cliffs, N.J.: Prentice-Hall, 1991.

Howell, John C. *The Guide to Business Contracts*. Boulder, Colo.: Hamilton Press, Inc., 1979.

Howell, Rate A., John R. Allison, and Robert A. Prentice. *Business Law Text and Cases*. 4th ed. Chicago: The Dryden Press, 1988.

Koren, Leonard, and Peter Goodman. *The Haggler's Handbook*. New York: W.W. Norton & Co., 1991.

Qubein, Nido R. *Communicate Like a Pro*. Englewood Cliffs, N.J.: Prentice-Hall, 1983.

Ries, Al, and Jack Trout. *The 22 Immutable Laws of Marketing*. New York: Harper Business, 1993.

Sitarz, Daniel. *Small Business Legal Forms.* Carbondale, Ill.: Nova Publishing Co., 1991.

Thorpe, E. Barrett. *Write Your Own Business Contracts: What Your Attorney Won't Tell You.* Oasis Press, 1994.

Consulting Books by Herman Holtz

The Consultant's Edge, John Wiley, 1985

The Consultant's Guide to Newsletter Profits, Business One Irwin, 1987

Expanding Your Consulting Practice with Seminars, John Wiley, 1987

The Consultant's Guide to Winning Clients, John Wiley, 1988

How To Succeed as an Independent Consultant, Third Edition, John Wiley, 1992

The Consultant's Guide to Proposal Writing, 2nd Edition, John Wiley, 1990

The Consultant's Guide to Hidden Profits, John Wiley, 1992

Enterprise•Dearborn *Complete Guide* Series

The Complete Guide to Business Agreements, Ted Nicholas

The Complete Guide to Consulting Success, Howard Shenson and Ted Nicholas

The Complete Book of Corporate Forms, Ted Nicholas

The Complete Guide to Nonprofit Corporations, Ted Nicholas

The Complete Guide to "S" Corporations, Ted Nicholas

The Complete Small Business Legal Guide, Robert Friedman

The Executive's Business Letter Book, Ted Nicholas

Computer Software To Create and Customize Contracts

Quickform Contracts, Invisible Hand Software, 3847 Whitman Road, Annandale, VA 22003; Telephone: 703-207-9353; Fax: 703-207-0343.

Writing Your Own Contracts, Cynthia Kolnick (text).

Consulting Forms: The Disk, computer program, Lucid Communications, 3145 Geary Blvd., Suite 230, San Francisco, CA 94118; Telephone: 415-239-5922.

Glossary

The following is not intended to be a complete glossary of legal terms. It includes terms that may arise in the course of dealing with contracts and other business matters related to the conduct of a consulting practice.

ab initio (From the very beginning, in Latin). Often used to refer to a contract that was void when written.

abuse of discretion Failure of a judge or administrator to use sound and reasonable judgment in making a decision.

acceleration clause A contract clause that provides for early payment under some condition, such as in a time-payment agreement when missing a payment causes the entire balance to become due immediately.

acceptance In contract law, agreement to the offer made; receiving goods with the intention of keeping them; or agreement to terms.

accommodation An arrangement done, without consideration, as a favor to someone.

accommodation party One who signs an instrument, usually financial, to lend his or her name/credit to the other party.

accord An agreement between two or more parties on the degree of performance that will satisfy and discharge an obligation.

accord and satisfaction A new agreement to settle a contract dispute by substituting a new performance to discharge a contracted obligation (although the obligation may also be satisfied by the original performance specified).

account receivable A record of a debt owed to someone but not yet paid.

acknowledgment A formal declaration made in the presence of a notary public that the statements contained in a document are true and that the signing of the document is the free act of the person making the statement. Also called a **notary statement.**

actionable Affording grounds for legal action, as a lawsuit.

action at law A civil suit where the plaintiff seeks a legal remedy (e.g., damages), contrasted with an equitable remedy, (e.g., an injunction).

action in equity A civil suit where the plaintiff seeks an equitable remedy, such as an injunction or decree of specific performance.

actual authority The express and implied authority of an agent.

adhesion contract A standard contract form that is nonnegotiable and offered on a take-it-or-leave-it basis.

adjudicate (adjudication) Determine through judicial proceeding.

adjudicatory power In administrative agency law, the right of an administrative agency to initiate actions as both prosecutor and judge against those thought to be in violation of the law (including agency rules and regulations) under the jurisdiction of the administrative agency. Also referred to as the quasi-judicial function of an agency.

administrative agency A board, commission, agency or service authorized to implement specific laws on local, state or national levels.

administrative law Public law administered and formulated by a government agency or commission to govern the conduct of an individual, association or corporation.

affidavit A statement made under oath before a person, such as a notary public, who is qualified in that state to administer oaths.

affirmative defense A defendant's claim to dissolve himself or herself of liability even if the plaintiff's claim is true.

agent One who is authorized by another, called the principal, to act for or on behalf of the principal.

a priori A Latin term used by both scientists and lawyers that refers to an assumption, rather than hard evidence. It is hazardous on which to base an argument.

arbitration The process for resolution of dispute by one or more private, unofficial (nongovernmental) persons whose selection is agreed to by the parties to the dispute and that is outside of the judiciary processes (the courts). As used both generally and in this book, the word implies the use of the rules and regulations of the American Arbitration Association.

assignee One who receives the title of ownership, right or interest from another party who is the owner of that title, right or interest.

assignment The act by an assignor of transferring the assignor's title of ownership, interest or right in real or personal property to another party. The assignor relinquishes his or her rights to and liabilities and responsibilities for the property. The recipient of the transfer is called the assignee.

assignor One who transfers his or her title of ownership, right or interest to another party.

bankruptcy The inability to pay one's debts because the debts and liabilities exceed one's income and assets. Also, legal proceedings brought in the U.S. Bankruptcy Court, which administers distribution of a bankrupt's assets to his or her creditors. Loosely termed *insolvency.*

best efforts A standard of performance or level of effort in a contract that obligates one party to use its best efforts in bringing about successful performance but that typically makes no warranty or assurance that the performance objectives will actually be met.

boilerplate Contract provisions used repeatedly as standard copy to include in agreements.

bona fide or bona fides (In good faith, in Latin). With integrity and honesty in dealing.

breach An intentional or unintentional violation of an obligation, contract or promise.

bulk transfers The transfer or sale of a major portion (more than 50 percent) of the materials, supplies, merchandise or other inventory of a business that is not in the ordinary course of the transferor's or seller's business, as governed by Article 6 of the Uniform Commercial Code. (Also known as bulk sale.)

bylaws The rules and regulations establishing the governing structure of a corporation or association.

certificate Written statement or testimony as to truth of a certain fact.

certified copy A copy of a document signed as a true copy of the original by the holder of the original.

certify To vouch for something in writing; to make known or establish something as fact.

choice of forum Parties to a contract have some freedom to choose what state's law will govern the contract as well as the place where any dispute must be litigated or arbitrated. Choosing the location—or forum—where any such proceeding must be initiated and maintained is called the "choice of forum." If a dispute erupts, a convenient forum can save thousands in legal fees and considerable travel, time and inconvenience. It's a provision worth negotiating to your advantage.

collateral Property given, designated or pledged as security or guaranty for the fulfillment or discharge of an obligation.

common law Legal rules and doctrine created by the courts, as opposed to statutory law created by legislatures, administrative law created by governmental agencies or constitutional law created under the Constitution. Common law may be purely of judicial origin, or it may be judicial interpretation or "gloss" added to statutory, administrative or constitutional law.

confidential information Any information that has some value and gives a business a competitive edge in the marketplace. In the computer industry confidential information or "trade secrets" includes functional and technical design of software, source code, know-how, ideas, concepts, customer lists, mailing lists, financial, accounting or other business information.

consequential damage Damage that results as an indirect consequence, rather than directly from failure to meet an obligation.

consideration Any benefit given to one party by another as an inducement to enter into a contract.

consignee A merchant who receives goods for sale on a commission basis but who does not actually take ownership of the goods.

consignment sale A form of sale in which goods are deposited by the owner (the consignor) with a merchant (the consignee), with the merchant to receive a commission on each item actually sold. The consignee does not own (take title to) the goods.

consignor The owner of goods who leaves the goods with a merchant for sale on a commission basis.

contingent fee The fee paid to an attorney as a percentage of the proceeds of a legal action or other proceeding.

contract A covenant or agreement between two or more parties to do or refrain from doing one or more things. The terms of the contract are expressed verbally or in writing, according to several specific requirements that make the agreement legally binding as a contract.

copyright The exclusive right granted by the government to original creative/artistic property.

corporation An artificial entity created or recognized by a state that acknowledges an association of one or more people. The association is separate and distinct from those people. Individual shareholders generally enjoy the protection of limited liability in that each is liable and at risk only to the extent of his or her investment to purchase the stock of the corporation.

counterpart A copy of an agreement that is executed by one or more of the parties to the agreement.

covenant A written pledge by one or more parties; an agreement.

custodian One who is entrusted, either by law or agreement, with the care, keeping, control or possession of a thing or person.

damages Monetary compensation paid to a person who has suffered loss, detriment or injury to his or her person, property or rights through the act or omission of another party.

dba A common abbreviation meaning "doing business as," usually in lower-case letters. Reveals who is the owner of a business (e.g., Joseph Jones dba JJ Associates).

declarant One who makes a declaration, generally not under oath and out of court.

de facto (In fact or deed, in Latin). Contrasted with *only in theory* or *in law (de jure)* as in *de facto standard.*

default Failure to meet a legal obligation, as in breach of contract.

escalation A contract clause providing for increases or decreases in price according to market changes, especially in long-term contracts.

escrow Money, property or document held by a third party until a specified event, when item will be delivered to seller. (If event does not occur, item is returned to owner.)

finder Anyone commissioned to find buyer, seller, source, financing or other item, usually for percentage of transaction.

f.o.b. (free on board). Shipment loaded without expense to buyer, usually at a designated point from which shipped, as in "f.o.b. plant."

force majeure An irresistible or overpowering force. A common contract clause that excuses breach or default when resulting from some major catastrophe beyond one's control, such as a flood or riot.

hold harmless See **indemnify.**

implied contract A contract not expressed but inferred from one's conduct or implied in law.

indemnify To save another harmless from loss or damage; to give security for reimbursement in case of anticipated loss.

independent contractor One who contracts to perform certain functions without being subject to the control of someone else, except for providing results agreed upon.

instrument Written document, formal or legal, such as a deed, contract, will or bond.

intangible property Property or right without physical existence, including such items as patents, copyrights and accounts receivable.

intellectual property The product of mental activity, such as copyrights and patents.

inter alia (Among other things, in Latin).

ipso facto (By the fact itself; by the mere fact, in Latin).

jurisdiction The power of a court to enforce laws or award remedies.

licensee One who receives a license from another.

licensor One who grants a license to another.

notary public A public officer with authority to certify signatures and statements.

offset A deduction; a counterclaim; a contrary claim by which a given claim may be reduced or canceled.

party One who undertakes an obligation under a contract and becomes thus a signatory to an agreement.

power of attorney An instrument authorizing a person to act as your agent or on your behalf. The person authorized need not be a lawyer.

premises That which is put before. In a contract the expression "in consideration of the premises" means "in consideration of the things stated before."

prima facie (At first sight, in Latin). On the face of it; presumably; so far as it can be judged from appearances.

pro rata Proportionately or in accord with a certain rate or ratio.

proprietary Per ownership. Often used in connection with intellectual property, as in *proprietary information*.

reduction to practice Often used in connection with inventions denoting the actual building or operating of the device or method embodying the invention.

retainer Money paid to a consultant or attorney in advance.

representation Statement in agreement that a certain fact or circumstance is true.

royalty Payment made for the use of a thing or a right, as for use of a patent or literary property.

subrogation The substitution of one person (or thing) in the place of another, with respect to rights, claims or securities.

survival of terms This usually refers to certain contract provisions or terms that will remain in force even after the agreement expires or is terminated.

term Length of time, especially with regard to duration of contract.

termination End of contract; conditions for ending.

trade secret Plan, process, tool, mechanism, compound, method or other proprietary information known only to its owner and those with a confidential obligation.

trust A right of property held by one entity for the benefit of another. Legal title is then held by the party holding property in trust, (i.e., the trustee).

trustee The person who holds the legal title to the trust property and holds it in trust for another.

Uniform Commercial Code (UCC) A set of laws adopted by the various states, with some variations to represent an almost uniform set of laws to govern business transactions.

venue The place or area where the court has jurisdiction; geographic location and jurisdiction of the court.

vested interest A present right or title to a thing with right to sell, trade or otherwise dispose of it, even if not in physical or immediate possession of it.

waiver Giving up some right.

warranty Undertaking or stipulation that certain facts are as stated.

Index